Hitler *and* Russia

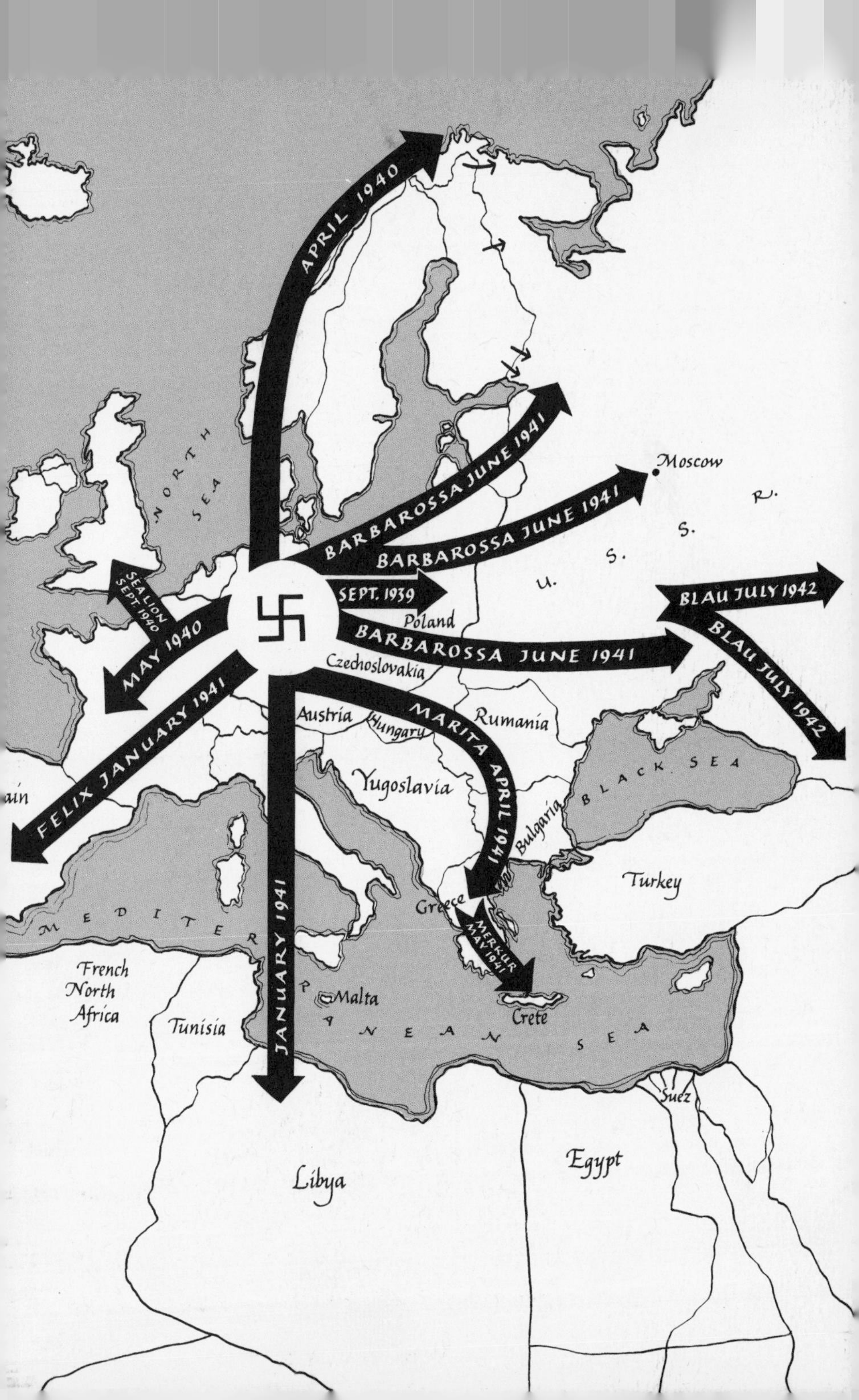
APRIL 1940
NORTH SEA
SEA LION SEPT. 1940
MAY 1940
BARBAROSSA JUNE 1941
BARBAROSSA JUNE 1941
SEPT. 1939
Poland
BARBAROSSA JUNE 1941
Moscow
U. S. S. R.
BLAU JULY 1942
BLAU JULY 1942
Czechoslovakia
FELIX JANUARY 1941
Austria
Hungary
MARITA APRIL 1941
Rumania
Yugoslavia
BLACK SEA
Bulgaria
Turkey
Greece
MERKUR MAY 1941
Crete
JANUARY 1941
MEDITERRANEAN SEA
French North Africa
Tunisia
Malta
Suez
Egypt
Libya
ain

Hitler *and* Russia

THE THIRD REICH IN A TWO-FRONT WAR 1937-1943

by Trumbull Higgins

NEW YORK: THE MACMILLAN COMPANY
LONDON: COLLIER-MACMILLAN LTD.

Library of Congress Catalog Card Number: 66-16705

FIRST PRINTING

The Macmillan Company, New York

Collier-Macmillan Canada Ltd., Toronto, Ontario

Printed in the United States of America

In Memory of

Mary Pinchot Meyer

Contents

"Only war with Russia is a war of revolutionary Germany, a war in which Germany can redeem the sins of the past, acquire virility . . . and liberate itself by liberating others."[1]

MARX AND ENGELS, 1848

"For it is in the East that our future lies, and we shall push back Russia's power and influence behind those borders from which, only through the weakness and disunity of earlier times, she has been able to advance so slowly and surely . . . to work for our ruin."[2]

KAISER FRANZ JOSEF

"I hate Slavs. I know it is a sin to do so . . . but I just can't help hating them."[3]

KAISER WILHELM II

"We terminate the endless German drive to the south and west of Europe, and direct our gaze towards the lands in the east. . . . If we talk about new soil and territory in Europe today, we can think primarily only of Russia and its vassal border states."[4]

HITLER, 1924

[1] E. H. Carr, *A History of Soviet Russia*, Vol. III: *The Bolshevik Revolution, 1917–1923* (New York, 1953), 549 n. 2.

[2] Edward Crankshaw, *The Fall of the House of Hapsburg* (New York, 1963), 127.

[3] Michael Balfour, *The Kaiser and His Times* (London, 1964), 71.

[4] Adolf Hitler, *Mein Kampf* (New York, 1939), 950–51.

Preface

DURING an interregnum of comparative peace, when in the open societies of the West the generals are automatically deemed mistaken and German generals particularly so, it is a relief to turn to Hitler's dilemma with respect to the problem of defeating the Soviet Union. Here, at least, popular opinion in the West may concede that such universally acknowledged monsters in the realm of state policy as Hitler and Stalin may have been somewhat lacking in strategical talents. It may, of course, be too much to expect any similar recognition of the military deficiencies of the political heroes of the West.

What Sir Winston Churchill once generously termed the main and decisive fronts in war have usually had a bad press. Men, in fact, are likely to hate war more for the bitter truths it reveals than for its all-too-obvious evils. But in war, as in any other aspect of man's social life, some armies and some generals have to do the dirty work of defeating the principal enemy forces and to pay the cruel price for such hard-won victories in lives and resources. To be sure, such commanders' names may only be Grant rather than Sherman, Bluecher instead of Wellington, or Zhukov rather than Eisenhower. Nevertheless, it remains an incontestable fact that in the Second World War the Eastern Front constituted the main and decisive theater against the Germans, the theater in which, as in 1914–18 in France, the backbone of the German Army was broken.

In addition to examining the origins and breakdown of Hitler's infamous crusade against the Soviet Union, the author is concerned with the two outstanding failures of the Allied coalition against Nazi Germany, the disastrous Soviet retreat to isolationism in 1939–41 and the closely connected theme of the comparative Western impotence in land warfare before 1944. While this account makes no pretense to exhaustiveness in source material, particularly on the Soviet side, material for the period following the completion of the great Stalingrad campaign in early 1943 is relatively thinner among all the belligerents. Thus, this appraisal of grand strategy terminates with the definitive collapse of Hitler's attempt to conquer the Soviet Union in February, 1943.

The author wishes to recognize his indebtedness to the unstinting assistance of the Cabinet Historical Office in London, and in Washington to the State Department, the National Archives and, especially, to the Office of the Chief of Military History of the United States Army. Acknowledgment is also due to the many scholars who devoted their time and resources to criticizing this manuscript with a dedication which may only be accounted for by the fascination and importance of the subject.

T. H.

New York City
October, 1965

Hitler *and* Russia

"Fascism is gaining victory after victory and finding its chief aid . . . [in] Stalinism. Terrible military perils knock at all the doors of the Soviet Union, and Stalin has chosen this moment to shatter the army and to trample on the nation."[1]

TROTSKY, 1938

"The Anglo-French bourgeoisie are laying a trap for us: 'Just come along, my little dears, and go to *war right now*. . . . We will profit magnificently from it. Germany will strip you bare . . . and will give us better terms in the West, and incidentally Soviet power will go to the devil. . . . Come on and fight, dear "allied" Bolsheviks, we will help you.' "[2] LENIN, 1918

"You know that I am like a wanderer who must cross an abyss on the edge of a knife. But I must, I just must."[3]

HITLER, September, 1938

"*Thus the fact of a conclusion of a treaty with Russia embodies the declaration of the next war*. Its outcome would be the end of Germany."[4] HITLER, 1924

[1] Isaac Deutscher, *The Prophet Outcast: Trotsky, 1929–1940* (London, 1963), 412.

[2] George F. Kennan, *Russia Leaves the War: Soviet-American Relations, 1917–1920* (Princeton, 1956), 486; cf. Carr, *The Bolshevik Revolution,* Vol. III, 23 n. 6.

[3] Andreas Dorpalen, "Hitler Twelve Years After," *The Review of Politics* (Notre Dame), October, 1957, 50.

[4] Hitler, *Mein Kampf*, 959.

CHAPTER I

The Fierce Friendship

1918–September 3, 1939

IN 1915, THAT HEADY YEAR of the early German victories in Poland during the First World War, in language remarkably anticipatory of a coming Fuehrer, General Hans von Seeckt wrote: "Separate peace with France and Belgium, on the basis of the status quo. Then all land forces against Russia. Conquest of ten thousand miles, expelling the population, except of course Germans. . . . We have the power to do it; and we have been plunged into conditions which in terms of blood and destruction leave the Voelkerwanderung far behind; therefore let us behave according to the customs of the Voelkerwanderung period."[5]

Five disillusioning years later, Seeckt, now Chief of the Truppenamt, the covert successor of the German General Staff (itself forbidden by the Treaty of Versailles), would record: "Only in firm cooperation with a great Russia does Germany have a chance of regaining her position as a world power. . . . It is quite immaterial whether we like or dislike the new Russia. . . . Our policy would have to be the same vis-à-vis a Tsarist Russia or a state under Kolchak or Denikin." And in 1922 in an official memorandum for the German Chancellor, Seeckt drove home his new and more modest

[5] Gustav Hilger and Alfred Meyer, *The Incompatible Allies: A Memoir History of German-Soviet Relations, 1918–1941* (New York, 1953), 191–92 n. 3. For that proto-Nazi, General Erich Ludendorff's, similar views, see Hajo Holborn, "Origins of Nazi Ideology," *Political Science Quarterly* (New York), December, 1964, 552.

realization when he declared: "The re-establishment of a broad common frontier between Russia and Germany is the precondition of the regaining of strength of both countries. Russia and Germany within the frontiers of 1914! This should be the basis of reaching an understanding between the two."[6] A fourth partition of Poland now constituted the acme of a still weak Germany's imperial dreams, and under these conditions the traditional Prussian friendliness toward her great Eastern Slavic neighbor would automatically reassert itself.

To be sure, the leaders of the new Bolshevik regime in Russia sustained few illusions concerning this drastic shift in German policy. When in the spring of 1918 Generals Max Hoffman and Erich Ludendorff forced through the predatory peace of Brest-Litovsk, stripping Soviet Russia of almost half her productive resources, Lenin checked an outraged revolt against such terms within his own Bolshevik Party by crying: "Revolutionary phrases will not do. . . . We have no army; we could not keep an army at the front. We need peace to gain a breathing-space to give the masses a chance to create new forces of life. In all probability that breathing-space will be of short duration. . . . We must prepare for the struggle."[7] With equal realism three years later, in December, 1920, Lenin would conclude: "Germany wants revenge and we want revolution. For the moment our aims are the same; but when our ways part, they will be our most ferocious and greatest enemies. Time will tell whether a German hegemony or a Communist federation is to arise out of the ruins of Europe."[8]

---

[6] From the "Seeckt Papers" in Freiburg, cited in F. L. Carsten, "The Reichswehr and the Red Army, 1920–1933," *Survey* (London), October, 1962, 115–16; cf. Carr, *The Bolshevik Revolution*, Vol. III, 438–39.

[7] John Wheeler-Bennett, *The Forgotten Peace: Brest-Litovsk, March, 1918* (New York, 1939), 303–4; cf. Wheeler-Bennett's *The Nemesis of Power: The German Army in Politics, 1918–1945* (New York, 1954), 120 ff.; General Max Hoffman, *The War of Lost Opportunities* (London, 1924), 235 ff.; Leon Trotsky, *My Life* (New York, 1960), 381–82.

[8] Gerald Freund, *Unholy Alliance: Russo-German Relations from the Treaty of Brest-Litovsk to the Treaty of Berlin* (New York, 1957), 83; cf. Carr, *The Bolshevik Revolution*, Vol. III, 330–31.

If after 1918 David Lloyd George's sharpest fear was that the "fierce friendship" of Germany and Russia would grant the Bolsheviks the means to world power, Lenin's chief anxiety at this time was that through a tacit understanding the Western Powers would foster or conclude a joint undertaking with Germany against the still floundering Soviet state. Certainly the violently anti-Bolshevik General von der Goltz took a disturbingly long time to give up German control of the Baltic States following the German defeat in 1918, and influential voices in France and Germany, such as those of Marshal Ferdinand Foch and General Max Hoffman, had been raised advocating a common enterprise against what, with Winston Churchill, then British Secretary of State for War, they deemed the Communist pestilence in the East.[9] We have seen, however, that Seeckt's postwar policy realistically had dropped the aspirations of the right-wing German Army romantics such as von der Goltz and that in collaboration with his fellow victim of the Versailles settlement—the U.S.S.R.—Seeckt contemplated a revival of German strength at the expense of Poland.

Following the conclusion of the Russo-Polish War in March, 1921, Lenin formally applied to the German Army for assistance in reorganizing and modernizing the Red Army. Seeckt promptly set up an organization within the German War Ministry to handle the ensuing training and economic-production program of the German Army in Russia. From 1922 until after Hitler's advent to power, the Germans trained the Red Army in the employment of tanks, poison gas, and planes, and in the process developed more up-to-date matériel for themselves in Soviet territory far from the eyes of prying Versailles inspectors. By 1931 the German Military Attaché in Moscow, Colonel Ernst Koestring, could report home that

[9] *House of Commons Debates*, Fifth Series, Vol. CLIV, 1457–58; cf. Isaac Deutscher, *The Prophet Armed: Trotsky, 1879–1921* (New York, 1954), 356; Freund, *op. cit.*, 40 ff.; John Wheeler-Bennett, "Twenty Years of Russo-German Relations: 1919–1939," *Foreign Affairs* (New York), October, 1946, 25–26; Carr, *The Bolshevik Revolution*, Vol. III, 111–12, 308–10; *Foreign Relations of the United States, 1919: Russia* (Washington, 1939), 56–67.

"our views and methods go through theirs like a red thread."[10]

In May, 1933, a few months after Hitler had become Reich Chancellor, a high-ranking German Army delegation was welcomed in Moscow by the Soviet Defense Commissar, Marshal Klimenty Voroshilov. Voroshilov expressed the hope that the ties linking the German and Red armies would remain intact. But on Hitler's orders in the summer and autumn of 1933 Soviet-German military cooperation was broken off, and to the openly expressed regrets of Voroshilov and of his deputy, the then General M. N. Tukhachevsky, all German Army installations in the U.S.S.R. were closed down.

In March, 1933, General Tukhachevsky had gone still further out of his way to thank the German Army for its "decisive" aid to the Red Army, and with almost equal nostalgia a year later at a customary banquet commemorating the October Revolution, the ardent Nazi War Minister, General Werner von Blomberg, toasted the Red Army for the last time.[11] The Weimar Republic's *de facto* reinsurance treaty with Russia was at last abandoned, and notwithstanding forebodings within the High Command of the German Army, Hitler's Reich was already embarked upon the fatal path of the Second Reich following Bismarck's dismissal in 1890.

During the autumn of 1936, Nazi-Soviet relations reached their lowest point of the prewar era. At the Nazi Party Rally at Nuremberg on September 12 of that year, Hitler pro-

---

[10] Hilger and Meyer, *op. cit.*, 207; cf. W. F. Hallgarten, "General Hans von Seeckt and Russia," *Journal of Modern History* (Chicago), March, 1949, 28 ff.; Ruth Fischer, *Stalin and German Communism* (Cambridge, 1948), 527 ff.; Carr, *The Bolshevik Revolution*, Vol. III, 436 ff., and his *German-Soviet Relations Between the Two World Wars, 1919–1939* (Baltimore, 1951), 56 ff.; Freund, *op. cit.*, 92 ff., 201 ff.; John Erickson, *The Soviet High Command: A Military and Political History, 1918–1941* (New York, 1962), 150 ff.

[11] Erickson, *op. cit.*, 348–93; cf. also 411–17; Hilger and Meyer, *op. cit.*, 256–71; Carsten, *op. cit.*, 131; Carr, *The Bolshevik Revolution*, Vol. III, 110–13; Walter Goerlitz, *History of the German General Staff, 1657–1945* (New York, 1953), 279; Telford Taylor, *Sword and Swastika: Generals and Nazis in the Third Reich* (New York, 1952), 153. For the lack of any change in Tukhachevsky's views as late as 1935, see *Documents on German Foreign Policy, 1918–1945* (cited hereafter as *G.D.*), edited by M. Lambert, P. Sweet, and M. Baumont, Series C, Vol. IV (Washington, 1962), 1–2, 18–20, 779–84.

claimed: "If we had at our disposal the incalculable wealth and stores of raw material of the Ural Mountains and the unending fertile plains of the Ukraine to be exploited, under the National Socialist leadership . . . our German people would swim in plenty." Five days later Marshal Voroshilov assured the Ukrainians in Kiev that the Red Army would be "fully able to meet the enemy wherever he prefers or whenever he turns his crazy attacks on Soviet territory."[12]

In reality, the Soviet regime was far less assured of being able to resist the rapidly waxing might of the Nazi Reich, despite the tripling of her production of planes and tanks in the three-year span 1934–37 and an almost comparable increase in artillery and rifle production. As the able German Ambassador to Russia, Count Friedrich von der Schulenburg, put it in a speech in 1937 to the Wehrmacht Academy, the two convictions lying at the root of all Soviet policy were, first, that the defeat of Czarist Russia in the First World War was due to the lack of an adequate war industry, and secondly, that the Soviets both respected and were intimidated by "the fearful strength of the German people." Schulenburg went on to warn that he doubted whether the current purges in the Soviet High Command would permanently cripple Russian military strength, however much they might temporarily weaken the U.S.S.R.[13]

Explanations for the appalling bloodletting within the Soviet Officer Corps during 1937/38 have varied over the years. In any event approximately half of the Officer Corps of the Red Army underwent punishments ranging from execution to degradation and imprisonment, including three out of five marshals, the great majority of general officers, and most tragically, almost all of the invaluable cadre of officers experienced in recent operations in Spain and the Far East. At the same time, that desperate Revolutionary device of

---

[12] Max Beloff, *The Foreign Policy of the Soviet Union, 1924–1941* (London, 1955), Vol. II, 58–64; cf. Wheeler-Bennett, *The Forgotten Peace*, xviii.

[13] *G.D.*, Vol. I, 899; cf. *History of the Great Patriotic War of the Soviet Union, 1941–1945* (cited hereafter as *The Great Patriotic War*), German-Language Edition (Berlin, 1962), Vol. I, 90 ff.

Soviet Civil War days—the assignment of political commissars to all military units as a check on their commanders—was reinstituted.

Since Nikita Khrushchev's famous speech to the Twentieth Communist Party Congress in 1956, the Soviet Government itself has no longer made any pretense that personal guilt among the executed and degraded officers was involved. From Marshal Tukhachevsky down, numerous Soviet military figures have been vindicated posthumously or released from imprisonment over recent years; many others, indeed, had been freed even under Stalin in time to participate in the Second World War. While in all probability the great purge may have commenced at the instigation of that malign genius of the Nazi S.S., Reinhard Heydrich (by forging evidence of continued collaboration between the German and Soviet General Staffs), soon enough both Stalin and Hitler saw in this supposed evidence an opportunity for eliminating their opponents within their respective High Commands. In fact, by 1944, following his officers' unsuccessful attempt on his life, Hitler would come to regret not having purged his Officer Corps before the war to the ferocious extent of his Soviet rival; unfortunately for him, during combat in 1944 his belated purge interfered with the conduct of military operations.[14]

Perhaps the most serious consequence of the Russian purges, which were soon extended with revolutionary and suicidal

---

[14] Erickson, *op. cit.*, 433–509; Victor Alexandrov, *The Tukhachevsky Affair* (London, 1963), 16 ff.; Nikita S. Khrushchev, "The Crimes of the Stalin Era," *New Leader* (New York), July 16, 1956, 539; Victor Serge, *Memoirs of a Revolutionary, 1901–1914* (London, 1963), 330–41; L. B. Atkinson, "Conflict of Command in the Red Army, 1918–1942," *Military Review* (Fort Leavenworth), July, 1952, 42; Walter Schellenberg, *The Labyrinth* (New York, 1959), 24–28; General A. V. Gorbatov, *Years Off My Life* (New York, 1965), chap. vii; Leonard Schapiro, "The Great Purge," in *The Red Army*, edited by B. H. Liddell Hart (New York, 1956), chap. vi; B. H. Liddell Hart, *The Other Side of the Hill* (London, 1956), 218; Werner Scharndorff, "The Bukarin Trial and Marshal Tukhachevsky's Rehabilitation," *Bulletin for the Study of the U.S.S.R.* (Munich), June, 1963, 3 ff.; see George Kennan's *Russia and the West Under Lenin and Stalin* (Boston, 1961), 255, 304–36, for the interesting argument that Stalin's purges necessarily led to the Nazi-Soviet Pact of 1939.

egalitarianism to all major facets of Soviet society, was that foreign countries tended hereafter to underestimate the still augmenting resources of the Soviet military machine. As a result, neither the French nor British governments, nor their General Staffs, were inclined to take very seriously the prospect of an alliance with the Soviets, nor would Nazi Germany fear potential Soviet counteractions nearly as much for several decisive years. In the words of General Maurice Gamelin, Commander in Chief of the French Army, so reflective of Western opinion at this juncture: "That's the ancient Russian Army, this time provided with matériel. But what can one expect from it after generals and higher officers have been put to death by the thousands?"[15] From overestimating Czarist Russia in 1914, the politically conservative generals of the French Army were about to underestimate Communist Russia during 1938/39 with still more disastrous consequences for France.

Although in 1934, following his assumption of the post of the German Presidency after Hindenburg's death, Hitler had extorted an oath of personal loyalty from the German Officer Corps, before 1938 the Officer Corps, as indicated in the postwar testimony of Field Marshal von Blomberg had found no reason to oppose Hitler in any event. Parallel to his many public professions of desire for international peace, the Nazi Fuehrer was realizing the program of large-scale armaments and growth of the Wehrmacht which the German military leaders so eagerly sought. To be sure, subsequent to his fatally easy reoccupation of the Rhineland in March, 1936, Hitler had stepped up the German rearmament program rather more rapidly than some of his more conservative military and political supporters favored, and in August, 1937 Hjalmar Schacht was allowed to resign as Minister of Economics in

---

[15] Pertinax, *Les Fossoyeurs* (New York, 1943), Vol. I, 16, n. 2; cf. Winston Churchill, *The Second World War*, Vol. I: *The Gathering Storm* (Boston, 1948), 289; Paul Reynaud, *Mémoirs*, Vol. II: *Envers et Contre Tous* (Paris, 1963), 153–68; Paul Marie De La Gorce, *The French Army: A Military Political History* (New York, 1963), 257–65; Joseph E. Davies, *Mission to Moscow* (New York, 1941), 168.

order to allow Hermann Goering to reorganize the Reich with the goal of establishing an effective war economy by 1940. Nevertheless, despite flamboyant threats to sacrifice butter to guns on the part of the porcine Chief of the Luftwaffe, in practice Goering only made preparations for a limited war by 1940, a limited war based upon a politically popular program of a rising civilian standard of living coupled with a dangerously modest armaments program, at least in terms of the eventual requirements of an absolute and general war.[16]

By November 5, 1937, concomitant with his decision to initiate building a Westwall in the Rhineland to guard against a French counterattack, Hitler revealed an increased impatience to exploit in the East what he now declared would, at best, be only a temporary superiority for the Reich in armaments. To the consternation of the Army members of his select audience on this occasion, Hitler affirmed that his aim now was to ascertain where Germany might make the "greatest possible conquest . . . at the lowest cost." If the Fuehrer's purpose was still dependent upon an inexpensive war, Hitler named 1943–45 as the last possible date for the completion of his program of conquest; after this date Germany could only expect a change for the worse in her relative position in armaments vis-à-vis her probable enemies. Hitler foresaw that Britain, and perhaps also France, had already silently written off Czechoslovakia, while any military aid by U.S.S.R. to the Czechs, if improbable because of the Japanese threat to the Soviet Far East, could be forestalled by the speed of German military operations in Bohemia.[17]

Whatever the ultimate implications of this much-debated

[16] Burton H. Klein, *Germany's Economic Preparations for War* (Cambridge, Mass., 1959), 16–27; *Nazi Conspiracy and Aggression* (cited hereafter as *N.C.A.*), (Washington: Office of United States Chief of Counsel for Prosecution of Axis Criminality 1946), Vol. II, 335, 852–53; Goerlitz, *The German General Staff*, 290.

[17] *N.C.A.*, Vol. I, 377–87, Vol. III, 295–305; cf. Major Robert Kennedy, *The German Campaign in Poland, 1939* (Washington: Dept. of the Army, April, 1956), 25.

speech recorded by Colonel Hossbach of the Fuehrer's personal military staff, it upset not only the soldiers in Hitler's audience but also Hitler's Foreign Minister, Baron Konstantin von Neurath, a diplomatic façade surviving from the less aggressive days of the Weimar Republic. In agreement with General Werner von Fritsch, Commander in Chief of the Army, and with General Ludwig Beck, Army Chief of Staff, Neurath complained that his whole foreign policy had been superseded by a program which the cautious generals were convinced would involve Germany in an all-out war long before the anticipated completion of her rearmament program in 1943–46. When at last in January, 1938, Neurath managed to see Hitler, he told the Fuehrer that should the latter persist in his new policy he would have to find another Foreign Minister to execute it.[18]

Hitler, who had long fancied himself as "a great strategist of a new kind, a future war lord in a sense and degree hitherto unknown," now decided to do not merely what Neurath advised, but while he was at it to make a clean sweep of the pessimistic Army High Command as well.[19] Consequently, on February 4, 1938, Hitler announced that henceforth he would "personally exercise immediate command over the whole armed forces." Thus, apart from dismissing Blomberg and Fritsch on irrelevant or fraudulent charges, Hitler assumed the powers of War Minister himself, like his future great antagonists in the Second World War, Winston Churchill and Joseph Stalin, with direct authority over the Army, Navy, and Air Force commanders.

Since Hermann Goering, now promoted to the rank of

[18] *Trial of the Major War Criminals* (cited hereafter as *T.M.W.C.*), (Nuemberg, 1947), Vol. XVI, 640–41; cf. General Franz Halder, *Hitler als Feldherr* (Munich, 1949), 9–21; A. J. P. Taylor, *The Origins of the Second World War* (London, 1961), 133–35; Goerlitz, *The German General Staff*, 299; E. M. Robertson, *Hitler's Pre-War Policy and Plans* (London, 1963), 106 ff.

[19] H. R. Trevor-Roper in the Introduction to *Hitler's Table Talk, 1941–1944* (London, 1953), xxv–xxx, an introduction which affords a notable contrast to the interpretation of A. J. P. Taylor; cf. the latter's *The Origins of the Second World War*, 133–49.

Field Marshal, and Grand Admiral Erich Raeder of the Navy were pliable enough subordinates, there remained for the Fuehrer only the question of finding a successor for Fritsch in the weak person of General Walther von Brauchitsch as Commander in Chief of the Army. To reinforce still further Hitler's control over strategy, a far more subservient Army officer was placed in charge of the new Oberkommando der Wehrmacht (O.K.W.) to supervise all interservice military planning, General Wilhelm Keitel. Keitel's most important assistant, Major General Alfred Jodl, Chief of the Operations Staff, was similarly an ardent admirer of the Fuehrer, if a great deal keener in intelligence than Keitel.[20]

After some hesitation, thanks to General Jodl's intervention, Ludwig Beck was allowed to stay on as Chief of Staff, largely because of Hitler's distrust of Beck's probable successor, General Franz Halder, as too orthodox a Roman Catholic, a sin in the Fuehrer's Weltanschauung almost as heinous as Beck's dedication to the more traditional Lutheran values of the Prussian General Staff. Moreover, with good reason Hitler disliked officers who, in his words later on, had "exaggeratedly theoretical minds," and observed with gratification the ambitious Jodl build up his Fuehrungsstab as a means of downgrading the Army General Staff still lower than the already subordinate, if no longer covert, status into which it had been relegated by the Diktat of Versailles. On the other hand, like Fritsch, the doleful Beck reflected no more faith in such revolutionary tactical innovations as the Panzer divisions favored by the more Nazi generals than he did in the Fuehrer's revolutionary methods in policy and strategy.[21]

[20] Gordon Craig, *The Politics of the Prussian Army, 1640–1945* (Oxford, 1955), 495 ff.; cf. T. Taylor, *Sword and Swastika*, chap. v; *N.C.A.*, Vol. II, 335–37, Vol. III, 682–83; William L. Shirer, *The Rise and Fall of the Third Reich: A History of Nazi Germany* (New York, 1960), chap. x; Major L. F. Ellis, *History of the Second World War: The War in France and Flanders, 1939–1940* (London, 1953), 333–35; Robertson, *op. cit.*, 112; Walter Warlimont, *Inside Hitler's Headquarters, 1939–1945* (London, 1964), 10–14.

[21] *Hitler's Table Talk*, 228; cf. Goerlitz, *The German General Staff*, 316 ff.; Hart, *The Other Side of the Hill*, 27 ff; Harold Gordon, Jr., *The Reichswehr and the German Republic, 1919–1926* (Princeton, 1957), 178.

With the purge of the Foreign Ministry and Army High Command almost complete, Hitler was at last in a position to undertake a politically popular Anschluss with Austria in March, 1938, simply by employing threats of force, notwithstanding the growing resistance of many higher officers to any such course of action. The nervous Chief of the Abwehr, or German Army Counter-Intelligence, Admiral Wilhelm Canaris, represented such military opinion when he welcomed his newly assimilated Austrian opposite number into his organization with the words: "Why didn't you people shoot? Then the Corporal [Hitler] would have known that things can't go on like this forever. However else is the man to learn any sense?"[22] Within the General Staff the former Corporal was already being compared to Charles XII of Sweden, the reckless eighteenth century monarch who finally destroyed Swedish pretensions to empire in a disastrous campaign in the Ukraine.

On May 5, General Beck addressed another of his anxious memoranda to the new Commander in Chief of the Army, General Brauchitsch, in which he emphasized that in the event of a German attack on Czechoslovakia, the still relatively weak Reich would encounter active Anglo-French hostility, supported by the United States and the U.S.S.R. In reality, as Hitler soon came to perceive with his customary political insight, in Prime Minister Neville Chamberlain's Britain public opinion would not allow the Government to risk war, even if the chances were one hundred to one against it. France had no intention whatsoever of assaulting the barely initiated German fortifications in the West for the sake of saving any of her small allies in the East; the United States was in the full throes of solving the problem of war with neutrality legislation, while the British Ambassador in Russia had just reported to London his, perhaps, wishful impression that the Soviet Government had no intention of going to war

---

[22] Goerlitz, *The German General Staff*, 325–26; cf. A. J. P. Taylor, *op. cit.*, 146–150; Karl Abshagen, *Canaris* (London, 1956), 126–27.

with Germany merely to aid the Czechs, and that in any event the Red Army was no better prepared for offensive war beyond its borders than were the French.[23]

As a result of a partial Czech mobilization on May 20/21, Hitler flew into a rage, real or simulated. On May 28 he informed his service chiefs and Foreign Ministry that Czechoslovakia must be "wiped off the map" by military action before October, 1938, and that the fortifications against France and general expansion of the Army should be speeded up. To console his shaken generals the Fuehrer offered no more than vague assurances that the day of reckoning with the West was still three or four years in the future.[24] Beck immediately replied that Hitler was moving rapidly toward "untenable positions" which might "seal Germany's fate," and Jodl noted that the conflict between the Fuehrer's intuition and the Army's calculations was again acute.[25]

In a final appeal to Brauchitsch against risking war over Czechoslovakia, in late July Beck demanded a meeting of the whole High Command of the Army in the hope of evoking a mass resignation of the generals in opposition to Hitler's plans. Although Beck was supported by most generals at a conclave held on August 4, Hitler managed to stall off the incipient rebellion of the General Staff by clever diplomatic tactics against the rapidly weakening statesmen of Britain and France. But as General Jodl remarked disapprovingly in his diary, the General Staff had still felt itself responsible for essentially political decisions since it lacked faith in "the genius of the Fuehrer."[26]

---

[23] *Documents on British Foreign Policy, 1919–1939* (cited hereafter as *B.D.*), edited by E. L. Woodward and B. Butler with A. Orde, Third Series, Vol. I, 148; Keith Feiling, *The Life of Neville Chamberlain* (London, 1946), 403; De La Gorce, *op. cit.*, 269 ff.; A. J. P. Taylor, *op. cit.*, 156–64, and T. Taylor, *Sword and Swastika*, 197.

[24] *N.C.A.*, Vol. I, 520–26; cf. General Alfred Jodl, *Diary* (MS in Princeton University Library), May 30, 1938.

[25] T. Taylor, *Sword and Swastika*, 197; cf. *N.C.A.*, Vol. IV, 363–64.

[26] Jodl, *Diary*, September 10–13, 1938; cf. *N.C.A.*, Vol. IV, 364; Wheeler-Bennett, *The Nemesis of Power*, 400–429; Shirer, *op. cit.*, 368 ff.; T. Taylor, *Sword and Swastika*, 198–233.

In the end Beck alone resigned, in late August, 1938. Safely after the Anglo-French capitulation at Munich in September, Hitler then dismissed several more of those he may have already surmised were active conspirators against him among the Army generals. Like Brauchitsch, Franz Halder—Beck's more easygoing Bavarian replacement as Chief of Staff—was not inclined to push conspiracy against Hitler to the point of action in the face of the latter's overwhelming political victory in what for the generals was the always somewhat alien realm of diplomacy.

Although Hitler was disappointed in his desire for a small war over Czechoslovakia, his momentary chagrin was nothing compared to the mortification and fear of the missing great European Power at Munich, the Soviet Union. Long dreading precisely this sort of settlement among the capitalist Powers of the West, the paranoid mentality of a Communist regime now had rational enough reasons to conclude that the Soviet garden was scheduled shortly to appear as the *pièce de résistance* on the menu prepared for an ever greedier Fuehrer by the seemingly complaisant chefs of London and Paris.

Although in 1938 there were no grounds for certitude among the Western Powers that the strong official Soviet line supporting Czechoslovakia would be followed by strong action in event of war, there can be no doubt that Soviet disappointment regarding Munich was real enough, even at the time. The bitter remark of Vladimir Potemkin, Maxim Litvinov's deputy as Soviet Minister of Foreign Affairs, to the French Ambassador on October 4, 1938, immediately after Munich, reflects the tone of the true Soviet position at this time more accurately than Stalin's subsequent similar semi-apology to Western statesmen at the Yalta Conference in 1945. Having complained that the Western Powers had deliberately excluded the U.S.S.R. from the Munich negotiations, emotion apparently overcame Potemkin and allegedly he cried out to Robert Coulondre, the French Ambassador:

"My poor friend, what have you done? For us I see no other way out except a fourth partition of Poland."[27]

Five months later, on March 10, 1939, in a speech to the Eighteenth Party Congress, Stalin himself reinforced the Potemkin *cri de cœur* with a warning whose significance was soon appreciated in Berlin, if not by the British Cabinet. After complaining about the remarks in the Western press regarding the supposed weaknesses of the Soviet Army and Air Force, Stalin went on to say that "one might think that . . . districts of Czechoslovakia were yielded to Germany as the price of an undertaking to launch war on the Soviet Union." Ominously, Stalin concluded that Russia must be cautious and not allow other countries to use her to pull their own chestnuts out of the fire.[28]

Hitler's reaction to Stalin's new posture became manifest within five days when on March 15 he felt so emboldened as to occupy Prague and the surviving rump of the Czech state, notwithstanding the recent Munich agreement to the contrary. Although on March 17 in Britain Prime Minister Neville Chamberlain at last openly asked whether this German action would soon again be followed by another such act of aggression at the expense of a small neighbor, Chamberlain's earlier attitudes died hard, as may be seen in a private communication to his sister in the next week. Here, obviously reluctant to abandon one of the essential postulates underlying

---

[27] Robert Coulondre, *De Stalin à Hitler* (Paris, 1950), 165–71; cf. Beloff, *op. cit.*, Vol. II, 155 ff.; Sir Lewis Namier, *In the Nazi Era* (London, 1952), 176 ff.; C. E. Schorske and F. T. Ford, "The Voice in the Wilderness: Robert Coulondre," in *The Diplomats, 1919–1939,* edited by G. Craig and F. Gilbert (Princeton, 1953), chap. xviii; James F. Byrnes, *Speaking Frankly* (New York, 1947), 283; Matthew P. Gallagher, *The Soviet History of World War II: Myths, Memories and Realities* (New York, 1963), 24–26; *Histoire de la Diplomatie,* edited by V. Potemkin (Paris, 1947), Vol. III, chap. xxiv.

[28] Gallagher, *Soviet History,* 24 n.; cf. *G.D.*, Series D, Vol. VI, 1–3; A. Rossi, *The Russo-German Alliance: August, 1939–June, 1941* (Boston, 1951), 7–9; *Nazi-Soviet Relations, 1939–1941: Documents from the Archives of the German Foreign Office* (cited hereafter as *N.S.R.*), edited by R. J. Sontag and J. S. Beddie (Washington, 1948), 76; Davies, *op. cit.*, 437–38; C. Poole De Witt, "Light on Nazi Foreign Policy," *Foreign Affairs* (New York), October, 1946, 141; Robertson, *op. cit.*, 168–69.

his appeasement policy, Chamberlain wrote: "I must confess to the most profound distrust of Russia. I have no belief whatever in her ability to maintain an effective offensive, even if she wanted to. And I distrust her motives, which seem to me to have little connection with our ideas of liberty, and to be concerned only with getting everyone else by the ears. Moreover, she is both hated and suspected by many of the smaller states, notably by Poland, Rumania and Finland."[29]

Nevertheless, fearing a prompt German assault upon Poland, and without waiting for a prior agreement with the Soviets—whom he so distrusted—or, indeed, even for the acquiescence of his French ally, on March 30 Chamberlain offered Poland a unilateral British guarantee of protection against Germany, a folly shortly to be followed by almost as provocative and futile guarantees for Rumania and Greece. Condemned in Parliament by both Winston Churchill and David Lloyd George, Chamberlain's act of weak defiance evoked a prompt and furious decision by Hitler on April 3 to attack Poland sometime after September 1 of this same year. The Fuehrer professed certitude that Soviet intervention to save Poland was unlikely, because any such intervention would be rejected by Poland as a consequence of her fear of Bolshevism. He also began to contemplate a subsequent German occupation of the Baltic States.[30]

Still more serious was the Soviet reaction to Chamberlain's extravagant slight in guaranteeing Poland and Rumania without a Russian agreement to give such promises a modicum of geographic or military reality. When Soviet Foreign Minister Litvinov's proposal for an Anglo-Russian-French mutual assistance pact on April 16 went by without the British Government evincing much interest, the Soviet Ambassador in Berlin on the very next day informed the German Foreign Office

---

[29] Feiling, *op. cit.*, 402–3; cf. Churchill, *The Gathering Storm*, 344 ff.; Herbert von Dirksen, *Moscow, Tokyo, London* (London, 1951), 229–30.

[30] *G.D.*, Vol. VI, 223–28; A. J. P. Taylor, *op. cit.*, 211–26; *T.M.W.C.*, Vol. XXXIV, 381–88; *House of Commons Debates*, Fifth Series, 345, 2500–2510; H. B. Gisevius, *To the Bitter End* (London, 1948), 362.

that there was no reason in the Russian view why Russo-German relations should not return to a more normal footing. "And," added the Soviet Ambassador, "from normal, [Russo-German] relations might become better and better."[31]

Hitler's rage against the British boiled over in an interview with Grigoire Gafencu, the Rumanian Foreign Minister, on April 19. After expressing his disappointment over his inability to reach agreement with the British on Poland, Hitler said that if England wanted war, she could have it. It would not be an easy war, as the British liked to think, the Fuehrer went on, nor one fought in the way the last war was. How, demanded Hitler, could the English imagine a modern war since they were unable to put two fully equipped divisions in the field?

Hitler would soon have an answer to his last question when on April 27 Neville Chamberlain reluctantly introduced peacetime conscription, a measure without precedent in British history. And, in a parallel dimension of military inadequacy, the German Naval Chief, Grand Admiral Erich Raeder, was preparing his small forces for a naval war with Britain, a war which Hitler had reassured him would not take place before 1945 at the earliest.[32]

As usual hereafter, the strengthening of British measures against Nazi Germany led to the weakening of Soviet reactions, and on May 3 the Minister for Foreign Affairs, Maxim Litvinov, was abruptly dismissed from his post by the Soviet Government. His non-Jewish successor, Vyacheslav Molotov, had the further advantage from the point of view of a possible rapprochement with Germany of not having been prominently associated with a policy of collective security in alliance with the Western Powers against Nazi expansionism.[33]

Nazi press attacks on the U.S.S.R. abruptly ceased, and

---

[31] *N.S.R.*, 1–2; cf. *The Great Patriotic War*, Vol. I, 165.

[32] Grigoire Gafencu, *Derniers Jours de l'Europe* (Paris, 1946); Grand Admiral Erich Raeder, *Struggle for the Sea* (London, 1939), 125–30.

[33] *N.S.R.*, 2–3; *G.D.*, Vol. VI, 419–20; Beloff, *op. cit.*, Vol. II, 239–40; Shirer, *op. cit.*, 478 n.

alarm grew in Britain that the Russians might be lost to the West. On May 4, Winston Churchill declared that no more time should be lost in negotiations with Russia since there was "no means of maintaining an Eastern front against Nazi aggression without the active aid of Russia." On May 11, the official Soviet newspaper, *Izvestia*, complained of a lack of reciprocity in the Western concept of a mutual assistance pact on the grounds that it left the Russians alone carrying the real military burden against Germany. On May 19, criticizing Chamberlain in the House of Commons, Churchill asked why the Prime Minister should oppose a peacetime alliance with Russia which would prevent war, when he now accepted the necessity for a wartime agreement with the Soviets.[34] As a military historian Churchill also dwelt upon the consequences to the West of the collapse of the Russian front in 1917, when as a result a million German soldiers and five thousand cannon were transferred to France for the final desperate German drive against the British Army in the spring of 1918. Neville Chamberlain, however, still preferred peace over what seemed to him a risky policy of embroiling all of Europe in a war against the Third Reich for the probable benefit of the Soviet Union.

Although Chamberlain continued to evade what Churchill justly termed the brutal facts, probably not even the latter surmised exactly how frantic Hitler had become in his new-found determination to expand at almost any risk. In a speech to his generals on May 23, perhaps calculated through leaks to frighten off the West, Hitler said:

> Further success cannot be attained without the shedding of blood. . . . Danzig is not the subject of the dispute at all. It is a question of expanding our living space in the East, and of securing our food supplies, of the settlement of the Baltic problems. Food supplies can be expected only from thinly populated areas. Over and above the natural fertility, thoroughgoing German exploitation

[34] Churchill, *The Gathering Storm*, 365–76; cf. Peter Kleist, *Zwischen Hitler und Stalin* (Bonn, 1950), 30–38.

> will enormously increase the surplus. There is no other possibility for Europe....
>
> We cannot expect a repetition of the Czech affair. There will be war. Our task is to isolate Poland. The success of the isolation will be decisive....
>
> It is not impossible that Russia will show herself to be disinterested in the destruction of Poland. Should Russia take steps to oppose us, our relations with Japan may become closer....
>
> The war with England and France will be a life-and-death struggle. The idea that we can get off cheaply is dangerous; there is no such possibility. We must burn our boats ... [and] be prepared for a war of 10–15 years duration.[35]

In accord with Hitler's hint that Soviet disinterest in the destruction of Poland might be hoped for, cautious feelers were extended by the German Foreign Office toward the U.S.S.R. during the next two months. Perhaps more effective as a spur to rapprochement with Russia was the successful Nazi pressure on Finland and the Baltic States to refrain from making any defensive arrangements with the U.S.S.R., as the latter was demanding as part of the price for a pact with the Western Powers. The Soviets had found no reason to forget Marshal von Hindenburg's notorious explanation to the German Foreign Office in 1917 that he needed to control the Baltic States for the maneuvering of his left wing in the next war with Russia.[36]

Equally cautious, the British Foreign Office continued to conduct negotiations with the Soviets at a relatively low level and with a complete unwillingness to cooperate with the Russians except upon terms satisfactory to the Poles. Although under French pressure to achieve an agreement with Russia before Hitler might do the same thing, the British Government was also most reluctant to grant the Soviet Union the guarantees in the Baltic States which it desired, guarantees

[35] *N.C.A.*, Vol. VII, 849–51; cf. *G.D.*, Vol. VI, 574–80; A. J. P. Taylor, *op. cit.*, 249–51; Raeder, *op. cit.*, 130–31; Robertson, *op. cit.*, 172–74; Hart, *The Other Side of the Hill*, 35.

[36] *N.S.R.*, 9 ff.; John Wheeler-Bennett, *Munich: Prologue to Tragedy* (New York, 1948), 395 ff.; Churchill, *The Gathering Storm*, 379–80; Shirer, *op. cit.*, 495.

which in all probability in the long run would have led to a Soviet absorption of these small states. Apart from the British inability to face offering Russia a still somewhat indeterminate slice of eastern Europe as part of the price for a Soviet alliance, the Germans had the still more crucial advantage of being able to grant Russia neutrality—and thus time for further military preparation against the onset of an ever more likely general war.

That this potential gift of German neutrality, as opposed to the unpromising prospect of launching an offense against Germany without much aid from the Western Powers, was hardly an offer to be easily rejected by the Soviet Union may be more readily seen when the German threats of an alternative deal with the Japanese are considered. Commencing on May 28, 1939, the Japanese Kwangtung Army in Manchuria renewed earlier unsuccessful probes of the Soviet Far Eastern frontier regions on a larger scale than before, in this case against the Soviet satellite state of Outer Mongolia. At the same time, as the Russians may have surmised, Japanese Premier Kiichiro Hiranuma opened negotiations with Germany for the transformation of the Anti-Comintern Pact of 1936 into a more effective military alliance against the Soviet Union. Here, perhaps more than anywhere else, lay the source of Russia's now desperate need for an active and powerful alliance with the Anglo-French coalition or, alternatively, for a bona fide neutrality pact with Hitler's ever more aggressive Reich.[37]

By the first week of August, Hitler's patience over the slow course of Nazi-Soviet negotiations was reaching its limit; his autumnal campaign deadline against Poland was almost at hand. As a result he stepped up the pace and significance of his solicitations to Russia in a frame of mind well illustrated by his statement on August 8 that while nobody could break

---

[37] *N.S.R.*, 18–34; *B.D.*, Vol. VI, 2–24, 50, 375–96; *The Great Patriotic War*, Vol. I, 166 ff.; Beloff, *op. cit.*, Vol. II, 248 ff.; Joseph W. Ballantine, "Mukden to Pearl Harbor: The Foreign Policies of Japan," *Foreign Affairs* (New York), July, 1949, 654–55; C. E. Schorske, "Two German Ambassadors: Dirksen and Schulenburg," in *The Diplomats*, 501–11; Erickson, *op. cit.*, 517 ff.

his nerves, nevertheless he was working on the assumption that Russia would not go to war with Germany. Hitler explained to a Hungarian guest that the Soviets would "not repeat the Czar's mistake and bleed to death for Britain. They would [instead] . . . try to enrich themselves, possibly at the expense of the Baltic States or Poland, without engaging in military action themselves."[38]

On the other hand, on August 12, to the anxious and distrustful Italian Foreign Minister, Count Galeazzo Ciano, Hitler maintained in accordance with the line of his Foreign Minister, Joachim von Ribbentrop, that in the last resort France and Britain would not go to war to save Poland. At least Hitler could gloss over his disappointment at learning from Ciano of Italy's relative unreadiness to enter a general war in 1939 with the news just received from Moscow that the latter was willing to commence high-level negotiations with the Reich on matters now suddenly equally urgent to the Soviets.[39]

Arriving in Russia by a slow boat, the comparatively low-level British and French military missions began negotiations on this same August 12 as the Soviet response to the Nazi higher-level bid. Nevertheless the Soviet military negotiations with the Anglo-French mission comprised the highest possible Russian military personnel, headed by Defense Minister Voroshilov and including General B. M. Shaposhnikov, Chief of Staff of the Red Army since the fall of Tukhachevsky.

The Western military missions were further inhibited by the distrustful attitudes of their political superiors toward the Soviet Union and also by the generally pessimistic opinion of Soviet military capacities then prevailing among the French and British military staffs. For example, British military estimates in the spring and summer of 1939 agreed that the Red Army, Navy, and Air Force were of such a low technical order, and had suffered so badly from the officer purge, that

[38] *G.D.*, Vol. VI, 973–74; cf. *N.S.R.*, 37 ff.

[39] *N.C.A.*, Vol. VII, 521–25; *The Ciano Diaries, 1939–1943*, edited by Hugh Gibson (New York, 1946), 119–20; Count G. Ciano, *Diplomatic Papers* (London, 1948), 302–3; Robertson, *op. cit.*, 177.

they were incapable of bringing any effective offensive aid to Poland or Rumania. Such an appalling misestimate is all the more striking in view of the recent consistent Soviet successes against Japan in the far less accessible areas of East Asia.[40]

If the Western Powers thought little of Soviet abilities, it soon turned out that the Russians had rather better cause for low opinions of Anglo-French military capacities and plans, especially those concerning the chances of any offensive in the West so essential to relieve the Eastern Front. Already on August 13, Marshal Voroshilov had crossed swords with Major General T. G. Heywood of the British Army regarding the immediate availability of only six British divisions for service in France. Heywood replied, as best he could under the circumstances, that in the First World War the British Empire had similarly commenced with only six active divisions, but had eventually contributed one hundred divisions to the Allied war effort. But, of course, it was precisely what happened to Russia before Great Britain was ready in the First World War that was disturbing Stalin.[41] Like France, Stalin was not fortunate enough to inhabit an island which could prepare for serious war in its own good time.

Following this inauspicious overture, an overture unhappily to be characteristic of the Anglo-Russian dialogue in the future, on August 14 Voroshilov got down to business. He asked whether the Red Army could operate against the Germans across Polish and Rumanian territory and declared that this was the cardinal point for the Soviet Union, "a point

---

[40] *B.D.*, Vol. IV, 183; Vol. VI, 782–86; Paul Reynaud, *In the Thick of the Fight, 1939–1945* (New York, 1955), 211 ff.; Erickson, *op. cit.*, 525 ff.; *The Ironside Diaries, 1937–1940*, edited by R. MacCleod and P. Kelly (London, 1962), 78; General Maurice Gamelin, *Servir* (Paris, 1947), Vol. II, 443–61.

[41] The Soviets have continued to belabor this issue of Britain's small contribution on land in 1939, as may be witnessed by Stalin's remarks to Churchill in 1942, and by the recent memoirs of General Vasili I. Chuikov, *The Beginning of the Road* (London, 1963), 352–53; cf. Churchill, *The Gathering Storm*, 391; L. F. Ellis, *op. cit.*, 2–8. While these are real arguments, reflecting sincere anxieties, Soviet historians have frequently been forced to overstate their military case against the West to the point of self-defeating absurdity. See, for example, examples cited by Kennan, *Russia and the War*, 40.

to which all other points were subordinate." The Soviet Defense Minister further stated that without a precise and unequivocal answer on this issue, further military conversations would be useless.[42]

As Hitler correctly informed an audience of high military officials on the Obersalzberg this same day, "the great drama" was indeed "approaching its climax." Stalin, who according to Hitler no longer had any intention of "pulling British chestnuts out of the fire," had nothing to gain and much to fear from war, including a victorious Russian Army in the event that he should win. As for the British, Hitler now implicitly conceded they might go to war, despite their military unreadiness, but he asserted that they still did not want a long struggle.[43] Only on this last matter may the reckless Fuehrer have been mistaken; here he evidently forgot that others, too, can plunge unprepared into desperate follies when trapped and stunned by the abrupt ambushes of their enemies.

Late that same evening of August 14, at Hitler's order, Foreign Minister Ribbentrop telegraphed Moscow requesting a personal interview with Molotov and Stalin. In a guarded reply the next day, Molotov asked German Ambassador Schulenburg about the chances of Germany lending her influence in behalf of a better Russian relationship with Japan as well as about the possibilities for the conclusion of a nonaggression pact between Germany and the U.S.S.R.[44]

The next day, on August 15, perhaps to impress the Western Powers with the seriousness of Soviet intentions and the magnitude of Russian resources, the Chief of Staff of the Red Army, General Shaposhnikov, outlined the Soviet plan to deploy 136 Russian divisions and over 9,000 tanks in the event of a German attack on the U.S.S.R. through the Baltic States. For this fairly remote contingency the distrustful Shaposhnikov demanded that the Western Powers employ

---

[42] *B.D.*, Vol. VII, 568–673.

[43] General Franz Halder, *War Diary* (MS), Vol. I, 6–22.

[44] *N.S.R.*, 51–56; *G.D.*, Vol. VII, 99; and especially, Robertson, *op. cit.*, 178–79.

70 per cent of this strength in an active offensive against the Reich, a task in any event beyond the capabilities of the British and French armies, still in almost no way organized for offensive operations. In this contingency, Poland, likewise, would have to commit her full strength against the Reich on Russia's behalf.

For the somewhat more probable circumstance of a German attack on France, in their turn the Soviets engaged themselves to providing 70 per cent of the strength of the Western Powers in a Russian offensive on Germany across Poland and Lithuania, the Western Powers guaranteeing the Soviet right to cross Polish and, if possible, Lithuanian territory. For the most probable contingency of all, namely a German attack on Poland, Shaposhnikov promised to match any Western forces directly employed against Germany, should Poland —and if possible Lithuania and Rumania—grant the Red Army passage across their territories.

Shaposhnikov's exercise in what John Erickson has justly termed the "categorical imperative" having evoked no immediate reply of a positive nature from the Poles, on August 17 Marshal Voroshilov adjourned the military meetings until August 21, whilst affirming that without a reply from Poland there was no need for further such meetings. With scarcely veiled sarcasm, Voroshilov advised the Western military delegates to amuse themselves with the sights of Moscow until their governments had obtained the Polish reaction.[45]

Notwithstanding such Soviet rebuffs, in a very fair explanation to the War Office on August 17, British General Heywood wrote of the Russian position that "for very sound military reasons they wish to take full advantage of cooperation with the Polish Army, rather than wait until that Army is defeated and they have to bolster up the remains of a defeated army, which might have a most unfortunate influence on their strategy and their own troops."[46]

---

[45] *B.D.*, Vol. VII, 575–78; Erickson, *op. cit.*, 528–29; Reynaud, *In the Thick of the Fight*, 212–14; De La Gorce, *op. cit.*, 269–80.
[46] *B.D.*, Vol. VII, 601.

That, characteristically, the Poles were not going to make matters any easier for potential allies than for enemies was evident the next day, when the Chief of Staff of the Polish Army declared that he believed the Russians wished to cross those parts of Polish territory which were formerly Russian only for the sake of their reoccupation, and not for mounting an offensive against Germany. Despite increasing pressure from the now thoroughly alarmed French, it would take several days before a somewhat less uncompromising posture would be grudingly accepted by the Poles and by then it was too late.[47] In short, the Poles believed that the Second World War was about to start as much over the question of their eastern frontiers as over their western, and, ultimately, over Poland's right to exist as a sovereign state at all.

The final undoing of the Poles came about on August 19, when as a consequence of renewed Nazi pressure in Moscow for a nonaggression pact, Stalin personally consented to receive Ribbentrop within a few days. With his deadline for military operations against Poland almost at hand, Hitler's relief was intense. Fresh warnings from General Georg Thomas, chief of the economics and armaments branch of the O.K.W., and from Admiral Wilhelm Canaris, head of the Abwehr, or Army Intelligence, between August 17 and 20 to the effect that Germany lacked ammunition and gasoline for a war of more than a few weeks' duration and that her Navy had only ten submarines ready for Atlantic operations, must have accentuated the Fuehrer's new-found eagerness to shake hands with his bitterest ideological enemy in the East.[48]

In his self-justification to his military chiefs on August 22, Hitler recapitulated, saying: "It was clear to me that a conflict with Poland had to come sooner or later. I had already made

---

[47] *B.D.*, Vol. VII, 25–26, 61, 141, 208–12, 347, 559–613. Reynaud, *In the Thick of the Fight*, 213–30; Leopold Labedz, "1939: A Backward Glance," *Encounter* (London), December, 1964, 89–90.

[48] Wheeler-Bennett, *The Nemesis of Power*, 432, 452; *N.C.A.*, Vol. III, 580–81; *N.S.R.*, 64–68; *G.D.*, Vol. VII, 121–68; R. Kennedy, *op. cit.*, 36–37; Hanson W. Baldwin, "Hitler's Power in 1939," *New York Times* (New York), May 9, 1948, 16; Hart, *The Other Side of the Hill*, 35–36.

this decision in spring, but I thought that I would first turn against the West in a few years, and only afterwards against the East. But the sequences cannot be fixed."

Hitler went on to explain that since no German again was apt to have more authority than himself, it was better to act now against opponents in the West still led by mediocre statesmen. Politicians, the Fuehrer asserted ominously, on occasion had to accept risks with the same "reckless resolution" as military leaders. In any event Hitler believed that Britain could only send a maximum of three divisions to aid France, and she was "still vulnerable from the air," a favorable situation which might change within two or three years. As for France, Hitler once again reassured his distrustful audience that the French not merely were lacking in manpower and modern matériel but also felt no desire to undertake an attack upon Germany in the West, a point of particular anxiety to the German generals in 1938 during the Munich crisis.

Hitler concluded with his bombshell: namely, that he had established personal contact with Stalin and a pact with the U.S.S.R. would be signed within forty-eight hours. Now Poland was "in the position in which I wanted her," and the Fuehrer's only remaining fear was that "some Schweinhund" would propose mediation (as had Mussolini at Munich).[49] Doubtless the Fuehrer reasoned that his generals would be as grateful for his abrupt reversion to the old Prussian tradition of friendship with Russia as the Western Powers would be shocked into inaction by such a staggering diplomatic *bouleversement*. With a few exceptions, Hitler knew his German generals at any rate.

On this same August 22, one day before Foreign Minister

---

[49] Cited from the safer *N.C.A.*, Vol. III, 581–86, 665–66, version in preference to the more suspect account in *N.C.A.*, Vol. VII, 752–54, and to Halder's incomplete record in the *G.D.*, Vol. VII, 551–56; cf. *T.M.W.C.*, Vol. XXV, 338–44, and T. Taylor, *Sword and Swastika*, 311–13; Robertson, *op. cit.*, 180, n. 3; Carr, *The Bolshevik Revolution*, Vol. III, 324 n. 2; Helmuth Greiner, *Die oberste Wehrmachtfuehrung, 1939–1945* (Wiesbaden, 1951), 39–43.

Ribbentrop's publicly announced arrival in Moscow, the British Military Delegation in the Russian capital noted:

The situation is now much clearer. The U.S.S.R. would appear to have [had] a leg in both camps for some time. They seem now to have come to the conclusion that Germany is in a strong position and that she will inevitably overrun Poland, in which case, if the Soviets make a pact with Britain and France, they will have committed themselves against Germany before they need [to do so]. The U.S.S.R., we think, realizes that her communications and equipment are still weak and her Staff and organization not yet fitted for a major war against a strong enemy, especially if they have a retiring Polish army to compete with.

The next day, August 23, Marshal Voroshilov informed the more sympathetic French Military Attaché that the Red Army needed better guarantees than simply a passive posture by the French Army, a posture which Voroshilov estimated would hold down only ten German divisions in the West while the bulk of the German Army was conquering Poland in the East. The bitterly disillusioned Chief of the British Military Delegation, Admiral Sir Reginald Plunkett-Ernle-Erle-Drax, consoled himself with the thought that the Soviets could be relied upon for dishonesty in carrying out a treaty as well as for duplicity in negotiating it. Indicative of the unfortunate Tory outlook of the chief British military negotiator, Admiral Drax finally reached the fantastic conclusion that in the long run it might prove fortunate that the Russians had allied themselves to Germany rather than to the West.[50]

Meanwhile, in two epochal meetings with Stalin and Soviet

---

[50] *B.D.*, Vol. VII, 594–609. By now the Soviet Government may have been in possession of the German military timetable for the invasion of Poland, information obtained through their remarkable agent in Tokyo, Richard Sorge: Labedz, *loc. cit.*, 86 n. 5. Not surprisingly, in 1942 Admiral Drax would turn into an advocate of bombing Germany instead of invading France: see his "The British War Effort," *Journal of the Royal United Service Institution* (London), November, 1942, 320, and Ivan Maisky's obviously biased but still useful *Who Helped Hitler?* (London, 1964), 165 ff.

Foreign Minister Molotov on August 23, with Hitler's ready acquiescence, Ribbentrop had come to a swift *quid pro quo* with the Soviets. Finland, Estonia, Latvia, eastern Poland, and the former Czarist province of Bessarabia, now in Rumania, would fall into the Soviet sphere of interest, leaving only Lithuania and western Poland for the Reich. In return the Russians guaranteed that they would not support the Western Powers over the Polish issue.

With respect to Japan, a problem as much on Stalin's mind at this juncture as the lack of an effective Western offensive to aid the Russians in Poland, the Soviet ruler observed to Ribbentrop that if Tokyo now desired war, she could have it. Stalin meant what he said. On August 19, within a few hours of the Soviet agreement to negotiate with Ribbentrop, General Zhukov had launched a spoiling attack against the Japanese Army in Outer Mongolia, forestalling a new Japanese offensive by barely four days. Owing to the unexpected superiority of Soviet artillery and tanks, the Japanese were to be completely expelled from Outer Mongolia by August 31, after suffering approximately 18,000 casualties. As Stalin would remark smugly soon thereafter to one of his new German friends: "That is the only language these Asiatics understand. After all, I am an Asiatic too, so I ought to know."[51]

So far as Britain was concerned, Stalin complained to Ribbentrop that the British military mission in Moscow had never really said what it wanted. In any event, Stalin deemed the British Army as weak, the British Navy as no longer deserving its previous reputation, and the Royal Air Force as still unready, although increasing in strength. Nonetheless, the Soviet dictator remained sure that despite her over-all

---

[51] Hilger and Meyer, *op. cit.*, 305; cf. Paul Schmidt, *Hitler's Interpreter* (New York, 1959), 139; Erickson, *op. cit.*, 532–36; Clark W. Tinch, "Quasi-War Between Japan and the U.S.S.R., 1937–1939," *World Politics* (New Haven), January, 1951, 184–86; *The Great Patriotic War*, Vol. I, 210; *New York Times* (New York), June 11, 1945.

military weakness, Great Britain would wage war "craftily and stubbornly."

When Stalin next proceeded to assert that the French Army was worthy of consideration, Ribbentrop hastily called attention to the great German superiority in manpower over France, if not to the fact that most of the Reich's trained effectives would have to be first employed in the East against Poland before they could be rushed back to hold the line in the West against the French Army. After mutual toasts to the respective heads of state, Stalin concluded his conversations with Ribbentrop by declaring that the Soviet Government took its pact with Germany very seriously. For what it was worth Stalin promised on his word of honor that the Soviet Union would not betray her partner in the new "non-aggression" pact, a pact so named as an unwitting tribute to the purportedly obsolete idealism of Woodrow Wilson.[52]

On August 24, Ribbentrop returned to Berlin from Moscow on the crest of the wave to be greeted by his grateful Fuehrer as a second Bismarck. Hitler had reasons for such gratitude: the until recently Germanophile British Ambassador, Sir Nevile Henderson, had just informed him of the British intention to honor her obligation to Poland regardless of the consequences of his pact with the U.S.S.R. Although Hitler had replied that an ensuing war would thus be Great Britain's fault and that in any event he preferred a war when he was only fifty years of age to one later on, the day when threats could frighten off British appeasers was done. Of more moment, Hitler also blamed Britain for forcing him into his agreement with Russia, concerning which Henderson did not consider the Fuehrer to be overly enthusiastic. But, as Hitler pointed out, Germany would no longer have to fight on two fronts. Even a final offer on Hitler's part to guarantee the British Empire with German military power only evoked a warning

[52] *N.S.R.*, 71–76; *G.D.*, Vol. VII, 220–46; *T.M.W.C.*, Vol. X, 269, Vol. XIV, 284, Vol. XL, 295–97; cf. Rossi, *op. cit.*, 38–48; *The Ribbentrop Memoirs* (London, 1954), 111–14.

from Henderson that while anyone might be able to predict the beginning of a war, nobody could correctly anticipate the surprises of a protracted struggle.[53]

To top off the unpleasant reaction of the British to the Fuehrer's Russian pact, under Ciano's pressure Mussolini wrote Hitler on August 25 that Italy would definitely not join the Reich in an alliance with Bolshevik Russia at the expense of Catholic Poland, officially on the grounds that he had previously been led to believe that Italy need not be ready for war until 1942/43. Considerably shaken by such a "base betrayal," Hitler raged that the Italians were behaving again just as they had in 1914, and at the last minute ordered a delay in the imminent German Army attack on Poland in order to gain time for another effort to bluff or buy off the British. The General Staff of the German Army also agreed with Italian Foreign Minister Ciano that Italy was in no position to conduct even a defensive war. The mortified Duce himself had real grounds for fearing that if the British and French would not attack Germany in the West to save Poland, they might well be inclined to assault a weak Italy instead as a cheap, if not essentially relevant, substitute for effective but costly action against the Reich.[54]

Hitler's astonishing reversal of alliances had similarly provoked consternation in still a third Great Power. Faced with what Tokyo termed a breach of faith by the Reich at a moment when Japan was heavily engaged in combat against the Russians in Outer Mongolia, the Japanese Cabinet was

---

[53] *B.D.*, Vol. VII, 162–63, 170–77, 201–2, 227–30, 257; cf. Alan Bullock, *Hitler: A Study in Tyranny* (London, 1958), 487–89; Sir Nevile Henderson, *Failure of a Mission: Berlin, 1937–1939* (New York, 1940), 260 ff.; Schmidt, *op. cit.*, 142–43.

[54] Fritz Hesse, *Hitler and the English* (London, 1954), 78–81; cf. *G.D.*, Vol. VII, 240–44, 281–82, 556–61; Major General I. Playfair, with G. Still, C. Molony, and S. Tormer, *History of the Second World War: The Mediterranean and the Middle East*, Vol. I (London, 1954), 23–39; T. Taylor, *Sword and Swastika*, chap. viii; *The Ciano Diaries*, 128 ff.; *B.D.*, Vol. VII, 221; *N.S.R.*, 80–83; Schmidt, *op. cit.*, 130–47; Robertson, *op. cit.*, 183–87; Abshagen, *op. cit.*, 135–37.

forced to resign and the Japanese Ambassador in Berlin, General Hiroshi Oshima, was ordered to protest to Hitler. The Japanese Army policy of realizing an effective military alliance with the European Axis at the expense of Russia, rather than against Great Britain as Hitler fervently desired, now seemed as discredited as Japanese equipment and tactics shortly would appear in the clash with the Red Army in the Gobi Desert.[55]

For that matter, within the Nazi Party incredulity and disgust regarding the pact with Bolshevik Russia was running high, and on August 28 Hitler had apologetically admitted to his old party comrades that a resulting war would be tough, that Germany might fail, but as long as he was alive there would be no talk of capitulation. Nevertheless, while he professed to be prepared to fight a two-front war if driven to it, Hitler still hoped that the British would only go through the motions of honoring their obligations to Poland and wage no more than a show war against Germany. As he said to Baron Ernst von Weizsaecker, the Undersecretary of State in the German Foreign Office, on August 29: "In two months Poland will be finished, and then we shall have a great peace conference with the Western Powers."[56]

By August 31, Hitler had finally resolved upon action against Poland for the next day regardless of what steps the Western Powers might take in consequence. On September 1, in a promise which he was to keep, the Fuehrer told the Reichstag that hereafter he would take off his uniform only after victory or he would not live to see the end. Two days later, on September 3, when the British ultimatum at last arrived requiring a German halt in Poland on pain of an immediate British declaration of war, Hitler appeared still more dismayed

---

[55] *G.D.*, Vol. VII, 224, 281–82; Robert J. Butow, *Tokyo and the Coming of the War* (Princeton, 1961), 138; *International Military Tribunal for the Far East* (cited hereafter as *I.M.T.F.E.*), (Tokyo, 1948), Exhibits 775, 782, 2735*A*; Herbert Feis, *The Road to Pearl Harbor* (Princeton, 1950), 34–37.

[56] *The Memoirs of Ernst von Weizsaecker* (London, 1951), 208–14; cf. Halder, *War Diary*, Vol. I, 32; *G.D.*, Vol. VII, 563–64.

by the dilemma into which he had worked himself. Savagely he demanded of the proud author of the pact with Russia, Foreign Minister von Ribbentrop, what he should do now. On this same occasion he told his collaborator on his famous autobiography, Rudolf Hess: "Now my whole world falls to pieces. My book [*Mein Kampf*] has been written in vain."[57] And Luftwaffe Chief Hermann Goering, who had struggled frantically in the last few weeks to make a private arrangement with Britain, admitted on the same day, September 3: "If we lose this war, then God have mercy on us." The Nazi leaders themselves, let alone the German people and the armed services, cannot be charged with eagerness for a general war with the West, regardless of any aggressive passions which they harbored in varying degrees toward the East.[58]

Perhaps to the Soviet Union went the last word. As Foreign Minister Vyacheslav Molotov proclaimed to the Supreme Soviet on August 31: "Is it really difficult to understand that the U.S.S.R. is following, and will continue to follow, its own independent policy, the aim of which is to further the interests of the peoples of the U.S.S.R. and these interests only? If these [other European] gentlemen have such an irresistible desire to fight, let them fight each other without the Soviet Union. We would look and see what sort of fighters they are." Once again Russia had gained a *peredyshka*, or breathing-space, with which to prepare for the future, but as in 1807 and in 1918, the time gained at the price of abandoning allies would be brief and Russia's own military preparations would prove grievously unrealistic or inadequate.[59]

---

[57] Albert Zoller, *Hitler Privat* (Dusseldorf, 1949), 156; cf. Schmidt, *op. cit.*, 155–58; Ribbentrop, *op. cit.*, 127; Hesse, *op. cit.*, 82–88; William L. Shirer, *Berlin Diary, 1934–1941* (New York, 1941), 197–201; Major General Bernhard von Lossberg, *Im Wehrmachtfuehrungsstab* (Hamburg, 1950), 36–37.

[58] Schmidt, *op. cit.*, 158; cf. Poole, *loc. cit.*, 142–43; Goerlitz, *The German General Staff*, 355; Raeder, *op. cit.*, 133; *The Memoirs of Field Marshal Kesselring* (London, 1953), 42; *B.D.*, Vol. VII, 176–512; G. M. Gilbert, *Nuremberg Diary* (New York, 1947), 335–37.

[59] *B.D.*, Vol. VII, 620–22; cf. Wheeler-Bennett, *The Forgotten Peace*, 279–80; Potemkin, *op. cit.*, 708–9.

"A conqueror is always a lover of peace (as Bonaparte always asserted himself); he would like to make his entry into our state unopposed."[1]

CLAUSEWITZ, with Lenin's marginal comment, "Ah, ah! Witty!"

"We must exploit the differences and contradictions between the two imperialisms, between the two groups of capitalist states, setting them at one another's throats. . . . If we had not adhered to this rule we should all long ago, to the satisfaction of the capitalists, have been hanging from so many aspen trees."[2]

LENIN, November, 1920

"Before the hour of Hitler's defeat strikes, many, very many in Europe will be wiped out. Stalin does not want to be among them and so he is wary of detaching himself from Hitler too early."[3]

TROTSKY, December 4, 1939

"To assume that there will be no breathing-space and that there will be constant ultimatums is to believe that there is no movement at all in the West. We assume that the Germans cannot do everything."[4]

STALIN, to TROTSKY, 1918

1 Byron Dexter, "Clausewitz and Soviet Strategy," *Foreign Affairs* (New York), October, 1951, 52.

2 V. I. Lenin, *Sochineniya,* Second Edition (Moscow, 1947), Vol. XXXI, 410–11; cf. Lionel Kochon, *The Struggle for Germany, 1914–1945* (Edinburgh, 1963), chap. ii.

3 Deutscher, *The Prophet Outcast,* 459.

4 Carr, *The Bolshevik Revolution,* Vol. III, 56.

CHAPTER II

The Wrong Wars

September 3, 1939–June 18, 1940

FOLLOWING the shock of the Anglo-French declaration of war on September 3, 1939, Hitler rallied his own confidence and that of his generals with the prediction, similar to the subsequent Soviet rationalizations for their betrayal of the West, that the Western Powers were merely making a token gesture toward their obligation over Poland and would soon welcome a negotiable peace with the Reich. Now the Fuehrer anticipated—correctly as it turned out—that the seventy-odd Anglo-French divisions eventually to be based in northern France would not attack the approximately thirty operative German divisions, mostly second-string, actually left guarding the Siegfried Line, while the bulk of the German Army overran Poland in the first of Hitler's Blitzkriegs.

In reality, the French High Command had consented to a declaration of war against Germany principally upon the grounds that the temporary diversion of the Reich's forces in the East would give the French Army time to mobilize at all; the last thing the French command wished to do, in honoring its promise to Poland to attack in the West, was to provoke a German reaction at this moment of extreme French weakness before even the four British divisions available had crossed the Channel or the slow-mobilizing reservist French Army of the 1914 variety had fully assembled. In addition, apart from the absence of any will to launch a costly assault against the German fortifications, the French Army lacked the means to do so in terms of armored divisions, air superiority or of an offensive dogma envisaging their employment.

In short, as Hitler had correctly surmised, by 1939 the French had utterly abandoned the disastrous offensive *à outrance* philosophy of 1870 and 1914, at a time when such a philosophy alone might have saved her and her allies. And in Great Britain Neville Chamberlain's reluctant acceptance of war was embodied in his conclusion that the best that could be hoped for was a gradual collapse of German morale, a military victory over the better-armed Reich being considered out of the question.[5]

Commencing on September 3, the day of the Allied declaration of war in the West, Ribbentrop began pressing for a rapid and public Soviet intervention in Poland. Soviet Foreign Minister Molotov cautiously demurred with respect to any such overt Soviet collusion with Nazi aggression while Poland was still reasonably intact, and on September 6 German Ambassador Schulenburg had to explain to Berlin that public opinion in Russia did not yet understand the pact with Germany very well and that, following the defeat of Poland, it feared the Reich might still turn against the U.S.S.R.

Alleging that the Wehrmacht had already reached Warsaw as early as September 8, the German Foreign Ministry soon renewed its pressure upon Molotov for a Soviet entry at the expense of the presumably expiring Polish state. After hasty congratulations to the Germans over their military achievements, on September 10 Molotov stalled for more time by explaining that the Red Army had been counting on several weeks before facing the need for intervention and now these weeks had shrunk to a few days. Still more infuriating to the Germans, Molotov declared that to avoid

---

[5] Gamelin, *op. cit.*, 29 ff.; Richard Challener, *The French Theory of the Nation in Arms, 1866–1939* (New York, 1955), 265 ff.; Feiling, *op. cit.*, 418; L. F. Ellis, *op. cit.*, 7–19; R. Kennedy, *op. cit.*, 76–77; *G.D.*, Vol. IX, 6; Wheeler-Bennett, *The Nemesis of Power*, 460–61; R. J. Minney, *The Private Papers of Hore-Belisha* (London, 1960), 222–45; Field Marshal Erich von Manstein, *Lost Victories* (London, 1958), 34–35; Reynaud, *Mémoirs*, Vol. II, 290–92.

giving the U.S.S.R. the appearance of being an aggressor, the Soviet Government proposed to announce that it was intervening for the sake of protecting the Ukrainians and White Russians in Poland from the German threat. The Nazis were learning, as later on the Western Powers and Chinese Communists would discover, that the Soviet Union was hardy a comfortable ally, whether as a *de facto* or *de jure* partner in conflict.

By September 14, Molotov informed the Germans that the Red Army "had reached a state of preparedness sooner than anticipated and that the Soviets would shortly enter Poland. In fact, both the rapid collapse of Poland and an armistice—now set for September 16—with the Japanese in Outer Mongolia had prepared Soviet policy to accept military operations in the West. Despite any pressure in the future, however, no consideration whatsoever would induce Stalin to accept more than one war or front at a time. To his own sorrow, in the long run Hitler would not reflect an equal determination to avoid a two-front war.

On September 17, a safe day after the armistice with the Japanese, at the urgent solicitation of its German colleague, the Red Army crossed the Polish frontier in the strength of approximately forty divisions, its first such incursion in the West since 1920. Stalin personally rewrote the joint Soviet-German communiqué announcing this event on the grounds that the German version was too frank, a customary Communist complaint concerning their stupider Nazi partners in chicanery. The Soviet dictator also reflected considerable doubt and anger regarding whether the German forces would retire from towns already seized within the Soviet-assigned zone of Poland following their completion of military operations, although he recognized that this might be due to the German generals' reluctance to surrender conquered territory rather than to a deliberate policy of the German Government.

To the great annoyance of the poorly informed O.K.H. and O.K.W., Hitler promptly ordered a German Army evacuation from Lemberg, the Drohobycz oil fields, and Brest-

Litovsk. With Tukhachevsky no longer able to thwart him, as in the previous Soviet invasion of Poland in 1920, at last Stalin was able to seize the West Ukrainian citadel of Lemberg (Lwów), although the anti-Communist German Army Intelligence chief, Admiral Canaris, was able to spirit away a few Ukrainian nationalist leaders from the eager clutches of the Soviet Secret Police.[6]

The Soviet entry into Poland, belated though it might have been from Ribbentrop's point of view, precipitated the first of many wartime rows between Hitler and the headquarters of the Army (O.K.H.). The Fuehrer now ordered that Warsaw be seized as rapidly as possible regardless of civilian or military casualties, so that the Red Army would find the Polish capital firmly in German hands. On the other hand, the Army High Command preferred slower siege operations against Warsaw, both to spare lives and artillery for the Western Front. In the words of many other chiefs of staff before and since 1939, General Halder lamented: "Strict separation between political and military establishment[s] has proved a great drawback. . . . The High Command of the Army must not be left at the vagaries of [foreign] policies. . . ."[7]

By September 25, second thoughts had assailed Stalin regarding a Soviet occupation of ethnic, as opposed to *de jure*, Poland. He proposed a new exchange of territory with Germany on the interesting grounds that, while the partition of Polish-speaking territory might cause friction between Germany and the U.S.S.R., a German surrender of most of Lithuania in return for the occupation of almost all of ethnic Poland would alleviate causes for tension between the two partners. Certainly such an exchange, more or less forced

[6] *N.S.R.*, 86–100; *G.D.*, Vol. VIII, 2–97; cf. R. Kennedy, *op. cit.*, 124–25; T. Taylor, *Sword and Swastika*, 354–55; John Armstrong, *Ukrainian Nationalism* (New York, 1963), 32; Leon Trotsky, *Stalin* (New York, 1941), 328–33, and his *My Life*, 458–59; Warlimont, *op. cit.*, 34–35; Carr, *The Bolshevik Revolution*, Vol. III, 214 n. 2; Abshagen, *op. cit.*, 143–49.

[7] Halder, *War Diary*, Vol. I, 60; Halder, *Hitler als Feldherr*, 27; Manstein, *Lost Victories*, 58.

upon the Reich at this moment of her engagement in the West, left Germany the sole onus of holding down the Poles and at the same time gave the Red Army a stronger and less exposed defensive line in the Baltic region against Germany.

In fact, once Ribbentrop had reluctantly arrived in Moscow on his second trip on September 27/28, he was to learn not merely that the Soviets demanded all the Polish oil fields (despite their own vast, and the Reich's negligible, resources in this respect) but also that they intended a military occupation of selected Latvian and Estonian bases in the immediate future. With a bleeding heart, Hitler accepted these terms, only insisting upon the withdrawal of the ethnic Germans in the Baltic States as a small consolation for the total abandonment of these regions so dear to the crusading Teutonic Knights of old.[8]

Hitler required Soviet diplomatic support at this moment, as much as her military and economic aid, to sustain either a peace offensive or, alternatively, a military offensive against the West. On September 28, in announcing the official demise of Poland, Germany and Russia declared that Great Britain and France would be responsible for any continuation of the war and that the German and Soviet governments would continue to engage in mutual discussions of measures necessary against any prolongation of the conflict. As it turned out, this threat, ostensibly uttered against the West, would rebound against its originators in the course of their uneasy collaboration.[9]

Opinion in the West was appropriately depressed by these events, but on October 1 Winston Churchill bravely proclaimed that at least "an Eastern Front had been created which Nazi Germany did not dare assault!" Privately the new First Lord of the Admiralty attempted to dispel pessimism, such as that of American Ambassador Joseph P. Ken-

[8] *N.S.R.*, 101–7; *G.D.*, Vol. VIII, 159–66; Hesse, *op. cit.*, 93–94; *The Initial Triumph of the Axis*, edited by A. Toynbee and V. M. Toynbee (London, 1958), 42 ff.

[9] *N.S.R.*, 108; *G.D.*, Vol. VIII, 167–75.

nedy, by asserting that the Germans would have to guard their conquests in the East with at least twenty-five divisions.[10] It would take more than whistling in the dark regarding implicit fronts in the East to protect the Allies in the West, as others less courageous than Churchill were soon to apprehend.

Spurred on by anxiety over the possible success of Hitler's peace offer to the West of October 6, the Soviets now hurriedly made claims upon Finland for territory, particularly territory covering the approach to the great exposed port and former Russian capital of Leningrad. In negotiations continuing for several weeks, the Soviet Government vainly offered the Finns face-saving concessions in eastern Karelia in return for their far more important posts on the Gulf of Finland, posts essential for Finnish defense against the Red Army, but also of some value for Soviet defense against the German Navy. Unfortunately for Finland, notwithstanding pressures inside the Reich as well as from the Italians, the Allied rejection of Hitler's peace offer on October 12 confirmed the Fuehrer's still cautious determination not to offend his Soviet partner at this juncture. As a result the Finns were to resist the U.S.S.R. without the aid of the only country in a position to defend them effectively.[11]

Professing a British threat to Norway and eager for the acquisition of German naval bases on both Norwegian and Soviet Arctic territory, Grand Admiral Raeder added weight to the influences already working to keep Hitler dependent upon good relations with the U.S.S.R. On October 10, the German naval chief proposed to Hitler the exploitation of Soviet pressure on Norway in order to acquire a German naval base in central Norway at Trondheim. Although this idea never materialized, Raeder did acquire a temporary base

---

[10] Churchill, *The Gathering Storm*, 448–49; cf. William Langer and S. V. Gleason, *The Challenge to Isolation, 1937–1940* (New York, 1952), 252.

[11] Vaino Tanner, *The Winter War: Finland Against Russia, 1939–1940* (Stanford, 1950), 27 ff.; *N.S.R.*, 121 ff.; Weinberg, *op. cit.*, 87–88; Langer and Gleason, *op. cit.*, Vol. I, 257–59; *The Memoirs of Marshal Mannerheim* (New York, 1954), 310 ff.

on Soviet soil near Murmansk, an Arctic substitute which served the German Navy until its acquisition of numerous better-situated Norwegian bases in the spring of 1940.[12]

Even before the rejection of his peace offer, over the bitter opposition of the conservative officers of the O.K.H., on October 9 Hitler had issued Directive No. 6 for the conduct of the war in the West. In, perhaps, the ablest of his war directives the Fuehrer concluded a historical analysis of Germany's relations with the West with a statement that time favored the Allies, especially Great Britain, rather than Germany which now at her relative peak of strength must attack France by way of the Low Countries as soon as possible. As one of the originators of this attack, to be imposed by Hitler upon a reluctant and, indeed, hostile Army General Staff, Lieutenant General (subsequently Field Marshal) Erich von Manstein, has observed, the eclipse of the O.K.H. had already commenced because the fact of the matter was that "the spring of 1940 was not only the earliest, but also the latest occasion on which Germany could have hoped to fight a successful offensive in the West."[13] So far as Russia was concerned, Hitler asserted that no treaty could insure the permanent neutrality of the U.S.S.R., but for the next few months or even years Germany might count on Soviet passivity, particularly if the Reich won more victories.

Opposition on the part of the unprepared Luftwaffe may have reinforced the objections of the Army to an immediate offensive against the West in the autumn of 1939, but not before General Alfred Jodl of the O.K.W. staff had written on October 15: "We will win this war, though it may be a hundred times contrary to the doctrines of the General Staff." On October 27, Hitler definitely ordered an attack on the West to be initiated within a fortnight; nevertheless,

---

[12] *G.D.*, Vol. VIII, 204–13, 277–88; *T.M.W.C.*, Vol. XIV, 97, and Documents 005C, 066C, 122C; T. K. Derry, *History of the Second World War: The Campaign in Norway* (London, 1953), 16–17; Raeder, *op. cit.*, 160.

[13] Manstein, *Lost Victories*, chap. iv; cf. *N.C.A.*, Vol. VII, 800–84; F. H. Hinsley, *Hitler's Strategy* (Cambridge, 1951), 38–42; *Hitler's War Directives, 1939–1945*, edited by H. R. Trevor-Roper (London, 1964), 12–14.

on November 5 the resistance of General von Brauchitsch, Commander in Chief of the Army, resulted in a terrible scene between him and the Fuehrer, an encounter from which the browbeaten Army chief emerged with his morale too shattered to undertake the strain of participating in any active military conspiracy against Hitler in addition to opposing his strategy.[14] Brauchitsch had particularly infuriated Hitler with his tactless argument that the hurriedly raised army of 1939 could not yet compare in combat endurance with the carefully constructed military forces of the old Kaiserreich.

Bad weather finally enabled the thoroughly discredited Army High Command to postpone, week by week, the proposed attack in the West; yet the old confidence between Hitler and the Army was never restored. For example, on what General Franz Halder described as a day of crisis, November 23, Hitler remarked that most of his earlier policies had been resisted by numerous prophets of misfortune, but he had gotten away with the supposedly impossible again and again between 1935 and 1938. Now, declared the Fuehrer to an audience of high military figures:

For the first time in sixty-seven years it must be made clear that we do not have a two-front war to wage. That which has been desired since 1870 and considered as impossible of achievement has come to pass. . . . But no one can know how long that will remain so. . . . Now the eastern front [in Poland] is held by only a few [German] divisions. . . . Russia is at present not dangerous. It is weakened by many incidents today. Moreover, we have a pact with Russia. Pacts, however, are only held as long as they serve the[ir] purpose. . . . Now Russia has far-reaching goals, above all the strengthening of her position in the Baltic. We can oppose Russia only when we are free in the West. Further, Russia is striving to increase her influence on the Balkans and is striving towards the Persian Gulf. That is also the goal of our foreign

---

[14] Jodl, *Diary*, October 15, 1939; cf. Telford Taylor, *The March of Conquest* (New York, 1958), 42–54; Halder, *War Diary*, Vol. II, 31 ff.; Wheeler-Bennett, *The Nemesis of Power*, 463 ff.; Hart, *The Other Side of the Hill*, 104–5; Gisevius, *op. cit.*, 388; Lossberg, *op. cit.*, Vol. II, 46–47; Warlimont, *op. cit.*, 58–61.

policy. . . . It is a fact that at the present time the Russian army is of little worth. For the next one or two years the present situation will remain.[15]

Hitler could hardly have been more explicit regarding the postulates underlying his basic policy of turning west before undertaking the more eagerly desired campaign in the East, and the favorable reaction of most of the generals present to this candid tirade bears witness to the Fuehrer's skill and subtlety in spurring on his fainthearted warriors.

That night the Commander in Chief of the Army, General von Brauchitsch, tendered his resignation, only to meet with Hitler's rejection of even this small assertion. Willy-nilly, the cowed Army High Command was ordered to continue preparing for an offensive in the West, and despite his objections to any such attack, Brauchitsch stayed on, evidently to some extent because the Fuehrer could find no more acceptable replacement for his Commander in Chief among the other leading officers of the Army.[16]

Two days later, on November 25, in a characteristically less frank discussion with Grand Admiral Raeder, Hitler amplified his earlier remarks to the generals in saying: "As long as Stalin is in power, it is certain that she [Russia] will adhere strictly to the pact made. Her political attitude may change after years of building up her internal strength, particularly if Stalin is overthrown or dies."[17] A fortnight earlier Hitler had turned down Raeder's suggestion of purchasing submarines from the Soviets, on the grounds of their poor quality and because he did not wish the Russians to perceive any weaknesses of the Reich.

---

[15] *N.C.A.*, Vol. III, 573–80; *G.D.*, Vol. VII, 439–46; cf. Halder, *War Diary*, Vol. II, 55–56; Ulrich von Hassell, *The Von Hassell Diaries, 1938–1944* (London, 1947), 106; for the parallel opinion of General Maurice Gamelin, the French Commander in Chief, two weeks before the Soviet-Finnish war, that the Red Army was "extraordinarily bad," see Gamelin, *op. cit.*, Vol. III, 194.

[16] Manstein, *Lost Victories*, 87–88; Hart, *The Other Side of the Hill*, 105–7; T. Taylor, *The March of Conquest*, 58–60.

[17] *Fuehrer Conferences on Matters Dealing with the German Navy* (cited hereafter as *F.C.G.N.*) *1939* (Washington, 1947), Vol. XLVII; cf. *N.C.A.*, Vol. VI, 980.

Negotiations between the Soviet Government and Finland having reached an impasse, on November 30 approximately thirty Red Army divisions, organized in three armies, attacked about nine somewhat smaller Finnish divisions at several points along the Russo-Finnish frontier. At the same time a Soviet-sponsored Finnish satellite government was proclaimed in the Finnish border town of Terijoki, an action which suggested a Russian assumption of a prompt and total Finnish defeat. In an explanation to Germany on December 3, Soviet Foreign Minister Molotov declared that a rapid solution of the Finnish problem was required by the U.S.S.R., so as to free Russian forces for the realization of the primary Soviet missions in the Balkans and Black Sea regions.[18]

Less constrained in their shock over Stalin's rapid exploitation of his pact with Nazi Germany, the Western Powers, including the neutral United States, emitted loud cries of distress over what President Franklin D. Roosevelt called "the dreadful rape of Finland." Conservative opinion in Great Britain and France was still more inflamed and plans were immediately launched for sending war matériel and other aid to the immensely popular Finns.[19] Worldwide reactions to the unprovoked Soviet assault culminated in the expulsion of the U.S.S.R. from the League of Nations on December 14, a final fling of that ill-fated organization's feeble attempts to uphold the status quo.

Fortunately for the Finns, their prolonged negotiations with the U.S.S.R. had gained time for the full mobilization of their army of 200,000 men, and at the last moment they had acquired some Bofors antitank guns, essential against the numerous Russian armored units soon to be thrown against them. On the other hand, the Finns had almost no planes and only a three-week supply of field-artillery ammunition with which to oppose the immense Soviet resources in these particular

---

[18] *N.C.A.*, Vol. VI, 980; Lieutenant General Kurt Dittmar, "The Red Army in the Finnish War," in *The Red Army*, 80–82; Mannerheim, *op. cit.*, 324–30; Erickson, *op. cit.*, 542–43.

[19] Langer and Gleason, *op. cit.*, Vol. I, 329–33; cf. De La Gorce, *op. cit.*, 285–86; Churchill, *The Gathering Storm*, 539–42.

categories. But high morale, difficult terrain, approaching winter, and the light field fortifications of the so-called Mannerheim Line were to afford the Finns initial advantages of a most embarrassing kind for the overconfident Red Army. It should be kept in mind, however, that in 1941 the equally overconfident Finno-German forces would find their offensives bogging down after comparatively modest advances in the almost roadless wilderness of northern and central Finland and Karelia.

If the Reich could take no steps at this stage to oppose Soviet activities in the regions once again assigned to the Russians by the 1939 version of the Tilsit Treaty of 1807, the German Navy, always strongly in favor of closer collaboration with Russia against Britain, sensed in the waxing tension in the Scandinavian regions a rare opportunity to overcome its grossly inferior geographic position as a prisoner of the North and Baltic seas. Given such an outlook, in early December the allegations of the Norwegian Nazi-sympathizer Vidkun Quisling that the British were already planning to enter Norway in order to help the Finns came as a most expedient weapon by which Grand Admiral Raeder might interest Hitler in German countermeasures, purportedly to forestall Allied action in Scandinavia. After some hesitation, on December 14 Hitler ordered the creation of an interservice planning staff within the more friendly atmosphere of the O.K.W. to investigate methods of seizing Norway.[20] As Raeder did not yet perceive, his Fuehrer had found a covert but effective riposte to Stalin's now unconcealed offensive toward the Baltic.

Already by December 17, it was becoming apparent that the Soviet invasion of Finland constituted no walkover. Admiral Raeder himself felt that the newly revealed inadequacies of the Red Army should make for a harder German posture in future negotiations with the demanding and often

---

20 *F.C.G.N.*, *1939*, 51–59; Jodl, *Diary*, December 12–13, 1939; *G.D.*, Vol. VIII, 519–20; *N.C.A.*, Vol. IV, 104–6, Vol. VI, 981; E. F. Ziemke, *The German Northern Theater of Operations, 1940–1945* (Washington: Dept. of the Army, 1959), 8–10; Derry, *op. cit.*, 16–18; Raeder, *op. cit.*, 168.

surly Russians. The day before, that eager advocate of amphibious action Winston Churchill had drawn a still harder conclusion from the Soviet threat in the North; the First Lord of the Admiralty now favored the landing of Allied troops in Norway in the hope of provoking a German counterattack into waters presumably dominated by the Royal Navy. Although enthusiastically supported by the violently anti-Soviet French Premier, Edouard Daladier, who, like the French military, sought to divert the Germans away from the Western Front, on December 22 the majority of the British Cabinet accepted action in Scandinavia, ostensibly to aid Finland, only in the event that the Norwegian and Swedish governments would agree to such measures. Facing simultaneous German and Soviet warnings, the terrified Scandinavian governments rejected all Western offers of such dangerous aid, and for the moment nothing was done.[21]

By the last week of December the fiasco of the first Soviet offensive in Finland was unmistakable; only one out of six separate assaults had manifested any sign of success at all and the Red Army was undergoing the first of several subsequent reorganizations as a consequence of its resounding failure. Mass Soviet attacks were discontinued throughout most of January, 1940, two new Soviet armies reinforced the original three, and as, perhaps, the most serious indication of Soviet concern, General Simyeon Timoshenko was nominated as the new *de facto* commander of the key front on the Karelian isthmus near Leningrad. Well might Stalin telegraph Hitler just before Christmas: "The friendship of the people of Germany and the Soviet Union, cemented by blood, has every reason to be lasting and firm."[22]

Enormous and renewed Soviet demands upon the Reich for military equipment, especially machinery for the manufacture of heavy-artillery ammunition with which to smash

---

[21] Churchill, *The Gathering Storm*, 543–48; Derry, *op. cit.*, 96–103; Langer and Gleason, *op. cit.*, Vol. I, 379–81; Feiling, *op. cit.*, 427–28.

[22] Isaac Deutscher, *Stalin: A Political Biography* (New York, 1949), 445; cf. Mannerheim, *op. cit.*, 350–52; Erickson, *op. cit.*, 545–48; Dittmar, *op. cit.*, 83; *G.D.*, Vol. VIII, 629–31.

the fortifications of the Mannerheim Line, hardly served to conceal from foreign eyes the extent of the Red Army's loss of prestige. As the General Staff of the German Army in an evaluation dated December 31, 1939, observed of the Red Army: "In quantity a gigantic military instrument. . . . Organization, equipment and means of leadership unsatisfactory—principles of leadership good; leadership itself, however, too young and inexperienced. Communication system bad, transportation bad; troops not very uniform; no personalities—simple soldier[s] good-natured, quite satisfied with very little. Fighting qualities of the troops in a *heavy* fight, dubious. The Russian 'mass' is *no* match for an army with modern equipment and superior leadership."[23] The events of the next year and a half were to provide no cause for the German Army to alter this smug estimate—quite the contrary, in fact, considering the dazzling victories of the Reich during this period.

On the third of January, Mussolini's mortified dissatisfaction over the increasingly intimate course of Nazi-Soviet collaboration overflowed in a letter which he dispatched to Hitler, writing as an equal to his fellow dictator almost for the last time. After a swift *tour d'horizon* of the European scene, Il Duce settled down on the subject of agreements with Russia in the following vein:

No one knows better than I, who have now had forty years of political experience, that politics—even revolutionary politics—has its tactical exigencies. I recognized the Soviets in 1924; in 1934 I concluded with them a treaty of commerce and friendship. So I realize that since von Ribbentrop's efforts toward nonintervention by the French and the British were not realized, you have avoided a second front. Without striking a blow, Russia has, in Poland and the Baltic, profited from the war.

But I, a born revolutionist who has not modified his way of thinking, tell you that you cannot permanently sacrifice the principles of your Revolution to the tactical exigencies of a certain

---

[23] *N.C.A.*, Vol. VI, 981–82; cf. *G.D.*, Vol. VIII, 591–96; and Feiling, *op. cit.*, 428, for Neville Chamberlain's parallel view at this date.

political moment. I feel that you cannot abandon the anti-Semitic and anti-Bolshevist banner which you have been flying for twenty years and for which so many of your comrades have died; you cannot renounce your gospel, in which the German people have blindly believed. It is my definite duty to add that a further step in your relations with Moscow would have catastrophic repercussions in Italy, where the anti-Bolshevik unanimity, especially among the Fascist masses, is absolute, solid as rock, and indivisible.

Permit me to believe that this will not happen. The solution of your Lebensraum problem is in Russia and nowhere else; in Russia, which has the immense area of twenty-one million square kilometers and nine inhabitants per square kilometer. Russia is alien to Europe. In spite of her extent and population, Russia is not a power but a weakness.

Mussolini concluded with a flourish which he would have cause to regret within another two or three years, saying: "The day when we shall have demolished Bolshevism we shall have kept faith with our two Revolutions."[24]

Eager to divert the Soviets away from the Balkans, so sensitive a region for German petroleum, Russian traditions, and Italian pride, on January 6 Hitler's O.K.W. issued a strategic study which favored a Soviet move south from the Caucasus into the Middle East. Such an action on the part of the U.S.S.R. would have an additional advantage from the German point of view in that it would tend to embroil the Russians with the Anglo-French forces protecting the crucial Allied oil fields in the Middle East. How serious the anti-Soviet French General Maxime Weygand, commanding vastly exaggerated forces in Syria, and the French Army General Staff actually were over the ensuing few months in their desire for air and naval operations against the Soviet Caucasian oil fields is still somewhat debatable, but the O.K.W. had every reason to whet Soviet anxieties in this respect, if only again as an

---

[24] *G.D.*, Vol. VIII, 608; cf. *Les Lettres Secrètes Echangées par Hitler et Mussolini* (Paris, 1946), 54–64; Schmidt, *op. cit.*, 167–72.

indirect method of aiding the Finns as well as the interests of the Reich.[25]

German hopes and Russian fears concerning the Western reactions to the Soviet embarrassments in Finland were still further accentuated on January 20, 1940, when Winston Churchill broadcast a statement that the Finns had "exposed for all the world to see the military incapacity of the Red Army and Red Air Force." Within the week the Soviet Government newspaper, *Izvestia*, replied, depicting Mr. Churchill as the greatest enemy of the Soviet Union, while the Communist Party newspaper, *Pravda*, went on to warn Anglo-French imperialists against any plans for extending the war in an exceedingly dangerous fashion.[26]

More concrete repercussions of these new Soviet fears were soon manifest, both in Moscow's abrupt elimination of its unsuccessful puppet regime for Finland under Otto Kuusinen, and in a renewal of the Red Army offensive on February 1 with a vastly increased artillery barrage against the fortified Karelian isthmus. At the same time, Stalin took pains to remind the Germans of his "very great service" to the Reich in selling her matériel not otherwise available to Germany because of the Allied blockade. Stalin added that although this Soviet policy had made enemies, Anglo-French pressure would not induce the U.S.S.R. to alter its policy of supplying Germany. Hitler was less forbearing, since he now hoped altogether to avoid having to give the gravely compromised Soviets a long-promised German heavy cruiser or even the blueprints for a battleship.[27]

Lending substance to *Pravda*'s charges, under strong domestic political pressure, on January 18 the French Govern-

---

[25] *G.D.*, Vol. VIII, 632–33; Halder, *War Diary*, Vol. III, 16; Dino Alfieri, *Dictators Face to Face* (New York, 1955), 59; Erickson, *op. cit.*, 548; Gamelin, *op. cit.*, Vol. III, 206 ff.; Major General Sir John Kennedy, *The Business of War* (London, 1957), 26, 41.

[26] Winston Churchill, *Into Battle* (London, 1941), 160; cf. *G.D.*, Vol. VIII, 742; Rossi, *op. cit.*, 82.

[27] *G.D.*, Vol. VIII, 721; cf. *ibid.*, 672 n. 2; Erickson, *op. cit.*, 548–50; Mannerheim, *op. cit.*, 353 ff.

ment had suggested to London not only a joint action against Narvik and the Swedish iron-ore fields but also the employment of Polish forces against Soviet bases in the Arctic for the sake of aiding Finland. Although subject to considerable criticism at home for inaction, most judiciously in early February the British Government eliminated the suggested Polish attack on the Soviet Arctic and confined what the doleful Lieutenant General Sir Alan Brooke termed its "wild projects" in subsidiary theaters of war to a so-called volunteer expeditionary force for Norway and Sweden alone. It is very possible that the order of the Soviet Secret Police dated February 12, 1940, for the liquidation of the Polish officers in their hands, was issued under the impetus of this threat of a Polish attack on Petsamo. In the event, well after the Allied threat to the Soviet Arctic had faded, the Polish officers were killed by the N.K.V.D. just the same.[28]

As usual, however, despite increasingly desperate appeals from the Finns, at the beginning of March the Norwegian and Swedish governments refused to allow themselves to become the cat's-paw of an Allied strategy ostensibly directed against Russia and actually against the Reich. Nevertheless, on February 16, Hitler, already much exercised by undue publicity in the Allied press regarding their Scandinavian plans, had been further outraged when the British Navy forcibly freed British captives from a German ship illegally using the cover of neutral Norwegian waters to transport their prisoners to Germany. The Fuehrer now ordered his reluctant Air Force and Army, as well as his more enthusiastic Navy, to prepare for an invasion of Norway under the direction of his personal staff in the O.K.W. On March 1, the final German directive for this operation was promulgated. But the sudden Finnish signature of a peace treaty with the U.S.S.R. on

[28] Arthur Bryant, *The Turn of the Tide, 1939–1943* (London, 1957), 75–77; cf. Sir Llewellyn Woodward, *British Foreign Policy in the Second World War* (London, 1962), 24–27; Derry, *op. cit.*, 12–13; *Die Geheimakten des franzoeischen Generalstabes* (Berlin, 1941), Nos. 18–38; Tanner, *op. cit.* 195 ff.; J. A. Zawodny, *Death in the Forest* (Notre Dame, 1962), 114 ff.; *Foreign Relations of the United States, 1942* (Washington, 1961), Vol. III, 150–51.

March 12 deprived Hitler as well as the Allies of any official pretext for occupying Norway.[29]

As Ambassador Schulenburg reported to Berlin, the U.S.S.R. may have decided to impose terms upon Finland short of her complete conquest because of Soviet fear of becoming engaged in a serious war with the Western Powers, for which it was "not prepared." Even so, the Finnish losses, involving the cession of more than 10 per cent of her inhabited territory accompanied by the complete flight of its population, were unexpectedly severe and, not surprisingly, left the Finns thirsting for the first opportunity to regain such regions.

On the other hand, the Soviet Union had sustained 200,000 admitted casualties in the course of its brief winter campaign and had been compelled to employ over 30 per cent of its Air Force and regular Army divisions for the sake of finally defeating the Finns. Under these circumstances Stalin deemed it wiser to make concessions to Red Army morale, and the successful commander of the Soviet offense, General S. K. Timoshenko, was now promoted to the rank of Marshal and made Defense Commissar in place of Voroshilov. A vigorous training program, more traditional ranks and discipline, and, at last, by August 12, 1940, a unitary command structure with the subordination of the political commissars to the military, marked the belated Soviet recognition of some of the lessons derived from her unhappy campaign in Finland.[30]

British and German anticipations that the victorious Soviets might next occupy northern Norwegian ports continued to focus attention on Scandinavia, and significantly, the Fuehrer did not share Admiral Raeder's willingness to have the Russians occupy the Norwegian port of Tromsoe in preference to the British. Hitler decided to seize Tromsoe as well as

---

[29] Jodl, *Diary*, February 19, March 13–14, 1940; *G.D.*, Vol. VIII, 779–833; Churchill, *The Gathering Storm*, 560 ff.; Lossberg, *op. cit.*, 58.

[30] *N.S.R.*, 139–40; cf. Erickson, *op. cit.*, 551–57; Mannerheim, *op. cit.*, 363–92; Robert Kilmarx, *A History of Soviet Air Power* (New York, 1962), 151–58; Atkinson, *op. cit.*, 44; *Foreign Relations of the United States, 1940*, Vol. III, 189–91; *Warfare in the Far North* (Washington: Dept. of the Army, October, 1951), 20.

Narvik himself, since he did not care for the Russians "so close" to the Reich as a mere two hundred miles north of the Arctic Circle.[31] Indeed, so offensive was the Soviet advance in Finland to Hitler that on March 18, in a meeting with Mussolini, he conceded that "only bitter necessity" had made him join Russia, a necessity which more privately Hitler hoped Italy's entry against the Western Powers would soon help to relieve.[32]

Still more acrid were the ashes of Finnish defeat to the French. In fact, on March 19, the Daladier Government resigned over the issue, and with the ardent support of the French Naval Chief, Admiral Jean Darlan, the new Government of Paul Reynaud felt impelled to demand bombing operations against the Soviet oil fields at Baku, purportedly to cut off German receipt of this vital ingredient supplied by the U.S.S.R. On March 28, the Supreme Allied War Council, sitting in London, deferred for further study this perverse fruit of the French determination to avoid war on the Western Front at any cost, including that of total defeat. But in an apparent effort to save the new French Government, the British did agree to lay down mine fields to interdict German use of Norwegian waters. Should the Germans react with force, the British agreed that the Allies would be prepared for limited landing operations in Norway.[33]

Much alarmed by rumors of these possible hostile Allied measures against her, the Soviet Government at the beginning of April hastily suspended its grain and petroleum shipments so crucial to the Reich, made difficulties regarding the promised German Arctic naval base, and assured the British Government that Soviet policy was independent from Germany. With the appearance of the German landings on April 9 along the entire Norwegian coast, however, Soviet policy

---

[31] *N.C.A.*, Vol. VI, 982; cf. *The Ciano Diaries*, 229.

[32] *G.D.*, Vol. IX, 8; cf. Ribbentrop, *op. cit.*, 145–47; Raeder, *op. cit.*, 193–95; Ciano, *Diplomatic Papers*, 361–65; Warlimont, *op. cit.*, 55.

[33] Reynaud, *In the Thick of the Fight*, 257–64; Gamelin, *op. cit.*, Vol. III, 206 ff.; Langer and Gleason, *op. cit.*, Vol. I, 419; Churchill, *The Gathering Storm*, 575 ff.; Woodward, *op. cit.*, 28–31.

underwent another *volte-face*. Economic and naval difficulties with the Reich abruptly vanished and Foreign Minister Molotov hurried to offer Germany wishes for "complete success in her defense measures" in Norway.[34] As always during the period of Nazi-Soviet collaboration, the greater the German threat, the more cordial the countenance directed toward Berlin by the Russians.

Less relieved by the German action in Norway, Winston Churchill nonetheless assured the House of Commons on April 11 that Hitler's invasion of Scandinavia was as great a strategic error as that of Napoleon's seizure of Spain in 1807. In the long run, the loss of much of the German surface navy in this operation, coupled with the tying down of 300,000 men of the German Army to guard this exposed conquest, may have validated Churchill's incautious remark. Even in the short run Grand Admiral Raeder has confessed that he did not have the chief eventual benefit of Norway for the Reich in mind when he sponsored the risky operation, namely its great value as a base for interdicting Western supplies to the U.S.S.R. in the future.

Such a future may conceivably have belonged to the subconscious aspirations of the Russophobe Fuehrer, rather than to those of a naval chief primarily concerned with his principal enemy at sea. And apart from this early manifestation of Hitler's growing tendency toward the unnecessary dispersion of his strength, the Norwegian campaign also first revealed an inclination toward panic in moments of operational difficulty on the part of the new successor to the almost equally febrile Ludendorff as military dictator of a wartime Reich.[35]

Oddly enough, as Churchill himself has recognized, on May 10 the Norwegian fiasco at last brought him to the top of Disraeli's greasy pole as Prime Minister, with greatly in-

---

[34] *N.S.R.*, 138–40; *G.D.*, Vol. IX, 134; cf. Woodward, *op. cit.*, 30; *N.C.A.*, Vol. VI, 983.

[35] Ziemke, *op. cit.*, 109–11; Raeder, *op. cit.*, 168, 200; Halder, *Hitler als Feldherr*, 31; Derry, *op. cit.*, 230–45; Jodl, *Diary*, April 17, 1940; Warlimont, *op. cit.*, 76–79, 95–96.

creased powers in his simultaneous role as Defense Minister over the British chiefs of staff. At the same time, Hitler finally forced his no longer reluctant soldiers to attack France and the Low Countries with a superiority in strength engendered by his ability to leave only between five and thirteen low-grade German divisions nominally guarding the German rear in Poland against the U.S.S.R. Certainly the desperate Schlieffen had not gambled on a much narrower margin or for higher immediate stakes.[36]

Within a week or ten days of the breaking of the German storm in the West, astonished at the speed and extent of his own victory, Hitler was already discussing an offer to Britain of peace terms, requiring from Britain only the return of former German colonies. Whether or not this new mood of magnanimity influenced the famous halt-order on May 24 to the Panzer divisions approaching the British escape route at Dunkirk is still a matter of controversy, but there is no doubt that to his generals at this time Hitler compared the British Empire to the Roman Catholic Church as an essential element in Western stability and showed very little desire to punish the British further.[37] In any event, the bulk of the British Army on the Continent managed to make its escape across the North Sea, leaving, however, most of its essential equipment behind on the beaches of Dunkirk.

Hitler's spirit of exaltation persisted through the French campaign, and his order on June 15, following the capture of Paris, to demobilize approximately forty Army divisions in order to strengthen the German war economy reveals no definite intention on the Fuehrer's part to undertake new enterprises until his anticipated settlement with Great Britian had been achieved. Meeting with that belated and unsuccessful entrant to the war Benito Mussolini on June 18/19, Hitler

[36] Churchill, *Their Finest Hour* (Boston, 1949), 16; Poole, *loc. cit.*, 17; *N.C.A.*, Vol. X, 525; Weinberg, *op. cit.*, 98.

[37] Halder, *Hitler als Feldherr*, 16–17, 29–30; Hart, *The Other Side of the Hill*, 145; General Guenther Blumentritt, *Von Rundstedt: The Soldier and the Man* (London, 1952), 78; Jodl, *Diary*, May 20–26; L. F. Ellis, *op. cit.*, 349–52; Rear Admiral Walter Ansel, *Hitler Confronts England* (Durham, 1960), 70–85; T. Taylor, *The March of Conquest*, 231–75; Warlimont, *op. cit.*, 97–99.

further humiliated the Duce by insisting upon easy armistice terms for the French at the expense of Italy. On the other hand, the already habitual Germanophobe Count Galeazzo Ciano was filled with admiration for Hitler, whom he described as a gambler who, rather to his own amazement, having made a "big scoop," now proposed to leave the gaming table and "risk nothing more."[38]

Some months before this crowning victory, in the autumn of 1939, Hitler may well have defined his true position to an important member of his S.S., Walter Schellenberg. On that occasion, in response to a question from the Anglophile Schellenberg, Hitler professedly had said: "Originally I wanted to work together with Britain. But Britain has rejected me again and again. It is true, there is nothing worse than a family quarrel, and racially the English are in a way our relatives. . . . It's a pity that we have to be locked in this death struggle, while our real enemies in the East can sit back and wait until Europe is exhausted. That is why I do not wish to destroy Britain and never shall"—here his voice became sharp and penetrating—"but they must be made to realize, and even Churchill must be made to realize, that Germany has the right to live too. And I will fight Britain until she has come down off her high horse. The time will come when they will be ready to reach an agreement with us. That is my real aim."[39]

In the middle of June, 1940, Hitler may reasonably have believed that with the destruction of French military power in the West an agreement with Britain was finally possible, and, as he had once predicted, he would now have a completely free hand for the long-deferred realization of his deepest and fondest desire, the destruction of Bolshevik Russia in the East.[40]

---

[38] *The Ciano Diaries*, 265–66; cf. Ciano, *Diplomatic Papers*, 373; Schmidt, *op. cit.*, 172–78; Ansel, *op. cit.*, 93–95; Halder, *War Diary*, Vol. IV, 72; J. R. M. Butler, *History of the Second World War: Grand Strategy*, Vol. II: *September, 1939–June, 1941* (London, 1957), 265–66.

[39] Schellenberg, *op. cit.*, 89; cf. *Hitler's Table Talk*, 12–13.

[40] *Mein Kampf*, 183, 963–66; Hermann Rauschning, *The Revolution of Nihilism* (New York, 1939), 195–219.

"The cooperation established between the Kings of Prussia and Russia for their respective aggrandizement cannot be of long duration. Their aggrandizement, by making them close neighbors, will also make them more redoubtable in each other's eyes; it will engender jealousy between them and jealousy soon degenerates into hostility."[1] VERGENNES, to LOUIS XV, 1768

"A way of atonement is open to Germany. By combating Bolshevism, by being the bulwark against it, Germany may take the first step towards ultimate reunion with the civilized world."[2]

CHURCHILL, 1919

"With England [in alliance] alone, one's back being covered, could one begin the new Germanic invasion [of Russia]."[3]

HITLER, 1924

"I can do everything now."[4] NAPOLEON, after Tilsit

[1] John Lukacs, *The Great Powers and Eastern Europe* (Chicago, 1953), 246–47.

[2] Fritz Stern, *The Politics of Cultural Despair: A Study in the Rise of the Germanic Ideology* (New York, 1965), 273 n.; cf. Carr, *The Bolshevik Revolution*, Vol. III, 111–12, 310 n. 2.

[3] Hitler, *Mein Kampf*, 183.

[4] Eugene Tarle, *Napoleon's Invasion of Russia, 1812* (New York, 1942), 52.

CHAPTER III

Aufbau Ost

June 14–November 14, 1940

HITLER's intention to exploit in the East the advantages of the French collapse may have been divulged to Generals Rundstedt and Jodl before the end of the German campaign in the West. In any event the automatic compensations of the balance of power were already asserting themselves elsewhere.

During the second week of June, 1940, over the protests of the Army General Staff, President Roosevelt had ordered the release of more than 20 per cent of the United States Army's reserves of artillery to Britain, despite both the questionable future of that heroic nation and the U.S. neutrality legislation still officially in force. For the Soviet Union, too, during the shattering week following the fall of Paris, in the words of the indiscreet Soviet Minister to Sweden, Madame Kollontai, it was now in "the common interest of the European powers to place themselves in opposition to German imperialism. It had become evident that the German danger was far greater than had been believed."[5]

Concerned since late May about the massing of Soviet troops against Rumania, Hitler must have been in no way pleased by an open Soviet warning on June 6 telling the Italians not to intervene at this favorable moment in the

[5] *N.S.R.*, 147; cf. *N.C.A.*, Vol. VII, 926; Wheeler-Bennett, *The Nemesis of Power*, 509–10; Richard Leighton and Robert Coakley, *United States Army in World War II: The War Department; Global Logistics and Strategy, 1940–1943* (Washington, 1955), 35; Lossberg, *op. cit.*, 83–85; Warlimont, *op. cit.*, 113.

Balkans. Whether anticipated or not by Germany, the rapid Soviet seizure of control of the governments of the Baltic States between June 15 and 19 reflected Moscow's determination to take advantage of at least the tag end of the German campaign in the West. And compliments from Foreign Minister Molotov regarding the "splendid successes" of the German Army in France in no way lessened the shock when on June 23 the Soviets demanded an immediate Rumanian cession not merely of the Bessarabian province previously assigned to her by the Nazi-Soviet agreements in 1939 but also of the province of Bukovina, not specifically assigned in 1939 to the Soviet sphere of influence.[6]

Rather heavy-handed Soviet denials that the eighteen to twenty Red Army divisions sent into the Baltic States were there for the sake of threatening the Reich had to be followed by a partial Soviet backdown on the question of Bukovina, leaving the southern half of this heavily German-ethnic province to Rumania when the rest was occupied by the U.S.S.R. on June 28. Yet, as the Italian Foreign Minister, Count Ciano, noted: "The capital in which there is the greatest amount of conspiracy against German victory is Moscow. The situation had appeared quite otherwise when, in August and September [1939], the Bolsheviks signed pacts with the Nazis. At that time they didn't believe in a German triumph."[7]

More than a century earlier the Austrian Foreign Minister, then Count Metternich, had warned an anxious Czar against aggrandizing himself at the expense of small and harmless neighbors, thus destroying bulwarks of Russia's own security against Napoleon. For, in the hopeful surmise of Winston Churchill on June 27: "*If Hitler fails to beat us here, he will probably recoil eastward. Indeed, he may do this even without*

---

[6] *N.S.R.*, 148–55; cf. *T.M.W.C.*, Vol. XV, 345; Beloff, *op. cit.*, Vol. II, 322 ff.; Ribbentrop, *op. cit.*, 145 ff.

[7] *The Ciano Diaries*, 269; cf. *N.S.R.*, 156–64; *G.D.*, Vol. X, 3–58; Halder, *War Diary*, Vol. IV, 90–98; Alexander Werth, *Russia at War, 1941–1945* (London, 1964), 87 ff.; A. Philippi and F. Heim, *Der Feldzug gegen Sowjetrussland* (Stuttgart, 1962), 22–23.

trying invasion [of Great Britain], to find employment for his Army, and take the edge off the winter strain upon him."[8] The Soviets, in short, were no longer in any position to offend small neutral neighbors, let alone to manufacture new enemies.

More pessimistic than his Fuehrer, Baron von Weizsaecker, Undersecretary of the German Foreign Ministry, had concluded by June 30 that "Britain will probably need one more demonstration of our military strength before she gives in and leaves us a free hand in eastern Europe." The next day, Stalin finally received the new British Ambassador, Sir Stafford Cripps, bearing a message from Winston Churchill dealing with the threat of a German hegemony to those peripheral European Powers Great Britain and the Soviet Union. Notwithstanding his subsequent mendacious report on this encounter to the Germans, Stalin appears to have admitted to Cripps the seriousness of the German danger, but to have reiterated his intention of avoiding conflict with the Reich even if this resulted in the Soviet Union having to fight Germany single-handedly in 1941.[9]

A day later, July 2, a day on which Hitler issued a half-hearted order to prepare for the invasion of England, General Halder was instructed to start thinking about an operation against Russia in order to compel her to recognize the dominant position of Germany in Europe. On July 3, Halder recorded that the strategic question of the moment was: "England or Russia?" In the postwar analysis of one of the first planners of the subsequent operation against the U.S.S.R., Field Marshal Friedrich Paulus, it was Hitler's fear that any attempt to invade Britain, whether successful or otherwise, would inevitably militate against his chances of conducting a

---

[8] Winston Churchill, *Their Finest Hour*, 228; cf. Erno Kraehe, *Metternich's German Policy*, Vol. I: *The Contest with Napoleon, 1799–1814* (Princeton, 1963), 66, 136.

[9] Halder, *War Diary*, Vol. IV, 98–99; cf. Langer and Gleason, Vol. I, 644–49; Eric Estorick, *Stafford Cripps* (London, 1949), 257; Churchill, *Their Finest Hour*, 135–45; *N.S.R.*, 166–68; Woodward, *op. cit.*, 140–42; J. M. Gwyer, *History of the Second World War: Grand Strategy* (London, 1964), Vol. III, Part I, 51; Philippi and Heim, *op. cit.*, 27.

campaign in the East. For this reason alone, quite apart from any latent Anglophilia, the Fuehrer's overwhelming antipathy to Soviet Russia clearly outweighed his more or less perfunctory hostility to Great Britain in the decisive summer of 1940.[10]

While the brutal British attack on the now neutral French fleet at Oran on July 3 may have diminished Hitler's hopes of peace with Britain, he remained as relatively cool to the recent unsolicited offers of the Japanese, Spanish, and Vichy French to assist in his war as he was to Mussolini's efforts to enlist German approval for sundry Italian enterprises in the Mediterranean. On July 11, Hitler agreed with Grand Admiral Raeder that a cross-Channel invasion should be undertaken against Great Britain only as a last resort, and two days later the Fuehrer finally hit upon a satisfactory rationalization for his dilemma: now it appeared that it was British hopes of Soviet intervention that were sustaining her otherwise inexplicable unwillingness to make peace. Ostensibly, this distressed Hitler on the grounds that Japan and America rather than the Reich would profit from the shedding of German blood for the sake of conquering Britain and the disintegration of her empire. Actually, as Hitler's simultaneous order to slow down the current demobilization of the German Army shows, the Fuehrer's anxiety over the fate of the British Empire was chiefly a cover for his real need for an excuse to his own staff to justify an immense new campaign against the Soviet Union.[11]

Hitler's characteristically German ambivalence toward Britain was again shown when, on July 16, he coupled a direction to carry out the invasion of Britain, "if necessary," with a public appeal on July 19 before the Reichstag for an

---

[10] Halder, *War Diary*, Vol. IV, 100 ff.; cf. Walter Goerlitz, *Paulus and Stalingrad* (London, 1960), 95–96; Peter Fleming, *Invasion 1940* (London, 1957), 41 ff.; Warlimont, *op. cit.*, 106–8.

[11] Lossberg, *op. cit.*, 87, 105; Greiner, *op. cit.*, 112; Halder, *War Diary*, Vol. IV, 117; *The Ciano Diaries*, 274; Ciano, *Diplomatic Papers*, 373–77; Ansel, *op. cit.*, 121–42; Playfair, *op. cit.*, Vol. I, 225.

end of the war with the British. In this remarkable oration the Fuehrer declared that it "almost" caused him pain to destroy an empire which he had never intended to harm. He saw "no reason why this war need go on," should the British be prepared to sacrifice Winston Churchill and their share of the former German colonies.[12]

Facing the lack of British response to his peace offer as well as his own doubts regarding the "very hazardous" invasion of Britain, on July 21 Hitler disclosed his basic inclination to his principal Army subordinates. Notwithstanding the Fuehrer's admission on this occasion that there were no indications of Soviet aggressiveness against Germany, Stalin's supposed flirtation with Britain, purportedly for the sake of gaining both time and territory, was advanced by Hitler as his real reason for initiating the planning of an attack on the U.S.S.R. during this very autumn of 1940.

The next day, General Halder was informed that the Fuehrer had ordered the assembly of eighty to a hundred divisions over the next four to six weeks in order to crush the Red Army (estimated at only fifty to seventy-five good divisions) and, in addition, to penetrate the Soviet Union deeply enough to prevent Russian air raids on the Reich and allow the Luftwaffe to bomb the industries of the Urals. Among his political objectives Hitler envisaged German-dominated Baltic, White Russian, and Ukrainian states. He admitted that any such campaign this autumn would weaken his current air attack upon Britain, but he was already discussing with Grand Admiral Raeder the prospect, equally agreeable to both, of postponing an increasingly hypothetical invasion of Britain until May, 1941.[13]

During the next week, while Halder discussed the possibili-

---

[12] Hitler, *My New Order: Speeches, 1922–1941*, edited by Raoul de Roucy de Sales (New York, 1941), 837; cf. Schmidt, *op. cit.*, 185–87; Hesse, *op. cit.*, 107; William L. Shirer, *Berlin Diary, 1934–1941* (New York, 1941), 452–57.

[13] Halder, *War Diary*, Vol. IV, 126–28; cf. *F.C.G.N.*, *1940*, 81; Erich Kordt, *Wahn und Wirklichkeit* (Stuttgart, 1947), 249; Philippi and Heim, *op. cit.*, 21–27.

ties of a hundred German divisions assaulting Moscow and from this central posture conquering the Ukraine, Field Marshal Keitel persuaded the Fuehrer that it was logistically impossible to return the German Army from France in time for an autumn campaign this same year. As the younger Moltke had been forced to explain to Kaiser Wilhelm II in 1914, the deployment of several million men could not be improvised at the last minute, however necessary or favorable the political circumstances.[14]

On July 29, General Jodl broke the news of Hitler's inclination to attack Russia in 1941 to Colonel Walter Warlimont and his staff in the O.K.W. To shocked inquiries whether this attack was to take place before the defeat of England, Jodl offered the rather lame explanation that the motive of the Fuehrer was to garner more resources for the conquest of Britain by destroying the Red Army, thus purportedly releasing men and matériel for a Channel crossing in the autumn of 1941 following the completion of a Russian campaign. At last Jodl had to inform the skeptical planners of his O.K.W. staff that the fundamental intention to attack the U.S.S.R. in 1941 was no longer a matter for discussion, Hitler's initial decision having already been made. The Army High Command (O.K.H.), which would have preferred to deliver "a decisive blow" against Great Britain in the relatively safe Mediterranean theater, instead had to assign the appropriately named Brigadier General Erich Marcks to the task of the preliminary planning for a campaign in Russia in the next year.[15] At this stage Grand Admiral Raeder and his Navy were left in complete ignorance of these plans for the East.

---

[14] *N.C.A.*, Vol. V, 741, VII, 249; George E. Blau, *The German Campaign in Russia: Planning and Operations, 1940–1942* (Washington: Dept. of the Army, March, 1955), 34; Poole, *loc. cit.*, 144–45; Captain B. H. Liddell Hart, *Reputations* (London, 1928), 58; Greiner, *op. cit.*, 116–18; *T.M.W.C.*, Vol. XV, 515–17; Warlimont, *op. cit.*, 112.

[15] Blau, *Russia*, 4–5; *T.M.W.C.*, Vol. XV, 390–91; Lossberg, *op. cit.*, 105–6; Ansel, *op. cit.*, 178–81; Halder, *War Diary*, Vol. IV, 141; General Heinz Guderian, *Panzer Leader* (London, 1952), 136–38; Weinberg, *op. cit.*, 112 n. 34; Greiner, *op. cit.*, 116–17, 288–90; Warlimont, *op. cit.*, 111-12.

On July 31, meeting with Army leaders at the Berghof, Hitler, following Raeder's departure, went into his proposals for Russia in some detail. Again he justified the operation because: "*Russia is the factor on which Britain is surely betting. Something has happened in London.* The British were entirely 'down'; now they are up again."

Hitler continued:

Should Russia, however, be smashed, then Europe's last hope is extinguished. Germany is then master of Europe and the Balkans.

Decision: In the course of this contest Russia must be disposed of. Spring '41.

The quicker we smash Russia the better. Operation only makes sense if we smash the state heavily in one blow. Winning a certain amount of territory does not suffice. A standstill during the winter hazardous. Therefore better to wait, but decision definite to dispose of Russia. Necessary also because of situation on the Baltic. No use for a second Great Power on the Baltic: May '41. Five months' time for carrying out. Preferable still in this year. Can't be done, however, if it is to be carried out as a single operation.

Aim: Annihilation of Russia's vital energy. Broken down in:

First drive Kiev resting on Dnieper. Luftwaffe destroys crossings Odessa.

Second drive Baltic States in direction Moscow.

Finally convergence from north and south. Later special operation against oil area Baku. To what extent Finland and Turkey can be interested remains to be seen.

In conclusion, Hitler decided to increase the Army by some 50 divisions, thus giving him 120 divisions for his eastern campaign, while leaving 60 divisions to stand guard upon his conquests in the West. The Fuehrer took pains to observe that the more units available for Russia the better; unlike the recently concluded operation in the West, there was to be no stinting on the campaign in the East, at least by the prevailing standards of Hitler's Reich.[16]

With regard to Hitler's argument that the Soviet Union

[16] *G.D.*, Vol. X, 373–74; Halder, *War Diary*, Vol. IV, 144–45.

was the country on which Britain was mainly relying, United States Ambassador Joseph P. Kennedy expressed an equally cynical, if rather more sincere, outlook when he telegraphed the State Department from London this same July 31 as follows: "Don't let anybody make any mistake; this war, from Great Britain's point of view, is being conducted from now on with their eyes only on one place and that is the United States. Unless there is a miracle, they realize that they haven't a chance in the long run."[17] Under these circumstances, Stalin's relative caution in the summer of 1940 is as intelligible as Hitler's overconfidence concerning an eastern campaign.

On August 1, General Halder briefed General Marcks on his planning for Russia, both in emphasizing a principal push in the direction of Moscow and by pointing out the inherent logistic weaknesses of any Rumanian-based campaign against the Ukraine. Halder would always play down operations on the periphery so that these would not cripple what from the beginning was his consuming point of interest, the drive on the Soviet capital. It should be noticed that Halder's emphasis on Moscow may have been a potential contradiction to Hitler's statement of July 31 that the first and second German drives would be against the Ukraine and the Baltic States respectively, with the junction on Moscow of these two divergent campaigns scheduled for a later date.

The Marcks plan, submitted to the O.K.H. on August 5, essentially embodied Halder's views with its main objective as Moscow and only subsidiary drives upon the Ukraine and Baltic regions. Marcks envisaged the deployment of a force of 147 German divisions, organized in 5 armies, of which 3 would be north of the Pripet Marshes. The line Moscow-Leningrad was to be achieved in between 6 and 12 weeks. The final-objective line of Archangel-Gorki-Rostov was estimated to require between 9 and 17 weeks to attain, depending upon Soviet resistance. In one respect, however, the Marcks plan was to prove fairly realistic; the Red Army was gauged

[17] Langer and Gleason, *op. cit.*, Vol. I, 712.

as comprising 150 divisions available against the Germans and Finns, while Marcks estimated that the Soviets would elect to hold rather advanced positions, thus giving the German Army an opportunity to destroy the Red Army before it could retire deeply into the interior of Russia.

Immediately after the submission of his plan, General Marcks discussed it with Major General Ernst Koestring, the able German Military Attaché in Russia. Sworn to keep the plan a secret from his more Russophile superiors, such as Ambassador Schulenburg, Koestring did not agree that the capture of Moscow would be decisive in the defeat of the Red Army. From his long experience in Russia the Military Attaché believed that Soviet resources in the Urals, plus the marked Russian facility for improvising new communications, would enable them to survive the loss of their capital despite its crucial role as the communications heart of so dangerously centralized a state as the U.S.S.R. Koestring did admit, however, that it would take four years for the Red Army to recover from the impact of Stalin's purges. In time Hitler would find certain facets of this Koestring argument invaluable in his debates with the O.K.H.[18]

The first directive for the logistic preparation for operations in the Soviet Union, camouflaged under the code name of *Aufbau Ost*, was issued on August 9. Whether he appreciated its significance or not, Grand Admiral Raeder must have begun to sense the new direction of the wind when on August 13 he was informed that the Fuehrer wanted stronger fortifications and larger Army forces in northern Norway in case of a Soviet attack. The German Army, Raeder was also told, would now occupy the valuable nickel mines near Petsamo in northern Finland in the event of renewal of the Russo-Finnish conflict.[19] The operation against Petsamo would be

---

[18] Blau, *Russia*, 6–12; *N.C.A.*, Vol. V, 734; Goerlitz, *The German General Staff*, 386; Erickson, *op. cit.*, 560; Ronald Seth, *Operation Barbarossa* (London, 1964), 94–95.

[19] *F.C.G.N.*, *1940*, Part I, 83; *N.C.A.*, Vol. VI, 986; Blau, *Russia*, 12–13; *G.D.*, Vol. X, 460; Ziemke, *op. cit.*, 114–15.

code-named *Renntier*, and would employ the German 2nd Mountain Division from a new advanced base at Kirkenes in Norway on the Finnish frontier.

The next day, General Thomas, the anti-Nazi Chief of the Army War Economy and Armaments Office, received orders from the Reichmarschall Goering that Hitler intended deliveries of German war matériel to the Soviets to go on only until the spring of 1941. This "allusion," as Thomas put it, to the still highly secret future, tipped off the Army Armaments Chief to give priority to supplies designated for the innocuous-sounding *Aufbau Ost*. This was just as well, since the chances of *Sea Lion*, the alternative and competitive invasion of Britain, were meeting with more and more difficulties in the face of the Fuehrer's and Raeder's mounting disinterest and the effective opposition of the Royal Air Force.[20]

On August 18, one of Goering's agents obtained Finnish permission to ship Luftwaffe supplies and personnel across Finland to northern Norway and at the same time the Reich was granted an option on the Finnish nickel mines now desired by the Soviet Union. In return the Finns were to receive war matériel from Germany. Desiring an ally to cover his northern flank, Hitler was already moving from the simple idea of defending Finland against any new Soviet threat toward an intention to reward the Finns with all of eastern Karelia if they would aid Germany in cutting the vital Soviet railway to Western supplies at Murmansk.[21]

The same tendency toward a Nazi intervention against the U.S.S.R. on the German flank in the Balkans was likewise becoming apparent in mid-August, 1940, if initially only as a means of keeping the Soviets and Italians out of this region. Needing an excuse with Ribbentrop, whose whole foreign policy was still based upon the Nazi-Soviet Pact of 1939, Hitler now alleged that should the Soviets renew their demands on Rumania, the ensuing threat to the Rumanian oil

---

[20] *N.C.A.*, Vol. IV, 1082; cf. Weinberg, *op. cit.*, 118–20.

[21] Mannerheim, *op. cit.*, 399–400; Ziemke, *op. cit.*, 115–22; Halder, *War Diary*, Vol. IV, 128–58.

fields at Ploesti would render the Reich dependent upon Stalin's good will for the further conduct of the war.[22]

As it turned out, the Hungarian desire to seize Transylvania from the weakened Rumanians afforded Hitler just as good a reason for German intervention. He explained to Count Ciano on August 28 that a war between Hungary and Rumania would necessarily interfere with Axis imports of Rumanian petroleum; moreover, such a conflict might evoke another Soviet advance in the Balkans "as far as circumstances permitted." In view of these possibilities, the Fuehrer had already reinforced his garrison in Poland by twelve new German divisions, including two armored divisions in the south well located for a rapid movement into Rumania in the event of a Soviet advance in that direction. The seriousness of Hitler's intention to thwart any Soviet action may be better seen in his simultaneous order stripping the supposedly imminent invasion of Britain of several hundred vital transport aircraft to reinforce a Rumanian operation more rapidly, should one prove necessary. For Hitler, *Sea Lion* could always wait.[23]

Following an Axis-imposed *Diktat* splitting Transylvania between Hungary and Rumania, on August 31 the German Ambassador in Moscow received the thankless task of explaining this unilateral Axis settlement to the slighted and outraged Soviets. Ribbentrop's argument that since the U.S.S.R. had already satisfied her demands on Rumania, she could not object to a German guarantee of the frontiers of the remainder of that unfortunate state, was probably the best line left open to him under the circumstances.

Nevertheless, replying to Ambassador Schulenburg for the Soviet Government the next day, Foreign Minister Molotov complained that Germany had violated Article 3 of its pact with the U.S.S.R., an article which provided for mutual consultation between the two powers before either took

[22] Ribbentrop, *op. cit.*, 145–47; *The Ciano Diaries*, 285; M. L. Simoni, *Berlino Ambasciata d'Italia, 1939–1943* (Rome, 1946), 161–62.

[23] *G.D.*, Vol. X, 539–70; cf. Ronald Wheatley, *Operation Sea Lion: German Plans for the Invasion of England, 1939–1942* (Oxford, 1958), 144 n. 3.

action in the area of eastern Europe. Ribbentrop thereupon rejoined that the Soviets had occupied territory in June, 1940, previously assigned to the Reich and that he had also received very short notice of the Russian occupation of Bessarabia and northern Bukovina in spite of the many ethnic Germans living in these two provinces. But it is perfectly clear that the fat was in the fire. As Count Ciano recorded somewhat later with his accustomed malice: "The Russian dream [had] vanished forever" following the drastic Nazi intervention in Rumania.[24]

The lack of illusion manifested hereafter, at least on the German Army side, is shown in a new directive issued on September 6 by General Jodl in the O.K.W. to Admiral Canaris' Abwehr (Army Counter-Intelligence). From now on it is essentially the Russians whom Hitler was trying to deceive, although, of course, he would continue to employ rationalizations for his actions to his own people as occasion demanded. Jodl's directive read:

> The Eastern territory will be manned more strongly in the weeks to come. . . . These regroupings must not create the impression in Russia that we are preparing an offensive in the East. On the other hand, Russia will realize that strong and highly-trained German troops are stationed in the Government-General [of Poland], in the Eastern provinces [of the Reich], and in the Protectorate [of Bohemia and Moravia]. She should draw the conclusion that we can at any time protect our interests, especially in the Balkans, with strong forces against any seizures by her. . . .
>
> The impression is to be created that the center of the troop concentrations is in the Southern part of the Government-General [of Poland], in the [Czech] Protectorate, and in Austria, and that the concentrations in the North are relatively unimportant.[25]

At the same time, the diversion of Luftwaffe attacks from British airfields to the night bombing of London reflected the

---

[24] *The Ciano Diaries*, 293; cf. *N.S.R.*, 178–84; *G.D.*, Vol. X, 570–90, Vol. XI, 1–10.

[25] *N.C.A.*, Vol. I, 796–97, Vol. III, 849–50; *T.M.W.C.*, Vol. III, 331–32.

increasingly obvious futility of *Sea Lion*, and Hermann Goering, for once, joined Grand Admiral Raeder in a desperate attempt to deflect the Fuehrer's eyes south, equally far away from the disappointments of the Channel or from the competitive service threat of an intrinsically Army theater of war, such as the Soviet Union. On September 6, Raeder recommended to Hitler, in the event that *Sea Lion* did not take place, the seizure of Gibraltar, Suez, and even the Canary Islands, as part of the war against Britain before the United States could intervene on her behalf.[26]

Although Hitler expressed the same approval regarding Raeder's far-flung Mediterranean schemes as he had previously demonstrated with regard to *Sea Lion*, the *Aufbau Ost* plan—which the new Deputy Chief of Staff of the Army, Major General Friedrich Paulus, was assigned to revise in the beginning of September—embodied the more bona fide interests and concerns of the Fuehrer. An expert in the use of armored formations, Paulus had been in agreement with his immediate superior, General Halder, in favoring operations against Great Britain in the Middle East in preference to adding the Soviet Union as a new burden to the Reich's strategic problems.

At the same time, as a check on the new assignment for Paulus, General Jodl had his own subordinates in the O.K.W. draw up an independent plan for an operation against the U.S.S.R. The O.K.W. plan, submitted to Jodl on September 19, stressed drives upon both Moscow and Leningrad to the exclusion of an assault on the Ukraine, without, however, definitely deciding in favor of either of the two northern operations. The Finns, also, in this preliminary O.K.W. conception, were to push directly for Leningrad instead of toward the Murmansk railway.[27]

With the waning of the chances for the invasion of Britain,

---

[26] *F.C.G.N., 1940,* Part II, 17–20; Denis Richards, *Royal Air Force, 1939–1945,* Vol. I: *The Fight at Odds* (London, 1953), 190; Bullock, *op. cit.,* 550–52.
[27] Blau, *Russia,* 12–13; Goerlitz, *Paulus,* 24–27.

Hitler's rage against the Soviets grew stronger. On September 14, he told Halder: "We did not 'bleed to death,' as Russia anticipated. We have achieved the greatest victories without great cost. . . . Russia's calculations went wrong." On the seventeenth, *Sea Lion* was indefinitely postponed, useful chiefly thereafter as a cover to conceal the real action to the East—again the Napoleonic analogy, here of 1805.[28]

The Germans now heard of a Red Army buildup in western Russia, totaling 120 divisions, and General Halder concluded that the Soviets probably expected a German attack in 1941. Anti-Nazi propaganda was reintroduced into the Russian military forces at the same time. But the re-equipping of the Red Army and Air Force with up-to-date tanks and planes lagged, and time was lacking to reintroduce the large independent tank units which German experience had so triumphantly vindicated in Poland and France. Finally Stalin was reluctant to drop entirely the purge of experienced senior Army officers, despite the lack of staff-college graduates as commanders of half the infantry regiments of the Red Army as a consequence of his earlier purges. Thus, in view of the desperate shortage of Soviet regimental officers, the heroic efforts of the new Defense Commissar, Marshal Simyeon Timoshenko, to reorganize and retrain the Red Army for the fast-moving type of warfare introduced by the Germans would require more time than Hitler would provide.[29]

Still other untoward consequences of Stalin's errors began to take on substance as German interest moved south and east. The new Fascist dictator of Rumania, General Ion Antonescu, informed the Germans that the Reich could and should attack the Soviet Union with Rumania's eager assistance in this endeavor. Although loath to disclose his intentions at this stage to his eventually favorite ruler in the Balkans, Hitler agreed to send a large German training mis-

---

[28] Halder, *War Diary*, Vol. IV, 193; cf. Ansel, *op. cit.*, 293–300.

[29] Erickson, *op. cit.*, 557–60; Halder, *War Diary*, Vol. IV, 213; *N.C.A.*, Vol. VI, 987; Labedz, *loc. cit.*, 87.

sion to prepare the Rumanian Army for a future role along the lines indicated by Antonescu, a training mission, moreover, with the immediate function of protecting the Ploesti oil fields against destruction or Soviet occupation. At the same time, on September 22, the German Foreign Ministry signed an agreement with Finland permitting the movement of all types of German Army and Air Force units across Finland. The incredulous Russians were informed that these German units were simply in the process of transit to Norway, an explanation which hardly served to save Soviet faces, let alone to assuage their anxieties.[30]

In mid-September, Spain recalled herself to Hitler's attention in the form of Generalissimo Franco's brother-in-law, Serrano Suñer. The Fuehrer agreed with Suñer that limited German aid to seize Gibraltar would padlock the Strait against the British, but Spain's enormous territorial ambitions in French North Africa dismayed Hitler because of the probability that the French would go over to General De Gaulle as a consequence. Spanish economic demands also irritated the Fuehrer in view of Germany's previous aid and the current needs of his war economy.

Similarly, Admiral Raeder's sly attempt on September 26 to draw out the Fuehrer on the subject of an eastern campaign by stressing the importance of the Mediterranean as an alternative met only with Hitler's bland agreement that the situation in the Mediterranean should be settled during the winter months. Nonetheless, as Raeder sourly confessed several years later, in practice Hitler remained so firmly resolved upon a surprise attack upon the U.S.S.R. that henceforth most of his glittering Mediterranean opportunities would reflect this basic determination.[31]

[30] *Germany and Her Allies in World War II: A Record of Axis Collaboration Problems* (Historical Division, H.Q. U.S. Army Europe, undated), Part I, 30; *N.S.R.*, 188 ff.; *N.C.A.*, Vol. VI, 877; *G.D.*, Vol. XI, 136–46.

[31] *N.C.A.*, Vol. VI, 988; *G.D.*, Vol. XI, 83–214; *F.C.G.N.*, *1940*, Part II, 20–24; *U.S. Dept. of State Bulletin* (Washington), March 17, 1946, 415–16; Ciano, *Diplomatic Papers*, 389–97; Serrano Suñer, *Entre les Pyrénées et Gibraltar* (Geneva, 1948), 150–62.

At a time when the intensity of Hitler's eastern bent was gradually penetrating the more peripheral members of the Fuehrer's entourage, the new course of American policy away from neutrality and in favor of Great Britain was becoming ever more openly apparent. With the United States' exchange of fifty destroyers in return for leases on British bases in the Western Hemisphere, the Axis partners could no longer afford to ignore the increasingly spectacular impact of Roosevelt's diplomacy upon British morale than they could gainsay the more covert resistance of the Soviet Union to their expanding designs. The Nazi leaders decided to answer the aroused American and surreptitious Soviet reactions in kind—that is, with an explicit warning to the United States and an implicit one to the U.S.S.R.

Officially, then, the Tripartite Pact of September 27, 1940, was not directed against the Soviet Union, as Ribbentrop explained to the suspicious Soviet Foreign Minister in his now customary last-minute telegram. Technically, this agreement between Germany, Italy, and Japan was undertaken to dissuade the United States from entering the war in either the Atlantic or Pacific by a threat of tripartite action everywhere against any such American action anywhere. In its actual effect, however, the Germans appear to have outsmarted themselves, since on the one hand the Pact enhanced the Japanese desire to move south against the Anglo-Saxon powers in the Pacific and on the other accentuated the Soviet and Japanese eagerness for a more reassuring relation between themselves in order to protect their common frontier while they were engaged elsewhere. Of course, at this stage, still an advocate of his 1939 pact with the U.S.S.R., Ribbentrop may have proposed this policy as an indirect method of committing the Axis more firmly to the existing war with the West rather than to a still avoidable conflict with Russia, but in the long run the influence of the Tripartite Pact was to be disastrous for Hitler's Russian campaign. Japan was now precipitated in the wrong direction for the Nazi Fuehrer's eventual grand strategy, and the Soviet Asian back door was being barred with the active assistance of Ribbentrop's misdirected diplomacy.[32]

On October 4, Hitler met Mussolini at Brenner Pass to explain, as he had already to General Halder, that Stalin's calculations regarding the length and nature of the war had gone wrong. After Ribbentrop had hastened to point out that the Russians were afraid of Germany and would not start anything unpleasant on their own accord, Hitler expressed doubt whether the Soviets could be successfully diverted away from Europe in the direction of India or the Indian Ocean. In any case Hitler believed that the Russians would not represent any problem for the Reich, even if the worst came to the worst. "Bolshevism," declaimed the Fuehrer, "is the doctrine of people who are lowest in the scale of civilization."[33]

A week later the German Foreign Ministry was given the futile job of explaining to the Soviets the unconcealed arrival of German troops in Rumania on the implausible grounds that these troops were to guard the Ploesti oil fields against the British. No longer polite, Foreign Minister Molotov refused to admit to any British threat to Rumania, saying that England was too busy fighting for her life to intervene in the remote regions of the lower Danube. Indeed, so sour was official Soviet policy becoming at this juncture that the British began to pluck up hope of a warmer rapport for themselves with the obviously frightened Russians.

Ribbentrop was at last up against it. Evidently desperate to shore up at least the façade of his crumbling pact with the Soviets, on October 13 he addressed a long apologia for German policy to Stalin. In the course of this *de facto* appeal for a restoration of their earlier relationship, the German Foreign Minister invited Molotov to Berlin for consultation with the Fuehrer concerning a lasting reconciliation of future

---

[32] *N.S.R.*, 195 ff.; *G.D.*, Vol. XI, 187–205; *F.C.G.N.*, *1940*, Part II, 19–20; F. C. Jones, *Japan's New Order in East Asia: Its Rise and Fall, 1937–1945* (London, 1954), chap. vii.

[33] *The Ciano Diaries*, 298–99; cf. *G.D.*, Vol. XI, 249.

Soviet policy with the policies of the three signatories to the Tripartite Pact.[34]

Almost as aghast as Stalin over the unexpected German intervention in Rumania, on October 12 Mussolini told Ciano that he was going to attack Greece to re-establish his competitive equilibrium with the Reich in the Balkans. The Germanophobe Italian Foreign Minister was delighted, notwithstanding the hostility of the chiefs of the Italian Army, Navy, and Air Force to this venture. Il Duce did not inform the Germans of the date of his proposed operation, but Hitler seems to have been pretty well aware of its imminence through his own Intelligence Service. Contrary to his subsequent *ex post facto* rationalization after the Greek expedition had gone badly, the Fuehrer on this occasion did not want to "cross" the Duce and made no open objection to an Italian action which was to contribute materially to the delay of his attack on Russia in the next year.[35]

On October 23, before matters came to a head with Italy over the Balkans, Hitler saw Generalissimo Francisco Franco at Hendaye on the Spanish frontier. Distrustful of playing another Godoy to the Nazi Bonaparte, Franco naturally reflected little interest in Hitler's opinion that the great problem in North Africa was to keep it from defecting to De Gaulle. Any such German policy would militate against Spanish colonial claims, and consequently Franco refused a commitment to enter the war or to seize Gibraltar with German aid in January, 1941, as Hitler proposed.

Leaving Hendaye in a huff, Hitler and the tactless Ribbentrop proceeded the next day to Montoire in France to try to persuade Marshal Philippe Pétain to support the Reich against Britain, if possible to the point of war. This Nazi attempt to induce another Latin nation to tie down the British in the Mediterranean having likewise failed, Hitler returned to Ger-

---

[34] *G.D.*, Vol. XI, 276–97; *N.S.R.*, 206–13; Ribbentrop, *op. cit.*, 148 ff.; Langer and Gleason, *op. cit.*, Vol. II: *The Undeclared War, 1940–1941* (New York, 1953), 123–32.

[35] Weizsaecker, *op. cit.*, 244; cf. *The Ciano Diaries*, 300–2, *G.D.*, Vol. XI, 324–52; Playfair, *op. cit.*, Vol. I, 225–26; Greiner, *op. cit.*, 182–85.

many to receive the yet more disagreeable word that the Italians were about to assault Greece.[36]

Arriving in Florence on October 28 in a last-minute effort to hold up Mussolini's invasion of Greece, Hitler was greeted at the railway station by a smug Duce with the news that the Italian Army in Albania had crossed the Greek frontier two hours earlier. Considering his chagrin over Mussolini's revenge, Hitler controlled himself surprisingly well; publicly he was always to make allowances for his jealous ally across the Alps. After discussing German assistance for the eventual occupation of Crete, Hitler asserted that, unlike his alliance with Italy, his partnership with Russia was based purely upon expediency. As "mistrustful" of Stalin as he believed the latter to be of him, the German dictator was still willing to receive Soviet Foreign Minister Molotov in the supposed hope of deflecting Russia away from Finland and the Bosporus toward India. Stalin, Hitler professed, was "shrewd" enough to appreciate the need for halting any further Soviet expansion in Europe.[37]

The next day, however, on October 29, Hitler's deeper and more sincere intentions vis-à-vis the Soviets emerged in the plan—now graduated to a full-fledged status under the more conventional code name of *Ost Fall* ("East Case")—submitted by General Paulus to Halder. The Soviet military assets, as listed by Paulus in this O.K.H. plan, included a slight superiority in strength: about 170 Red Army divisions in western Russia against a proposed 145 German divisions, apart from the Finns and Rumanians. The vast extent of Russian terrain, involving a rapid German advance of approximately five to six hundred miles over an increasingly poor road network within the five months, May to October, 1941, also would impose upon the invading army the terrible pressure of time from the very onset of the campaign.

Among the German advantages anticipated by the O.K.H.

---

[36] *G.D.*, Vol. XI, 371–90; Schmidt, *op. cit.*, 193–99; Lossberg, *op. cit.*, 95–98.
[37] *G.D.*, Vol. XI, 417–20; *N.C.A.*, Vol. I, 636–37; Schmidt, *op. cit.*, 199–200; Ciano, *Diplomatic Papers*, 401–4; Greiner, *op. cit.*, 186.

were the higher training and leadership of the Wehrmacht, at least some degree of surprise, the unpopularity of the Soviet regime in the Baltic, Ukraine, and Caucasus regions, and the supposedly low morale of the Red Army, as revealed by the purges and the Finnish campaign. Paulus stressed that substantial Soviet forces had to be cut off from retreat as near to the frontier as possible and compelled to fight on reverse fronts without being permitted to retire upon their own communications. The O.K.H. still upheld Halder's emphasis upon a principal thrust toward Moscow so as to achieve a military victory over the Red Army as soon as possible; the economic benefits of the Caucasus and the Ukraine could wait as ripe plums to be easily plucked following the defeat of the Red Army.[38]

During the first week of November, the stubbornness with which Hitler adhered to his Russian plans, despite the difficulties caused by the undesired Italian gambol in the Balkans, became more apparent than ever. After declaring on November 4 that "Russia remains the great problem in Europe; everything must be done to be prepared for the great reckoning," Hitler went on to plan a brief campaign in the Balkans for the next spring in order to aid Italy and thwart any British bombing of the Ploesti oil fields from Greece before he undertook the invasion of the Soviet Union. But in this plan, soon to be code-named *Marita*, the Fuehrer warned no action against Turkey, let alone Suez, was to be contemplated because any such operation would be too lengthy and would have to wait for the autumn of 1941 following the completion of his Russian campaign.[39]

By November 12, in his War Directive No. 18, the Fuehrer summed up his complex and somewhat dissonant planning for the spring of 1941. The French role was seen as purely

---

[38] Blau, *Russia,* 14–16; Goerlitz, *Paulus,* 28; *N.C.A.*, Vol. VI, 989.

[39] *F.C.G.N., 1940,* Part II, 32–33; Halder, *War Diary,* Vol. V, 7; *T.M.W.C.*, Vol. XV, 391–92, Vol. XXXIV, 691; Lossberg, *op. cit.*, 98–99; Andreas Hillgruber, *Hitler, Koenig Carol und Marschall Antonescu, 1938–1944* (Wiesbaden, 1954), 112–13.

defensive—to guard France's colonies against Churchill's occasional incursions upon the African periphery. In Operation *Felix*, Spain was still scheduled to drive the British from Gibraltar and the Strait with German aid. A German armored division was now contemplated to assist Mussolini's stalled campaign in Libya against Egypt; while for the Balkans Hitler was willing to commit ten divisions to occupy northern Greece, but not Yugoslavia or Turkey, as a guard against the British. It should be kept in mind that German troops in the Balkans were fairly well situated for a rapid movement northward into the Ukraine, after having employed a limited operation in Greece as a most convenient cover for moving to the southeast in the first place.

Concerning the fifth and most important point of Directive No. 18 Hitler minced no words, whatever confusion may have subsequently eventuated on this score. Following a statement that political conversations were about to open with the Soviets, Hitler affirmed that "regardless of what results these discussions will have, all preparations for the East which already have been orally ordered, are to be continued. Directives on this will follow as soon as the outline of the Army's plan of operations is submitted to, and approved by me."[40]

On the same day as War Directive No. 18, Foreign Minister Molotov arrived in Berlin at Ribbentrop's invitation. The German Foreign Minister opened the epochal conversations with Molotov with his usual statement that Britain was already beaten, although inconsistently Ribbentrop went on to assure the Soviet emissary that Britain could not land on the Continent again, even if backed by the United States. The Reich Foreign Minister then modestly assumed some credit for having helped in directing Japan away from the Soviet Union toward the south, a particularly effective cover plan in the short run for concealing Hitler's real intentions toward Russia,

---

[40] *G.D.*, Vol. XI, 527–31; *N.C.A.*, Vol. I, 797–98, Vol. III, 403–7; cf. Weinberg, *op. cit.*, 137–39; *Hitler's War Directives*, 38–43.

if a disastrous diversion of strength in the long run. Then, as with Napoleon's innuendoes to more than one Czar, Ribbentrop suggested a similar Soviet movement in the direction of a southern sea.

Molotov coolly inquired regarding which sea the Germans had in mind; it soon transpired the Russian was thinking of the Black Sea and the Germans of the Arabian. Nevertheless, as with Talleyrand, Ribbentrop was willing to grant freer Russian use of the Dardanelles Strait to the Mediterranean than the Montreux Convention had permitted in the past. Beyond that the German Foreign Minister refused to commit himself at the expense of the Turks. Later on this day, Hitler reiterated this same theme to Molotov, only to meet with a direct question concerning Finland's continued status within the Soviet sphere of interest by the terms of the 1939 Pact as well as a query concerning the possible role of the U.S.S.R. in the new Tripartite Pact.

The next day, November 13, the going got tougher between Molotov and the Fuehrer, whom Molotov persisted in treating as an equal. The whole of the borderland disputes between Germany and Russia was discussed, with particular emphasis upon the presence of German troops in Finland, not to mention the almost equally offensive German guarantee to Rumania. Hitler evaded positive answers on these issues and also on the question of a similar Soviet guarantee to Bulgaria. In his turn, Molotov manifested little response to the Fuehrer's enthusiasm for parceling out the "bankrupt estate" of the British Empire. As he subsequently told Ribbentrop, the Germans were "assuming that the war against England had actually been won." And for the Germans, even Ribbentrop was forced to break out with a protest against the overly close questioning on the part of the relentless Soviet statesman.

The following day, November 14, Franz Halder was informed that his civilian superiors remained sure that the Soviets had no intention of breaking with the Reich at this juncture and, in fact, still desired to enter the Tripartite Pact, albeit on their own terms.[41] For Hitler the situation was most satisfactory; Stalin was to be lulled as long as possible with Ribbentrop's irrelevant diplomatic ploys, while under the cover of rescuing a properly chastened Duce, the Fuehrer was rapidly completing his preparations for fulfilling what he would subsequently describe as "the ambition of my life and the *raison d'être* of National Socialism—the destruction of Bolshevism."[42]

---

[41] *G.D.*, Vol. XI, 533–70; *N.S.R.*, 247–54; cf. *N.C.A.*, Vol. VI, 989–90; Schmidt, *op. cit.*, 214–15; Poole, *loc. cit.*, 147–50; Halder, *War Diary*, Vol. V, 24–26.

[42] *The Testament of Adolf Hitler: The Hitler-Bormann Documents, February–April, 1945*, edited by François Genoud (London, 1961), 34.

"You are just like the Russians; you can see nothing but threats, nothing but war, whereas this is just a disposition of forces necessary to make England sue for terms before six months have passed."[1] NAPOLEON, to CAULAINCOURT, 1811

"It is not negotiations with Trotsky, nor the Reichstag's Peace Resolution . . . but the advances of the unbroken military might of Germany which has brought us peace in the East."[2]
STRESEMANN, February, 1918

"If a war were to begin, we would not sit with idle hands. We will have to come out, but to come out after the others. And we shall come out for the purpose of throwing the decisive weight into the scales of fate."[3] STALIN, 1925

"We don't know what strength we shall find once we have really had to push open the door to the East."[4]
HITLER, to RIBBENTROP, April, 1941

[1] General de Caulaincourt, *With Napoleon in Russia* (New York, 1935), 23.
[2] Wheeler-Bennett, *The Forgotten Peace*, 263.
[3] Nathan Leites, *A Study of Bolshevism* (Glencoe, 1953), 509. See Stalin's recitation of this theme again on March 10, 1939: *G.D.*, Vol. VI, 1–3.
[4] Ribbentrop, *op. cit.*, 153; cf. Dorpalen, *op. cit.*, 503.

CHAPTER IV

Barbarossa

November 14, 1940—June 22, 1941

FOLLOWING the somber departure of the Soviet Foreign Commission from Berlin, Grand Admiral Raeder, on November 14, recorded of his conference with Hitler that day: "Fuehrer is still inclined to instigate the conflict with Russia. Naval Supreme Commander recommends putting it off until the time after the victory over England since there is heavy strain on German Forces and the end of warfare is not in sight. According to the opinion of the Naval Supreme Commander, Russia will not press for a conflict within the next year, since she is in the process of building up her Navy with Germany's help . . . thus, during these years she continues to be dependent upon German assistance."

Not put off by Hitler's increasingly open disinterest in his discussions of the Mediterranean, Raeder dwelt upon the recent series of Italian military fiascos at the hands of the British and Greeks as a further cause for a German offensive toward the Middle East.[5] Hermann Goering likewise advised Hitler to concede everything to the Russians except the Baltic region, asserting that they could not attack Germany before 1942. Hitler's reply revealed his real motives when, according to Goering, he said: "My Army is free now. Only the Navy and Air Forces are engaged with England. It is necessary to

[5] *N.C.A.*, Vol. II, 860; cf. *F.C.G.N.*, *1940*, Part II, 50–52; Greiner, *op. cit.*, 318–19.

strike while it is possible to do so. I want to destroy the Russian armed forces before they become dangerous."[6]

Four days later, on November 18, Hitler made clear to Serrano Suñer, once again in Berlin, his own conception of who was to take care of the Mediterranean during the next year. By entering the war as soon as possible, the Fuehrer informed the dubious Suñer, the easier would be Spain's success against Britain. Hardly reassured by the unhappy example of Italy, Suñer took refuge in his usual demands for heavy economic assistance and French North African territory, the latter an aspiration already rejected by Hitler as likely to embroil German forces in regions in which the Fuehrer still preferred to let others carry on the burden of the war against Britain. To revert to the Napoleonic analogy, Hitler could not muster much enthusiasm over the prospect of complementing his embryonic Russian campaign with what Bonaparte had termed "the Spanish ulcer."

And on November 20—in a letter in which Mussolini was to admit he had been rapped over the knuckles like a schoolboy—Hitler reiterated that Spain must be immediately persuaded to enter the war. Complaining about the difficult season during which the Italians had launched their campaign against Greece, Hitler warned that the German air and transport forces which he was rushing to Italy's aid must be returned north by May 1 and, therefore, that the conquest of Egypt would have to wait for the autumn of 1941. No word was vouchsafed to the Duce concerning the real employment the Reich was to make of such an intense concentration of its strength in the north during the ensuing summer.[7] As with Raeder, France, and Spain, Hitler preferred to have the Duce pursue the clever deception of an offensive war against England as long as possible.

To return to a blunter level of reality, on November 23

---

[6] Poole, *op. cit.*, 145–50.

[7] *G.D.*, Vol. XI, 598–606; Suñer, *op. cit.*, 205 ff.; *Les Lettres Secrètes*, 81–92; *The Ciano Diaries*, 314.

Hitler offered both the Finns and Rumanians promises of full German support against any new Soviet demands, while on the twenty-fourth Hitler told General Halder that Germany could seize the Dardanelles "only after Russia has been beaten."[8] At this stage Hitler and Halder were in complete agreement regarding the possibility of an effective attack on Egypt by no other means than the safe overland route from the Balkans through Turkey and Syria.

If potential German allies against the U.S.S.R. were to be relieved of their anxieties concerning a new Nazi deal with Moscow, on November 25 Foreign Minister Molotov spelled out to the Germans the Soviet terms for a renewal of their 1939 rapport. Molotov's requests included the immediate withdrawal of German troops from Finland and the conclusion of a Soviet mutual assistance pact with Bulgaria, as well as granting Russia a military base within Turkey on the Dardanelles. Further Soviet claims on Japan and Persia were, of course, less offensive to Hitler,[9] but any argument that by this period a Soviet movement across his shortest land route to the Middle East was evoking Hitler's plans to attack the U.S.S.R. is absurd. On the contrary, Hitler had long intended to invade Russia in any case, and the Soviet Caucasus afforded the Germans almost as convenient a land route to the oil fields of the Middle East as did the Balkans and Turkey, with the additional advantage of a great deal of Caucasian oil on the way.

On December 5, General Halder submitted the O.K.H. plan for Russia to Hitler for his unofficial approval. The Fuehrer agreed with the Army plan's stated purpose of crushing the Red Army as close to the frontier as possible in a campaign now scheduled to commence about May 15, but he reiterated that "Moscow was of no great importance" as

[8] Halder, *War Diary*, Vol. V, 34; cf. *G.D.*, Vol. XI, 662–68; Ziemke, *op. cit.*, 117; George Blau, *The German Campaign in the Balkans: Spring, 1941* (Washington, 1953), 5–10.

[9] *N.S.R.*, 255–59; *G.D.*, Vol. XI, 647 ff. If the Russians were really as alarmed over the prospects of a joint German-Japanese attack on the U.S.S.R. in the next spring as German diplomatic sources believed at this time, Soviet policy appears extraordinarily rash vis-à-vis the Reich. *G.D.*, Vol. XI, 941–43.

the goal for the strong central German Army Group. In the opinion of both Hitler and his Army planners, 130 to 140 divisions seemed adequate for the operation.

In spite of the conclusion from several war games held by General Paulus of the O.K.H. to the effect that the expanding funnel of the Russian theater of operations would demand more German troops than the 130 to 140 divisions so far envisaged, like Paulus, the O.K.H. itself, remained optimistic. The conclusion of the O.K.W. planners that Germany was already too short of oil to engage in any large-scale campaign for indefinite objectives similarly had no chastening effect upon Jodl or Keitel. By mid-December, opinion in the Army High Command was that the Soviet Union would be defeated in a campaign not exceeding eight to ten weeks in duration.[10] When the professionals of the previously pessimistic Army were entertaining such inconsistent conclusions, it is not surprising that a Fuehrer determined upon the campaign in any event was waxing more confident all the time.

Meanwhile, Hitler's autumnal hopes that Spain would enter the war—and thus padlock the Strait of Gibraltar against any Allied or Gaullist incursions—had begun to fade. Although he sent the enigmatic and probably hostile Admiral Canaris to Madrid in a final plea to Franco to participate in Operation *Felix* against Gibraltar, by December 11 Hitler recognized that, whether from economic conditions bordering upon famine or for other reasons, Spanish assistance could no longer be awaited. Instead, in War Directive No. 19, he made plans for a speedy seizure of unoccupied France (Operation *Attila*) if the Allies should strike Northwest Africa, and on December 13 in War Directive No. 20 (Operation *Marita*), Hitler replaced *Felix* with a large-scale German campaign in

---

[10] Halder, *War Diary*, Vol. 5, 55–56; cf. Greiner, *op. cit.*, 322–29; *N.C.A.*, Vol. IV, 374–75; Goerlitz, *Paulus*, 28, 99–105; Blau, *Russia*, 20; Vice Admiral Kurt Assmann, "The Battle for Moscow: Turning Point of the War," *Foreign Affairs* (New York), January, 1950, 310; Warlimont, *op. cit.*, 114–15, 137.

the Balkans, ostensibly to relieve Il Duce.[11] Unlike *Felix*, *Marita* would take place in eastern Europe and, Halder currently estimated, would delay the proposed attack on the U.S.S.R. in May, 1941, only by about two weeks.

Operation *Marita* involved the assembly of up to twenty-four German divisions in Rumania, divisions most of which were scheduled to traverse Bulgaria and drive the British out of all the Greek mainland and immediately adjacent islands during the spring of 1941. As Hitler explained to his intimates in the next month, the German buildup in Rumania served the dual purpose of safeguarding that country and Bulgaria from the Russians as well as procuring a convenient base for a land operation against Greece. Nevertheless, the estimate of no more than a fortnight's delay which this still somewhat limited campaign in the Balkans had already imposed upon the subsequent Russian assault was entirely dependent upon the presumed neutrality of Yugoslavia and Turkey, two rather bold assumptions of which only one would be upheld in practice.[12]

Three days later, on December 16, the O.K.W. staff presented to General Jodl their revised version of the O.K.H. plan for the Russian assault. Following some discussion between Generals Jodl and Warlimont regarding the dangers of a two-front war, on December 17 the O.K.H.-O.K.W. plan was handed up to Hitler for his final approval. After the Fuehrer had raised the advance upon the Baltic States and Leningrad to first priority, leaving the attack upon Moscow to later, the Commander in Chief of the Army, Field Marshal von Brauchitsch, objected that such a delay would result in the failure to destroy the heavy concentration of the Russian forces east of Bialystok on the central German front. Hitler

---

[11] *G.D.*, Vol. XI, 782–853; Suñer, *op. cit.*, 224–25; *F.C.G.N.*, *1940*, Part I, 5–7; Halder, *War Diary*, Vol. V, 60–69; Hillgruber, *op. cit.*, 115–16; *Hitler's War Directives*, 46–48.

[12] *G.D.*, Vol. XI, 867–86; *N.C.A.*, Vol. IV, 101–2, and "Opinion and Judgment," 41; Playfair, *op. cit.*, Vol. I, 348–49; Lossberg, *op. cit.*, 108–9.

angrily turned down this argument of Brauchitsch's, claiming that it was based upon outdated considerations. It is possible, as General Adolf Heusinger has suggested, that the Fuehrer feared to travel in precisely the same path as Napoleon—Moscow may already have represented something sinister and threatening to him.[13]

Without further ado, on December 18 in War Directive No. 21, Adolf Hitler promulgated the formal plan for his grand assault upon the Soviet Union in the next spring. Under its final code name of *Barbarossa*, this decisive war plan embodied, as its opening sentence made apparent, Hitler's most decisive error during the Second World War. Symbolically, Friedrich I of the Hohenstaufens, popularly known as Barbarossa (Red Beard), had been the great German emperor of the Middle Ages. He had died from drowning in the course of leading all the Germanic peoples on a vast, if somewhat amorphous, expedition to the East. To this day—or so the myth has it—the corpse of Barbarossa is supposed to be slumbering in the Harz Mountains along the Soviet-N.A.T.O. demarcation line in the very center of the Reich, waiting for the proper moment to rise again and lead the hosts of Europe on a new crusade against the infidel East.

The directive for Operation *Barbarossa*, signed by Hitler, read as follows:

The German Wehrmacht must be prepared to crush *Soviet Russia in a quick campaign* even before the conclusion of the war against England. For this purpose the *Army* will have to employ all available units, with the reservation that the occupied territories must be secured against surprises.

For the *Luftwaffe* it will be a matter of releasing such strong forces for the eastern campaign in support of the Army that a quick completion of the ground operations can be counted on and that damage to eastern German territory by enemy air attacks will be as slight as possible. This concentration of the main

[13] Blau, *Russia*, 21–22; Greiner, *op. cit.*, 329–31; for the war-game studies, and incorrect assumptions of Soviet inferiority in armor and artillery upon which these games were based, see Goerlitz, *Paulus*, 99–120.

effort in the East is limited by the requirement that the entire combat and armament area dominated by us must remain adequately protected against enemy air attacks and that the offensive operations against England, particularly her supply lines, must not be permitted to break down.

The main effort of the *Navy* will remain unequivocally directed against England even during an eastern campaign.

I shall order the *concentration* against Soviet Russia possibly 8 weeks before the intended beginning of operations.

Preparations requiring more time to get under way are to be started now—if this has not yet been done—and are to be completed by May 15, 1941.

It is of decisive importance, however, that the intention to attack does not become discernible.

The preparations of the High Commands are to be made on the following basis:

I. *General Purpose:*

The mass of the Russian *Army* in western Russia is to be destroyed in daring operations, by driving forward deep armored wedges, and the retreat of units capable of combat into the vastness of Russian territory is to be prevented.

In quick pursuit a line is then to be reached from which the Russian Air Force will no longer be able to attack the territory of the German Reich. The ultimate objective of the operation is to establish a cover against Asiatic Russia from the general line Volga-Archangel. Then, in case of necessity, the last industrial area left to Russia in the Urals can be eliminated by the Luftwaffe.

In the course of these operations the Russian *Baltic Sea Fleet* will quickly lose its bases and thus will no longer be able to fight.

Effective intervention by the Russian *Air Force* is to be prevented by powerful blows at the very beginning of the operation.

II. *Probable Allies and Their Tasks:*

1. On the wings of our operation the active participation of *Rumania* and *Finland* in the war against Soviet Russia is to be expected....

2. It will be the task of *Rumania* to support with selected forces the attack of the German southern wing, at least in its beginnings; to pin the enemy down where German forces are not committed; and otherwise to render auxiliary service in the rear area.

3. *Finland* will cover the concentration of the German *North Group* (parts of the XXI Group) withdrawn from Norway and will operate jointly with it. Besides, Finland will be assigned the task of eliminating Hango.

4. It may be expected that *Swedish* railroads and highways will be available for the concentration of the German North Group, from the start of operations at the latest.

III. *Direction of Operations:*

A. *Army* (hereby approving the plans presented to me):

In the zone of operations divided by the Pripet Marshes into a southern and northern sector, the main effort will be made *north* of this area. Two Army Groups will be provided here.

The southern group of these two Army Groups—the center of the entire front—will be given the task of annihilating the forces of the enemy in White Russia by advancing from the region around and north of Warsaw with especially strong armored and motorized units. The possibility of switching strong mobile units to the north must thereby be created in order, in cooperation with the Northern Army Group operating from East Prussia in the general direction of Leningrad, to annihilate the enemy forces fighting in the Baltic area. Only after having accomplished this most important task, which must be followed by the occupation of Leningrad and Kronstadt, are the offensive operations aimed at the occupation of the important traffic and armament center of Moscow to be pursued.

Only a surprisingly fast collapse of Russian resistance could justify aiming at both objectives simultaneously.

The most important assignment of the XXI Group, even during the eastern operations, will still be the protection of Norway. The additional forces available are to be employed in the north (mountain corps), first to protect the Petsamo region and its ore mines as well as the Arctic Highway, and then to advance jointly with Finnish forces against the Murmansk railroad and stop the supply of the Murmansk region by land.

Whether such an operation with *rather strong* German forces (two or three divisions) can be conducted from the area of and south of Rovaniemi depends upon Sweden's willingness to make the railroads available for such a concentration.

The main body of the Finnish Army will be assigned the task, in coordination with the advance of the German northern wing, of pinning down as strong Russian forces as possible by attacking west of or on both sides of Lake Ladoga, and of seizing Hango.

By converging operations with strong wings, the Army Group committed *south* of the Pripet Marshes is to aim at the complete destruction west of the Dnieper of the Russian forces standing in the Ukraine. The *main effort* for this is to be made from the area of Lublin in the general direction of Kiev, while the forces in Rumania, crossing the lower Prut, form a widely separated enveloping arm. The Rumanian Army will have the task of pinning down the Russian forces in between.

Once the battles south and north of the Pripet Marshes have been fought, we should aim to achieve as part of the pursuit operation:

in the south, the prompt seizure of the economically important Donets Basin;

in the north, rapid arrival at Moscow.

The capture of this city means a decisive success politically and economically and, beyond that, the elimination of the most important railway center.

B. *Luftwaffe:*

Its task will be to paralyze and to eliminate as far as possible the intervention of the Russian Air Force and also to support the Army at its main points of effort, particularly those of Army Group Center and, on the main wing, of Army Group South. . . .

In order to concentrate all forces against the enemy Air Force and to give direct support to the Army the armament industry will not be attacked during the main operations. Only after the completion of the mobile operations may such attacks be considered—primarily against the Ural region.

C. *Navy:*

The Navy's role against Soviet Russia is, while safeguarding our own coast, to prevent an escape of enemy naval units from the Baltic Sea. As the Russian Baltic Sea fleet, once we have reached Leningrad, will be deprived of its last base and will then be in a hopeless situation, any larger naval operations are to be avoided before that time . . .

IV. All orders to be issued by the Commanders in Chief on the basis of this directive must clearly indicate that they are *precautionary measures* for the possibility that Russia should change her present attitude toward us. The number of officers to be assigned to the preparatory work at an early date is to be kept as small as possible; additional personnel should be briefed as late as possible and only to the extent required for the activity of each individual. Otherwise, through the discovery of our preparations—the date of their execution has not even been fixed—there is danger that most serious political and military disadvantages may arise . . .[14]

Apart from many doubts within the O.K.W. concerning this fundamental decision, General Halder's hesitations on *Barbarossa* were also to boil over within the privacy of his war diary during the next month. For example, on January 28 Halder would observe: "The purpose [of *Barbarossa*] is not clear. We do not hit the British that way. Our economic potential will not be substantially improved [by it]." Moreover, Halder feared that if Italy collapsed, and the British created a new southern front against Germany in the Mediterranean while the Reich was still tied up in Russia, "a bad situation" would be made "much worse."[15]

Nevertheless, although Halder was pessimistic as regards Italy, his confidence with respect to defeating the Soviet Union was immense. Furthermore, the confidence of his mili-

[14] *G.D.*, Vol. XI, 899–903, taken from the files of the Naval War Staff, has been cited as the fullest recent version of this famous directive; cf. *N.S.R.*, 260–64; *T.M.W.C.*, Vol. XXVI, 47–52; Lossberg, *op. cit.*, 112–16; *Hitler's War Directives*, 48–52; *N.C.A.*, Vol. III, 407–9.

[15] Halder, *War Diary*, Vol. V, 98–100; cf. *T.M.W.C.*, Vol. XV, 519–20.

tary concerning the purely physical problem of disposing of the U.S.S.R. was the only consideration Hitler deemed at all relevant. With good reason he had long since held in contempt the cautious, but rather ingenuous though obsolete, political judgments of his military advisors.

Whatever may be said about the overoptimism of the Fuehrer and of the military services most concerned with *Barbarossa*, for Grand Admiral Raeder, at least, the now-decided-upon campaign in Russia represented the downfall of all his hopes for a peripheral maritime war against Great Britain and her still more vulnerable empire and shipping lanes. Two days after Christmas, Raeder lamented that the threat to Britain in Egypt and the Middle East had now been eliminated in one stroke. To Hitler the German naval chief courageously declared that the strict concentration of the entire war effort against England as Germany's main enemy was the most urgent need of the hour. Hitler replied to Raeder's objections to a Russian campaign before the completion of the war against Britain with the claim that he could no longer wait to deal with the renewed Soviet threat to the Balkans.

Of course, *Marita* alone could have coped with any possible Soviet threat to the Balkans, but to defend the necessity for *Barbarossa*, Hitler naturally used any argument suitable to the occasion. A day later, December 28, Raeder had to accept the transfer of top production priorities to the German Army, although a face-saving clause was added to the effect that the previous emphasis upon the naval and air war against Great Britain would not be reduced. From Raeder's own arguments with Hitler on December 27, however, he knew that such priorities could not be maintained, given the needs of an all-out campaign in the East. Doubtless the German naval chief consoled himself with the more sincere assurances of his Fuehrer that, following the swift completion of *Barbarossa*, he would regain his lost priorities for the German Navy.

In this almost final attempt to deflect Hitler from his

eastern campaign, Raeder may have rendered the Soviets at least one other service. With the exuberance of overoptimism, the normally cautious planners of the German war economy took such detailed measures for the cutback in Army priorities in favor of the Navy and Air Force, now scheduled for the autumn of 1941, that many of the most crucial of these cutbacks would automatically take place at that later date regardless of the small detail that the Soviet Union had not yet been conquered in October, 1941.[16]

Hitler's growing confusion over the dazzling array of opportunities open to him came to a head in a general meeting of his military advisors held on the Obersalzberg on January 8/9, 1941. After admitting to Grand Admiral Raeder that it was vital that Italy should not collapse, the Fuehrer got down to the more serious business at hand. Stalin, declared Hitler, if intelligent and shrewd, was also a cold-blooded blackmailer who would repudiate any treaty to suit his own advantage. More to the point, Hitler asserted that a German victory was incompatible with Soviet ideology and that Russia must be smashed before the British had rebuilt their army up to forty or fifty divisions by 1943. Hitler added that another reason for taking immediate action against the Soviets was that the Red Army was still "like a headless Colossus with feet of clay," but that it should not be underestimated for the future, when better leadership and up-to-date matériel could make predictions dangerous. For the present, Hitler concluded that all of Germany's reserves would be needed to defeat Russia.[17]

Less perceptively, Hitler now made another concession to Raeder's maritime concept of the war, a concept essentially incompatible with his own Continental outlook. Japan, Hitler said, "should be given a free hand" against Singapore, notwithstanding the risk that the United States might then take "drastic steps," evidently in Raeder's hopeful interpretation,

---

[16] *F.C.G.N., 1940*, Part II, 68–72; Lossberg, *op. cit.*, 107; Klein, *op. cit.*, 189–91.
[17] Warlimont, *op. cit.*, 140.

exclusively against Japan.[18] Hitler's developing grand strategy for the war, namely that the Italians and Japanese should tie down the British and Americans respectively until he had disposed of Russia, had much to be said for it in terms of timing, always Hitler's particular forte. Happily for his enemies, the Fuehrer was taken in by the overwhelming consensus of professional opinion that the Reich had the capacity to defeat the U.S.S.R. in 1941, and if necessary in 1942, long before the Western Powers could mobilize effective strength and come to the Soviets' aid.

Two days later, on January 11, in War Directive No. 22, Hitler ordered the O.K.H. to send a "blocking unit" to reinforce the Italians in Libya with German armor. This unit, eventually to expand into a formidable corps under Major General Erwin Rommel, was, however, not yet envisaged as capable of taking an offensive against the British across the Mediterranean, a dangerous and a difficult supply route for the Germans so long as the Mediterranean remained a secondary theater of war for the Reich. *Marita* in the Balkans, securely sustained by land routes, was still seen as the basic offensive operation against the British pending completion of *Barbarossa* in the autumn of 1941.[19]

During the next week of January, the Soviets publicly and privately protested to the Germans concerning the latter's anticipated entry into Bulgaria, a country now defined by the Russians as essential to the interests of Soviet security. In practice, Ribbentrop denied this Soviet interest in his reply on January 21, announcing that the Germans would transverse Bulgaria anyway, should it prove necessary to drive the British out of Greece. Hitler's statements to Mussolini at the same time were almost as blunt, the Fuehrer particularly warning against the supposed Soviet threat to the Balkans. Hitler qualified these hints to his Italian partner regarding the future

---

[18] *F.C.G.N.*, *1941*, Part I, 1–13; Halder, *War Diary*, Vol. V, 83–85; *N.C.A.*, Vol. VI, 992; *G.D.*, Vol. XI, 1057–60; Greiner, *op. cit.*, 340–45, 374–76.

[19] *N.C.A.*, Vol. III, 413–15; *G.D.*, Vol. XI, 1073–75.

by adding that, while the "shrewd and cautious" Stalin lived, the Soviets would not take action against Germany, but that with his unknown successors, the situation would become more problematic.[20]

Although the British Ambassador to Russia, Sir Stafford Cripps, remained pessimistic concerning the future course of Soviet policy, on January 21 the United States State Department, informed through an intelligence leak of the German plans to attack Russia, lifted its so-called moral embargo on the shipment of American war matériel to the U.S.S.R. Unfortunately the needs of the American defense program, and those of its new allies under the Lend-Lease Act, precluded major shipments to Russia, even of such relatively abundant items as aviation gasoline in this period of comparative maritime impunity. As a result, in the summer of 1941, what survived of the Soviet Air Force would be further enervated because of a chronic shortage of fuel.[21]

On the last day of January, as his operational plans for *Barbarossa* were about the crystallize, in a public *cri de cœur* in the Berlin Sportspalast, Hitler demanded: "Does England think I have an inferiority complex with regard to her? . . . I have offered Britain my hand again and again. It was the very essence of my program to come to an understanding with her."[22] Four days later, on February 3, 1941, his disappointment with Great Britain somewhat assuaged by his plans for the East, Hitler gave his approval to the detailed O.K.H. plan for Aufmarschanweisung *Barbarossa.*

Even before Hitler's formal approval of the *Barbarossa* operational plan, on February 2 Field Marshal Fedor von Bock, slated as commander of the presumably decisive Army Group Center, had asked the Fuehrer how the Russians could be compelled to seek peace, although Bock expressed his confidence in the achievement of a military victory in the event

---

[20] *G.D.*, Vol. XI, 1122–56; cf. *N.C.A.*, Vol. VI, 939–46, 993; *N.S.R.*, 268–74; Greiner, *op. cit.*, 346–49.

[21] Langer and Gleason, Vol. II, 335–40; Mannerheim, *op. cit.*, 374.

[22] Hitler, *My New Order*, 914.

the Red Army chose to fight near the frontier. Hitler replied that if the seizure of Moscow, Leningrad, and the Ukraine did not force the Russians to sue for terms, he would advance to the Urals. Reflecting his customary intoxication with technology, Hitler concluded the conversation by asserting: "In any event . . . our war production is equal to any demand. We have such an abundance of matériel that we had to reconvert some of our war plants."[23] The difference between the overconfidence of the Fuehrer and that of his generals was that his was far more universal, not to say damaging.

The next day, February 3, in a conference of the chiefs of both the O.K.W. and the Army, Hitler was briefed by the Army Chief of Staff, General Halder, on the *Barbarossa* operations plan. Halder opened the discussion by stating that the German Army was so superior to the Red Army in quality that this would outweigh an estimated Soviet quantitative superiority of 3 or 4 to 1 in armored strength, let alone in the 125 Soviet, as against 104 German, infantry and cavalry divisions currently estimated as available for *Barbarossa*. Of course, at this stage none of the Germans had heard of the new Soviet T-34 and KV tanks.

Halder then explained that the return of the six German armored divisions allocated to *Marita* in time for *Barbarossa* depended upon the attitude of Turkey. At this juncture Hitler broke in to assure his audience that there would be no danger from the Turks, thus freeing the German Army from any serious anxiety in the Balkans after the British had been expelled from Greece.

In further discussion, Hitler and Halder both displayed doubts concerning the chances of surrounding all of the Soviet forces in the west before the latter could effect a retreat. The Fuehrer, however, continued to emphasize advances on the flanks as opposed to the overwhelming thrust in the center favored by Halder as a means of destroying the Red Army as quickly as possible. It would seem that in common with

[23] Blau, *Russia*, 30.

many rulers of keen political insight, Hitler was confusing his policy aims, such as conquering the Baltic States and establishing a land route via Leningrad to Finland, with the very different needs of an effective strategic plan for the military defeat of the Soviet Union.

In conclusion, Hitler grandiloquently declared that when *Barbarossa* was finally unveiled, "the world will hold its breath and make no comment," while the Soviets would collapse "like a soap bubble." For the Mediterranean, Hitler admitted that the Duce had to be given support, since the loss of North Africa would enable the British to "hold a pistol to Italy's head" and force her to seek peace.[24]

As an important adjunct to the German plan of attack, discussions with the Finnish General Staff had been initiated in December, and by January 30, in Operation *Silberfuchs*, the Germans were contemplating the employment of three and a half of their divisions from Norway to cut the Murmansk railway and, if possible, to seize the vital Russian supply port itself. This operation was heavily dependent upon obtaining transit rights from neutral Sweden, as well as upon the last-minute mobilization of the principal Finnish forces in the south near Lake Ladoga in order to avoid alerting the Russians. It goes without saying that the capture of Murmansk was one of the few objectives of the eastern campaign accepted by the German Navy with much enthusiasm.[25]

---

[24] *N.C.A.*, Vol. III, 626–33; *T.M.W.C.*, Vol. XXVI, 392–99; cf. Manstein, *Lost Victories*, 175–78; Halder, *Hitler als Feldherr*, 22–24; Philippi and Heim, *op. cit.*, 45; Kordt, *op. cit.*, 305–6; Goerlitz, *The German General Staff*, 388–90; Greiner, *op. cit.*, 350–60; Blau, *Russia*, 26 ff. The German armored divisions available at this time for *Barbarossa*, numbering seventeen, included about 3,300 tanks, against the current German estimate of approximately 10,000 Russian tanks. Against the advice of his experts on armor, in part for the sake of a better bluff, Hitler had insisted upon doubling the number of his Panzer divisions without increasing their over-all strength in tanks. Hart, *The Other Side of the Hill*, 41, 91–92; Guderian, *Panzer Leader*, 143–44; *The Red Army*, chap. x. The estimated fifteen Soviet divisions on the Finnish frontier are excluded from the figures cited in Halder's précis. Goerlitz, *Paulus*, 104 n. 1.

[25] Ziemke, *op. cit.*, 124–27; *N.C.A.*, Vol. VI, 993; *G.D.*, Vol. XI, 1231, Vol. XII, 122–26; Lossberg, *op. cit.*, 114; Greiner, *op. cit.*, 354.

As a cover for *Barbarossa*, what the naval staff called the "greatest undertaking of deception in the history of war" was set up over the next three months. Not merely would *Barbarossa* continue to be described as purely a precautionary measure against a possible Soviet attack, but also both the actually intended *Marita* and the long since moribund *Sea Lion* operations, the latter now ostensibly revivified for the spring of 1941, were to be used as elaborate ploys to divert attention from the proposed Russian campaign.[26]

Another casualty of *Barbarossa* not even dignified with the status of a cover plan was that special baby of Admiral Raeder's, if not of Admiral Canaris', Operation *Felix*. Since the artillery and troops reserved for this operation against Gibraltar were now urgently required in the East for *Marita-Barbarossa*, Hitler accepted his frustration by the Spaniards with unusual grace. But his annoyance crept out in a complaint to Franco on February 6 to the effect that "the closing of the Straits would have changed the Mediterranean situation in one stroke." Still more important to the Fuehrer, however, were the implications of his warning to Franco that time lost in war often could not be regained; time lost for *Barbarossa*, that is, since there was still no particular cause for haste in seizing Gibraltar.[27]

The Nazi Fuehrer may have at last recognized that what he termed the long Spanish rigmarole was about played out for the moment. Perhaps, as his Napoleonic mentor had remarked to Caulaincourt during his retreat from Moscow, "it would have been better to have wound up the war in Spain before embarking on this Russian expedition–though there is much room for discussion on the point."[28] On the other hand, Hitler had little reason to spread himself still thinner in southern

---

[26] *N.C.A.*, Vol. VI, 848, 994; cf. Lossberg, *op. cit.*, 116–18; Greiner, *op. cit.*, 151; Wheatley, *op. cit.*, 97–98.

[27] *The Spanish Government and the Axis* (Washington: Dept. of State, March, 1946), 28–33; *G.D.*, Vol. XII, 36–42; cf. *N.C.A.*, Vol. I, 801; Greiner, *op. cit.*, 171.

[28] Caulaincourt, *op. cit.*, 302; cf. *Les Lettres Secrètes*, 115–16.

and western Europe in early 1941 when he needed as many resources as possible for the East; he could always take care of Spanish procrastination later on when his Army was free of the Russian incubus.

In fact, even without Spain, Hitler's ambitions were already vaulting so far over German capacities by this February of 1941 that on the seventeenth of the month he asked the O.K.W. to draw up plans for the invasion of India from Afghanistan for the sake of an eventual meeting with the Japanese. On February 18, Grand Admiral Raeder made another effort in behalf of the Mediterranean, insisting upon the occupation of that efficient British submarine base, Malta, athwart the main Axis convoy lane to Africa, before the *Barbarossa* operation. Hitler turned Raeder down, decreeing that, as with Spain, all such operations in the Mediterranean had to wait until the autumn of 1941.[29]

So determined now was Hitler for his Russian assault that on February 17 he told General Halder that so "stunning" were the latest intelligence reports on the growth of the Soviet Air Force that a conflict with Russia was "inevitable." Furthermore, Hitler reasserted, once the war against England was finished, he would no longer "be able to rouse the German people to a fight against Russia; consequently Russia would have to be disposed of first."[30] As we have seen, where justifications for *Barbarossa* were concerned, any argument would serve Hitler's purpose.

On February 22, Ambassador Schulenburg in Moscow was ordered to bare the Reich's teeth in no uncertain manner; he was to inform the Russians that in Rumania there were already 680,000 German troops, probably an overestimate but a figure well designed to discourage Soviet counteraction beyond the purely verbal. On February 27, Molotov was told that Bulgaria would accede to the Tripartite Pact, and on March 1 came the anticipated Soviet protest. It was perfectly

29 Blau, *Russia*, 37; *N.C.A.*, Vol. VI, 994, and "Supplement B," 1108.
30 Halder, *War Diary*, Vol. V, 117.

clear to all concerned that the Balkan door to the Dardanelles had been slammed shut against the Russians, following upon the German barriers raised in Rumania and Finland in the previous autumn.[31]

Complementing the German movement into Rumania was an agreement with Bulgaria allowing the Wehrmacht to enter that country at the end of February. As a result, the Greek Government finally gave in to the injudicious British offers of troops, and despite second thoughts among the British military, Winston Churchill and his War Cabinet called off General Sir Archibald Wavell's promising offensive in Libya in order to bring succor to the Greeks.[32]

If in the middle of February the Spanish card appeared to be useless pending the completion of *Barbarossa*, the possibility of diverting the Americans from the still exposed entrance of the Mediterranean at Gibraltar toward the Pacific tempted Foreign Minister Ribbentrop more and more. In no way desirous of *Barbarossa*, Ribbentrop may have hopefully imagined that by spurring the already eager Japanese Government in the direction of Singapore, he might also influence the Fuehrer in a manner favorable to re-emphasizing the war against Ribbentrop's particular enemy, Great Britain. What the Reich Foreign Minister did not grasp during his gauche attempts to tie the Americans down in the Pacific was that the secretive Japanese not merely were contemplating what he wanted but, indeed, were already planning such an inflammatory attack upon the United States Navy at Pearl Harbor that they would thereby resolve the Roosevelt Administration's problem of how to proceed more effectively against all of the Axis partners, including Germany herself.

Abetted in this dangerous game of a global diversionary strategy by Grand Admiral Raeder, Ribbentrop's maneuvers culminated in Hitler's War Directive No. 24 of March 5

[31] *N.S.R.*, 274–79; *G.D.*, Vol. XII, 126–216.

[32] *G.D.*, Vol. XII, 99–100; Woodward, *op. cit.*, 133 ff.; J. Kennedy, *op. cit.*, chap. xi; Churchill, *The Grand Alliance*, 64 ff.; Playfair, *op. cit.*, Vol. I, 374 ff.; Blau, *Balkans*, 17 ff.; Butler, *op. cit.*, Vol. II, chap. xix.

regarding collaboration with Japan. "The common aim" of the war for the Axis was stressed as forcing Britain to her knees before the United States could fully participate. Although *Barbarossa* was seen as a great advantage to the Japanese in securing their northern flank against Russia and thereby releasing the Japanese Army against Singapore in late 1941, Hitler, contrary to the wish of Raeder, would allow no hint of his Russian plans to reach the Japanese.[33] In time the distrustful Fuehrer would learn that Oriental as well as European allies could reciprocate his own style of insulting deception, particularly when misled on fundamental issues by the Third Reich until almost the last moment.

Meanwhile, in early March, a small British commando raid on the Lofoten Islands off northern Norway alarmed Hitler to such an extent that, saying Norway represented the best British target available once his *Barbarossa* campaign commenced, the Fuehrer canceled his earlier orders for the movement of 40 per cent of his Norwegian garrison to the operation against the Russians in northern Finland. As a result, to the great disappointment of the German Navy, the planned assault against the vital Soviet supply port of Murmansk was curtailed to the point of impracticality—although, if granted transit rights by Sweden, a weaker offensive might still be mounted. Already the British were directly aiding the Soviet Union, although at this stage neither at a Soviet request nor of their own deliberate intention.

As another fringe benefit for the Soviets of Hitler's excessive reaction to this minor British raid, the Army of Norway was transferred in its offensive Finnish role from the jurisdiction of the O.K.H. (Headquarters of the Army) to that of the O.K.W., thus placing Hitler's personal headquarters directly in charge of both the defensive Norwegian and offensive Finnish theaters of war. All this might have been very fine from the Fuehrer's political point of view, but for the O.K.H.,

---

[33] *G.D.*, Vol. XII, 219–20; *N.C.A.*, Vol. I, 847–49, Vol. IV, 469–75, Vol. VI, 966–95; cf. Raeder, *op. cit.*, 219; Ballantine, *loc. cit.*, 660; Greiner, *op. cit.*, 376–78; *Hitler's War Directives*, 58–59.

solely responsible for the principal Russian theater of war under *Barbarossa*, the reconciliation of the direction of common operations against Leningrad from Finland and the Baltic States with the Finnish theater no longer under its operational control, was to prove difficult, to say the least.[34]

Further indicative of Hitler's acute personal interest in matters pertaining to the East, on March 13 a supplement to the *Barbarossa* order was sent out by the O.K.W. transferring all anticipated conquests of Soviet territory upon the cessation of hostilities from the jurisdiction of the Army to three civilian administrators directly responsible to the Fuehrer. Still more ominous for the unfortunate residents of these prospective German colonies—e.g., the Baltic States, White Russia and the Ukraine—Reichsfuehrer S.S. Heinrich Himmler was to exercise authority independent of the civilian administration in preparing these eastern regions to reap the fullest benefits of Nazi liberation. It is possible that Himmler may have already expressed the opinion that an essential purpose of the *Barbarossa* campaign was the extermination of some thirty million Slavs.[35]

Hitler's increasingly overt intentions regarding the fate of the Soviet Union were manifested to General Halder on March 17, when he said that "the ideological ties holding together the Russian peoples are not yet strong enough and the nation would break up once the [Communist] functionaries are eliminated." The Ruthenians, or Ukrainians formerly in Poland, Hitler felt, accurately enough as it turned out, "will welcome us with open arms." The Soviet Ukrainians from before 1939 and the Don Cossacks were less certain to accept the Reich, so "the intelligentsia put in by Stalin must be exterminated" *in toto* for the sake of creating several Socialist republics isolated from all Soviet influences.[36]

Hitler repeated these views in an address he gave to his

[34] Ziemke, *op. cit.*, 127–28; *N.C.A.*, Vol. VI, 995; Halder, *War Diary*, Vol. VI, 26–27; Greiner, *op. cit.*, 361–68.

[35] *T.M.W.C.*, Vol. IV, 482; Lossberg, *op. cit.*, 119; Greiner, *op. cit.*, 369–70; Warlimont, *op. cit.*, 148–60.

[36] Halder, *War Diary*, Vol. VI, 29.

principal commanders on March 30. After conceding the Soviet numerical supremacy in tanks, Hitler asserted that most of these were obsolete, a point confirmed by recent official Soviet sources. Getting down to the policy objectives to be upheld by the German Army in the forthcoming campaign, the Fuehrer declaimed: "The war against Russia cannot be conducted in a knightly fashion." Unlike the more gentlemanly conflicts in the West, in the East it was "a struggle of ideologies and social differences and will have to be conducted with unprecedented, unmerciful, and unrelenting harshness. All officers will have to rid themselves of obsolete ideologies. I know that the necessity for such means of waging war is beyond the comprehension of you Generals, but I cannot change my orders and I insist absolutely that my orders will be executed without contradiction." To ensure that there could be no evasion of his intentions, Hitler then declared that all captured Soviet political commissars should be promptly killed, if necessary by the German Army itself.

Following the departure of this self-proclaimed Attila, his outraged generals turned to the Commander in Chief of the Army, Field Marshal von Brauchitsch, to express their shock over this attempt by their Fuehrer to implicate them in his more barbarous schemes. The weak Brauchitsch temporized, and with the aid of Halder and the Army group commanders involved, may have alleviated considerably the application of the order for the execution of political commissars. Of course, to the Soviet commissars, as to the several other rapidly expanding categories to whom this order would soon come to apply, it made little difference whether they died under S.S. or German Army bullets, but for the German military, still operating under the more Christian ethics of earlier eras, Hitler's new-found candor was as embarrassing as it was repugnant. Illusions regarding their own virtue are necessary to most men and to soldiers more than most.[37]

[37] *N.C.A.*, Vol. VIII, 645 ff.; cf. Halder, *War Diary*, Vol. VI, 41–42; *T.M.W.C.*, Vol. XXI, 32–40; Alexander Dallin, *German Rule in Russia, 1941–1945* (London, 1957), 30; Lossberg, *op. cit.*, 118–20; Greiner, *op. cit.*, 370–73; Warlimont, *op. cit.*, 160–70; Philippi and Heim, *op. cit.*, 50–51.

In this same month that Hitler unveiled his intentions to his generals, the United States Government officially informed the Soviet Union of the *Barbarossa* plan, the existence of which the Americans had learned through an intelligence leak as early as January, 1941. Although Stalin's reactions to this early American warning are not yet known, in the forthcoming months when informed again of the impending German attack both by Winston Churchill and by his own Intelligence Service, he would dismiss such warnings as a British provocation. At least on April 10 a secret alert was sent out to the vital Soviet West Front in White Russia. Probably the explanation for his conduct which Stalin would offer Lord Beaverbrook later in the year has as much truth in it as any: namely, that he expected war, but had hoped to gain another six months or so by various expedients.

At any rate, during March and April the Red Army gradually increased its frontier garrisons and resumed the building of fortifications in the recently acquired Baltic regions. Unfortunately, the Soviet Government or the Army Command seemed unable to decide whether to abandon entirely the dismantled fortifications of the once strong Dnieper River line and to take up more advanced positions in the new conquests in the West. As a consequence, its troop concentrations were not firmly seated within any operative defensive positions throughout the fateful spring of 1941. For that matter, as postwar Soviet admissions have revealed, the Red Army did not yet admit the necessity for any doctrine for a general defensive against a superior enemy.[38]

---

[38] *Foreign Relations of the United States, 1941*, Vol. I, 712–13; Winston Churchill, *The Second World War*, Vol. IV, *The Hinge of Fate* (New York, 1950), 493; Erickson, *op. cit.*, 566–77; Gallagher, *Soviet History*, 160–61; Khrushchev, *op. cit.*, 536–37; Langer and Gleason, *op. cit.*, Vol. II, 337–42; General Alexei Markoff, "How Russia Almost Lost the War," *Saturday Evening Post* (Philadelphia), May 13, 1950, 175 ff.; For the inadequacies of Soviet Military Intelligence since Stalin's purge, see David Dallin, *Soviet Espionage* (New Haven, 1956), 134–48, 194–211. For the somewhat absurd efforts of the once-burnt-twice-shy British Ambassador to Moscow, Sir Stafford Cripps, to stall on delivering Churchill's warnings to Stalin, see Churchill, *The Grand Alliance*, 354–61; Woodward, *op. cit.*, 147–49; Estorick, *op. cit.*, 241–70; Gwyer, *op. cit.*, 81; Werth, *op. cit.*, 276–77.

Even before the Serbian officer coup of March 27 against Yugoslav participation in the Tripartite Pact, Hitler had been watering down the southern component of Operation *Barbarossa* on behalf of extending and strengthening *Marita* against the British Army, now at last disembarking in Greece. In War Directive No. 20, issued on March 22, Hitler ordered that the Twelfth German Army be employed to occupy the whole of Greece and thus no longer be available for an early armored thrust from Rumania into the Ukraine in accord with the dictates of the original *Barbarossa* operational plan. The Italians were also requested to tie down as many British troops in North Africa as possible.

Taking off from this most tenuous authorization, the new German corps commander in Africa, Erwin Rommel, decided on March 24 to jump the gun and exploit the British lack of preparations for a defensive in the Libyan Desert. To the disgust of his cautious and far more continently-inclined superior, General Franz Halder, Rommel, with a tactical panache which the world would learn to respect, promptly pushed the British back to the Egyptian border almost before anybody knew what was happening. To be sure, this premature German action had the effect of slowing down the unwary British movement into Hitler's more dangerous trap in Greece, but it so established Rommel's reputation that hereafter he would become a perennial problem and annoyance for an Army General Staff about to become utterly embroiled in the ever more insistent demands of *Barbarossa*.[39]

Hitler reacted violently to the unexpected Serbian officer coup of March 27, primarily, it would appear, because this new development threatened to throw his already complicated series of expedients reconciling *Marita* with *Barbarossa* completely off balance. Already short of time due to the recent extension of *Marita* to southern Greece, the sudden need on

---

[39] *G.D.*, Vol. XII, 338–42; Blau, *Russia*, 34–35; Halder, *Hitler als Feldherr*, 33–34; *The Rommel Papers*, edited by B. H. Liddell Hart (London, 1953), 111–21; Warlimont, *op. cit.*, 141–42; Philippi and Heim, *op. cit.*, 49.

March 27 to improvise an emergency operation against Yugoslavia resulted in Hitler's immediate recognition in War Directive No. 25 that *Barbarossa* would have to be postponed "up to four weeks." Although heavy rains in Poland may have helped in delaying the overture of *Barbarossa* still another ten days, there is little doubt that Hitler's excessive anxiety concerning a recrudescence of the Allied First World War front at Salonika had contributed to this postponement of *Barbarossa* until late June, 1941.[40]

The Fuehrer's fears concerning the Balkans were further whetted when he learned on April 5 that the Soviet Government was about to sign a nonaggression pact with Yugoslavia, clearly an act of calculated provocation which precipitated a decision on the part of the infuriated Nazi dictator to attack Yugoslavia the very next day. In a desperate gesture designed to achieve what subsequent British rationalizations similarly professed to have done, the Russians evidently hoped to entangle the Germans in the mountainous Balkans throughout the spring of 1941. Given Hitler's traditional Austrian paranoia regarding this region, to some extent they succeeded, since the date for *Barbarossa* was now tentatively pushed back to June 22, or five and a half weeks after the original target date of May 15.[41]

Hitler's savage and swiftly successful invasion of Yugoslavia and Greece brought about an equally speedy Soviet retreat into a revival of politics designed to placate the Reich. On April 10, the German Navy diarist noted that a state of emergency in the U.S.S.R. had been declared, involving increased military preparations for all units on Russia's western front. Within another fortnight the Germans were receiving

---

[40] *G.D.*, Vol. XII, 372–96; cf. *N.C.A.*, Vol. IV, 275–79, and Vol. VI, 938–39; Lossberg, *op. cit.*, 110–12; Greiner, *op. cit.*, 382–83; *Hitler's War Directives*, 60–62.

[41] *G.D.*, Vol. XII, 451–76; *N.S.R.*, 316–70; *Foreign Relations of the United States, 1941*, Vol. I, 135 ff.; Fitzroy Maclean, *The Heretic: The Life and Times of Josip Broz-Tito* (New York, 1957), 81–82; Butler, *op. cit.*, Vol. II, 540–41; Blau, *Balkans*, 150; *The Memoirs of Anthony Eden: The Reckoning* (Boston, 1965), 266–76.

well-authenticated rumors from Moscow that a German attack was now expected, with the startling, if somewhat less accurate, information from their Naval Attaché that the British Ambassador, Sir Stafford Cripps, had predicted the precise day of their assault as June 22, 1941.[42]

It was under the influence of this Balkan imbroglio that the famous trip to Europe of Yosuke Matsuoka, Foreign Minister of Japan, took place. Paralleled in this same spring by the simultaneous conclusion of the Anglo-American military staff planners in Washington to emphasize action against the European Axis regardless of what the Japanese might do, Matsuoka's epochal voyage was presumably designed from the beginning to free Japan's hands from any commitments to the Axis for the sake of an independent Japanese offensive in the Pacific.

Stopping off in Moscow on his way to Berlin, on March 24 Matsuoka lectured Stalin and Molotov on how the moral Communists of Japan were unalterably opposed to the individualistic ideals of the Anglo-Saxon peoples. Not to be outdone in Oriental persiflage, Stalin replied that the Soviet Union had never gotten along well with Great Britain and "never would."[43] Tentative Japanese feelers aimed at the conclusion of a nonaggression pact were less successful at this juncture with the Soviets.

Three days later, Matsuoka arrived in Berlin in an atmosphere which, notwithstanding the tension evoked by the abrupt defection of Yugoslavia from the Tripartite Pact, increasingly resembled that of a Gilbert and Sullivan operetta. There the wandering minstrel from Nippon was promptly warned by Hitler and Ribbentrop that in the event of any new Soviet opposition to German interests, the German Army would crush Russia without hesitation. Ignoring this broad

---

[42] *N.C.A.*, Vol. VI, 996–97; *G.D.*, Vol. XII, 604–32; Hesse, *op. cit.*, 130; *Foreign Relations of the United States, 1942*, Vol. III, 587; Ilya Ehrenburg, *Men, Years–Life*, Vol. IV, *Eve of War, 1933–1941* (London, 1963), 274–75.

[43] See n. 44. For further evidence of the intensity of Stalin's Anglophobia, see *Foreign Relations of the United States, 1941*, Vol. I, 166-67.

hint regarding future German intentions, Matsuoka replied with one of his own to the effect that Japan, too, might find herself involved in war with the United States in the course of her proposed attack upon Singapore.

At first, the Axis partners chose to overlook the implications of each other's allusions, but a week later, on April 4, following Matsuoka's return from a brief sojourn in Rome, Hitler promised that should Japan come into conflict with either the United States or the Soviet Union, Germany would join her in the struggle. In return, Matsuoka said that he agreed with Mussolini's argument that America was the principal enemy of the Axis, while the Soviet Union only constituted a secondary rival. And despite the reluctance of the Germans openly to oppose any prospective pact between the Japanese and the Russians, Matsuoka appears to have understood well enough the reasons behind the Reich's unavowed distaste for such an agreement.[44]

As he may well have anticipated as a consequence of his prolonged and suspicious conversations in Berlin and Rome, upon his return passage through Moscow, Matsuoka encountered a distinctly warmer Soviet reception, a warmth in no way abated by the currently impressive German victories in the Balkans. For whatever reasons, in negotiations lasting a week, the Soviet Government dropped its previous insistence upon the immediate termination of Japanese economic concessions in northern Sakhalin, while Matsuoka settled for a simple Neutrality Pact with the Russians. Both sides appreciated the importance of this step, Stalin going so far as personally to bid farewell to the Japanese Foreign Minister at the railroad station. As Czar Alexander had done when facing imminent attack in the spring of 1812, Stalin had bought off at least one potential enemy at a relatively negligible price.

Nevertheless, to demonstrate that his pact with Tokyo was

---

[44] *N.S.R.*, 280–316; *G.D.*, Vol. XII, 349–474; cf. Schmidt, *op. cit.*, 222–31; Hesse, *op. cit.*, 132–33; Weinberg, *op. cit.*, 157–60; Kordt, *op. cit.*, 303; Greiner, *op. cit.*, 379–81.

in no overt sense an anti-German gesture, at the station Stalin also went out of his way to embrace German Ambassador Schulenburg, and to him declared in a loud voice for all to hear: "We must remain friends and you must now do everything to that end." Then, turning to the new Acting German Military Attaché, Colonel Hans Krebs, the Soviet dictator uttered the still more significant remark: "We will remain friends with you—in any event."[45]

Hitler concealed his mortification concerning this logical denouement of his overly clever machinations, giving Grand Admiral Raeder the pleasing misinformation that the Russo-Japanese pact had been concluded with German approval in order to encourage the Japanese to attack Singapore rather than Vladivostok. As the future would reveal, however, in his desire to camouflage Operation *Barbarossa* all the more effectively, Hitler had only succeeded in deceiving himself rather than the subtler Russians or Japanese.[46] With rational Soviet and irrational Nazi encouragement, the Japanese were now liberated to attack the United States, thus bringing an additional Great Power into the war against Germany. On the other hand, despite all subsequent American pressure to the contrary, the Soviet Union was to be enabled to concentrate upon the Germans alone. In all probability the Russians avoided defeat in the Second World War because for reasons of their own the Japanese honored their pact with the Soviet Union.

Following Matsuoka's departure, as anticipated by the infuriated Army General Staff, General Erwin Rommel's rapid advance in Cyrenaica was checked, as much from the difficulty of supplying his forces across the Mediterranean and the Libyan Desert as from British resistance. Both to relieve Rommel's logistic problems and to gain a base for eventual operations against the Middle East, the Luftwaffe on April 20 talked Hitler into Operation *Merkur*, the seizure of Crete by predominantly airborne means. Nevertheless, with Hitler's full

[45] *G.D.*, Vol. XII, 495–537; *N.S.R.*, 321–26; cf. Jones, *op. cit.*, 213–14.
[46] *N.C.A.*, Vol. VI, 997; *F.C.G.N.*, *1941*, 47–53; *G.D.*, Vol. XIII, 84–86.

approval, the reluctant German Army had insisted that Operation *Merkur* should not lead to any additional delays in the strategic concentration for *Barbarossa*.[47]

Crete was not captured by the Germans until June 1, after a hard struggle, and thenceforth Hitler was to refuse any further attempts of the Luftwaffe or Navy to inveigle him into further Mediterranean operations, whether when necessary, as at Malta, or merely tempting, as on the occasion of the Arab revolt against the British in Iraq at the end of May. *Marita-Merkur* had already amply served its subsidiary function as a cover for the immense *Barbarossa* buildup, and both the planes and the seven armored divisions eventually employed in the Balkans were now urgently needed in eastern Europe unless the invasion of Russia was to be delayed once again.

As it was, two of the German armored divisions so vital to speedy and successful operations in the Ukraine had not yet returned from Greece by June 22. Moreover, most of the five armored divisions which had already gone back to Poland and Rumania needed rest and refitting before undertaking another arduous campaign. Luftwaffe Air Fleet Four, likewise, had comprised approximately one-third of the air forces assigned to *Barbarossa*, and operations against Crete proved very costly and especially delayed the transfer of Air Fleet Four back to Rumania.[48]

Thus, not merely the delay in, but also the weakening of the southern wing of *Barbarossa* were real—if not very serious—by-products of Hitler's extended operations in the Balkans. The opportunity thus afforded both Hitler and Winston Churchill—when *Barbarossa* had failed to achieve its stated goals at the end of 1941—to claim that their unnecessary campaigns in the Balkans had thereby saved Moscow and Russia

---

[47] Blau, *Balkans*, 120 ff.; *G.D.*, Vol. XII, 636–37; Playfair, *op. cit.*, Vol. II, 41; Hart, *The Other Side of the Hill*, 173 ff.; Goerlitz, *Paulus*, 30–32; Halder, *War Diary*, Vol. VI, 97–98; *Hitler's War Directives*, 68–69.

[48] Asher Lee, *The German Air Force* (New York, 1946), 109–10; Blau, *Balkans*, 151–52; *G.D.*, Vol. XII, 925–33; Playfair, *op. cit.*, Vol. II, 540–41; Halder, *Hitler als Feldherr*, 38–39; Greiner, *op. cit.*, 383.

was too good to be overlooked. After all, Churchill would require some explanation, however *ex post facto*, to account for his disastrous intervention in Greece, while after *Barbarossa* had gone sour Hitler conveniently discovered that, but for Mussolini's "idiotic campaign in Greece," he would have assuredly destroyed the Red Army when this was still possible during the brief summer and autumn of 1941.

All such explanations doubtless console those who employ them. Few professional military historians are much impressed, however, if only because Hitler was to throw away far more valuable time in Russia in July, August, and September, 1941, in the course of his prolonged row with his Army General Staff over the direction of the main German attack. Fundamentally, it was Hitler's and Churchill's political motives for tangential operations in the Balkans that were responsible for their ensuing military difficulties, but it is generally as useless to expect statesmen to repudiate politics as to anticipate that their military critics will embrace such all-too-often disastrous considerations of prestige.[49]

As the last stage before *Barbarossa* approached, final preparations and final thoughts began to appear on the German side. For example, on April 20 the erstwhile Baltic German and long-time advocate of a German annexational program in the East, Alfred Rosenberg, received an appropriately ambiguous appointment as Reich Commissioner for Eastern European Questions. In sundry memoranda during these blissful spring months, Rosenberg outlined a program of ruthless Germanization of racially promising areas of the Soviet Union, coupled with semistarvation for the remainder through the removal of any food surplus from the Ukraine for the sole benefit of the Reich. Hitler himself had long perceived Rosenberg's ambivalence regarding Russia, and for that, among other reasons, had never taken him very seriously, as may be seen in his remark to Hermann Rauschning before the war

[49] *The Hitler-Bormann Documents,* 65; cf. Hart, *The Other Side of the Hill,* 180–82; Blau, *Balkans,* 152; Churchill, *The Grand Alliance,* 354; J. Kennedy, *op. cit.*, chap. xi; Major General Sir Francis de Guingand, *Operation Victory* (New York, 1947), 77 ff.; Butler, *op. cit.*, Vol. II, 457 ff., 554–62.

that Rosenberg was "rabid against the Russians only because they would not allow him to be a Russian."[50]

Evidently at Ribbentrop's instigation, on April 28 Hitler reluctantly received the aristocratic German Ambassador to Russia, Count von Schulenburg, to discuss a memorandum submitted by the German Embassy in Moscow regarding the strength of the Soviet Union. To Hitler's annoyance, the Ambassador explained that Germany was probably obliged by the terms of the Nazi-Soviet Pact to consult Russia over her invasion of Yugoslavia and for that reason each German action in the Balkans had been met with a Soviet counter-action. As for the present, Schulenburg emphasized that it was Soviet anxieties concerning a German attack that had evoked the Russian military buildup in the Baltic States, but that Stalin was prepared to make additional economic concessions to the Reich for the sake of avoiding war.

According to one account, Schulenburg returned to Moscow convinced that, notwithstanding the Fuehrer's specific denial to the Ambassador of any such intent, Hitler now planned to attack the Soviet Union. Schulenburg told another colleague that any discussion with Hitler concerning Soviet power was useless since the Fuehrer had his own completed image of the U.S.S.R. from which he would not deviate.[51]

Complementing Schulenburg's efforts in behalf of peace with the Russians, on this same April 28 Ribbentrop's deputy, State Secretary Weizsaecker, wrote another memorandum which must have proved equally unpalatable to Hitler—in the event that Ribbentrop had the courage to submit it. In an almost classic preface to the *Barbarossa* campaign, Weizsaecker had written: "If every Russian city reduced to ashes were as valuable to us as a sunken British warship, I should advocate the German-Russian war for this summer; but I

[50] Hermann Rauschning, *The Voice of Destruction*, 132; cf. *N.C.A.*, Vol. III, 674 ff., 832–33; A. Dallin, *German Rule*, chap. iii; Walter Laquer, "Hitler and Russia, 1919–1923," *Survey* (London), October, 1962, 104–13, and his *Russia and Germany: A Century of Conflict* (London, 1965), 56–78.

[51] *G.D.*, Vol. XII, 666–69; *N.S.R.*, 330–32; Hilger and Meyer, *op. cit.*, 328–29; Lossberg, *op. cit.*, 108; Hesse, *op. cit.*, 130–31; *The Goebbels Diaries, 1942–1943*, edited by Louis Lochner (New York, 1948), 87.

believe that we would be the victors over Russia only in a military sense, and would, on the other hand, lose in an economic sense."

Taking it for granted that the German Army would "advance victoriously" beyond Moscow, Weizsaecker nevertheless warned that the survival of the Soviet regime beyond the Volga would involve the German Army in a summer campaign in the East again in 1942. Thus, not merely would undertaking *Barbarossa* raise British morale in the short run but also it "might actually prolong" the war for Germany "instead of shortening it."[52] Whatever Ribbentrop's motives in prompting such prophetic professional insights from his deputies, it cannot be said that Hitler was let down by his diplomatic servants on the great question of attacking the U.S.S.R.

Hitler's real, if not avowed, answer to his diplomats may be seen in his formal decision on April 30 to commence *Barbarossa* on June 22, a decision impending, in practice, ever since the Serbian officer revolt. Of the three German Army Groups scheduled to operate the main Russian theater, a decisive German superiority in strength was seen only for the Center Group aimed at Moscow. In fact, thanks to the Balkan campaign, in the Ukraine the Soviets at first were expected to have a considerable superiority in numbers, while in the Baltic region a rough equality was supposed to prevail between the two contestants. Field Marshal von Brauchitsch anticipated violent frontier battles lasting up to four weeks, followed, despite Russian courage, by much weaker Soviet resistance. For concealment, conversations with Hungary and Rumania regarding their military collaboration were to be postponed to the last moment.[53]

Again, on May 2, the plans for the economic exploitation of the Soviet Union, which had been developing under the code name *Oldenburg*, were summarized in the highly questionable statement that Germany could continue the war for another

---

[52] *G.D.*, Vol. XII, 661–62; *N.S.R.*, 333–34.
[53] *N.C.A.*, Vol. III, 633–34; *T.M.W.C.*, Vol. XXVI, 399–401.

year only if her armed forces were to be fed by Russia. "There is no doubt," ran this unvarnished memorandum, "that as a result many millions of people will be starved to death if we take out of the country the things necessary for us."[54] Since Germany was already being adequately fed, in part by Russian deliveries throughout the period of the Nazi-Soviet Pact, a true motive for this rationalization presumably was prompted by the recurrent Nazi desire to cut down the Russian population as much as possible in any event. Under the all-encompassing cloak of a general war, an infinity of unnecessary horrors are rather easily justified, as, unfortunately, many besides the much-tried peoples of the Soviet Union were about to rediscover during the next four years.

In the Soviet camp, evidence of mounting Russian nervousness continued to accumulate. Already the Soviet Government may have gone beyond futile protests against Luftwaffe reconnaissance flights over Russia with similar flights of their own over German-held territory. On May 1, the Soviet Defense Commissar, Marshal Timoshenko, warned publicly against the dangers of capitalist encirclement. On May 5, Stalin was reported to have told graduates of the War Academy that despite reorganization and re-equipment the Red Army was not yet ready for war with Germany, an opinion parallel to that of Colonel Krebs, the optimistic new Acting German Military Attaché in Moscow. The next day in an unprecedented step, Stalin took over from Molotov the post of head of the Soviet Government, leaving the latter, however, his old position as Commissar of Foreign Affairs. Schulenburg felt this "extraordinary" event was caused by Stalin's determination to preserve the Soviet Union at any cost from a conflict with Germany.[55]

---

[54] *N.C.A.*, Vol. V, 378; cf. *N.C.A.*, Vol. I, 811–14, *Vol.* III, 811–16.

[55] *N.S.R.*, 329–39; cf. *G.D.*, Vol. XII, 730, 964–65; *Foreign Relations of the United States, 1942,* Vol. III, 587; Halder, *War Diary*, Vol. VI, 100; Hilger and Meyer, *op. cit.*, 330–31. For the unfortunate influence of Krebs as the replacement for the probably too experienced and pessimistic General Koestring as Military Attaché, see Milton Shulman, *Defeat in the West* (New York, 1948), 62–64.

New gestures of appeasement toward the Reich, ranging from the denial of troop concentrations in western Russia to the withdrawal of Soviet recognition of several exiled European governments (including that of Yugoslavia), make it easy to agree with Schulenburg's despairing explanation of Soviet policy on the eve of the catastrophe. Certainly it is an overstatement to say, as Churchill and others have suggested, that Stalin and his aides had shown themselves at this moment to be "the most completely outwitted bunglers of the Second World War." Granted that the Soviets, like everyone else, had too long seriously underestimated Hitler, at this juncture what else could the Soviet Government have done, apart from stalling off the forthcoming German attack as long as possible? Stalin could hardly have hoped to assault the main elements of the German Army with his own forces still unready even for defense, however eagerly Churchill may have desired such an outcome. Soviet strategists and tacticians had much to learn in the future; nevertheless, in this final period before attack, Stalin's foreign policy, both in the West and in the Far East, was as realistic as it was egocentric.[56]

Stalin's distrust of British motives and German intentions could hardly have been assuaged when he learned that on the evening of May 10, Hitler's erstwhile intimate and nominal chief of the Nazi Party organization, Rudolf Hess, had mysteriously flown to Scotland. Whether or not this mission was undertaken with Hitler's tacit consent, the Soviets had little reason for accepting at their face value either the embarrassed German or noncommittal British announcements concerning the Hess flight. Although, both publicly and to Mussolini, Hitler eventually decided to describe Hess's abortive effort to reach an agreement with the British as the act of a madman, there is no doubt that the Fuehrer would have gladly accepted any reasonable opportunity to obtain a free hand in eastern

[56] Churchill, *The Grand Alliance*, 353; cf. his *The Hinge of Fate*, 493, and *N.S.R.*, 339–42, for Stalin's probable motives. For an eloquent expression of the Stalin-as-a-bungler thesis, see the unsympathetic appreciation by the Turkish Ambassador on May 24, 1941: *G.D.*, Vol. XII, 873–76.

Europe on the very eve of *Barbarossa*. For example, on this occasion General Halder heard Hitler's by no means unsympathetic private description of Hess's "grief over the fratricidal struggle between the two Germanic nations," a struggle which the Fuehrer had every reason to wish to terminate more than ever before.[57]

If Hitler remained acquiescent with respect to arrangements with the British, his ferocity toward the East went unabated. On May 13, he broadened and strengthened his earlier decrees for the immediate execution of political officers and commissars with orders permitting, and indeed encouraging, the employment of the most brutal military methods against any resistance on the part of the civilian population of the Soviet Union as a whole. Attempts by the generals to water down these new orders met with subsequent instructions to conceal, but nevertheless to enforce, them. At the same time, the deception operations for *Barbarossa* went into a more advanced stage, now emphasizing that the airborne assault upon Crete was simply a rehearsal for such an attack on a larger scale upon Britain.[58]

German deception operations to cover *Barbarossa* were urgently needed with the spate of German troops from all over Europe, including the Balkans, at last pouring toward the Soviet frontier. At least in retrospect, few seem to have been much deluded regarding Nazi intentions any longer, although the possibility that a last-minute deal—on terms far more favorable to the Germans than before—distracted all potential belligerents on the Axis side and in all probability simultaneously whetted Stalin's hopes for further procrastination with the Reich.

---

[57] Halder, *War Diary*, Vol. VI, 117; cf. *Foreign Relations of the United States, 1941*, Vol. I, 143, 314; *The Ciano Diaries*, 361; *N.C.A.*, Vol. VIII, 37–46; *T.M.W.C.*, Vol. VII, 143, Vol. XL, 280; *G.D.*, Vol. XI, 15–61, Vol. XII, 797–99, 1043; Churchill, *The Grand Alliance*, 48–55; James Leasor, *Rudolf Hess: The Uninvited Envoy* (London, 1962), 146–74.

[58] *N.C.A.*, Vol. III, 635–39, Vol. VI, 871–76; *T.M.W.C.*, Vol. XXIV, 252–57, Vol. XXVI, 401–8.

Already in early May, rumors in Berlin of an impending German attack on Russia were too widespread and persistent for foreign observers to discount, whatever the official postures of the German and Soviet governments might be. Certainly by the middle of May, the British Prime Minister in all sincerity had reached such a conclusion, since he privately informed his old friend General Jan Christiaan Smuts that he suspected a German attack on Russia in the near future. The Soviets themselves cannot have entirely discounted these rumors, not to mention reports from their own intelligence services, because on May 17 the movement of diplomats to western Russia was prohibited owing to the heavy Russian troop movements taking place there. On May 20, among many other such reports from its agents and military attachés, one of the oldest and most trusted espionage operatives of the Red Army, Richard Sorge, evidently warned from Tokyo that on June 20 approximately 180 German divisions would attack Russia, with their first thrusts aimed in the direction of Moscow and Leningrad. In both May and June the Red Army would receive specific information on *Barbarossa* directly from informants within the German Army General Staff and the O.K.W., the last only a week before the German attack.[59] Truly, despite the ravages of the great purge, the Soviet Union was not let down by its intelligence agencies in the relatively simple task of observing the immense German tactical preparations essential for *Barbarossa.*

At this unfavorable moment, Grand Admiral Raeder chose to make another attempt to protect his preferred Mediterranean theater. Supporting Mussolini and Erwin Rommel, Raeder urged the Fuehrer to allocate twelve divisions in the autumn of 1941 to the capture of Suez. The German naval

---

[59] Churchill, *The Grand Alliance*, 364–65; Khrushchev, *op. cit.*, 537; *G.D.*, Vol. XII, 981–82; Major General Charles Willoughby, *Shanghai Conspiracy: The Sorge Spy Ring* (New York, 1952), 105; Raymond Garthoff, *Soviet Military Doctrine* (Glencoe, 1953), 260–61, 434–35; Alexander Foote, *Handbook for Spies* (New York, 1949), 113–15; Alfieri, *op. cit.*, 120; Chalmers Johnson, *An Instance of Treason* (London, 1965), 155–56.

chief assured Hitler that such a stroke "would be more deadly to the British Empire than the capture of London." Perhaps Raeder did not yet fully grasp that Hitler had little enough eagerness to go against London, and still less to destroy the British Empire. As Hitler had always maintained, his India was in Russia, and in War Directive No. 30, issued on May 25, the Fuehrer had already instructed that operations against the Middle East must wait upon the conquest of Russia.[60]

The time had come at last to inform the Reich's allies, active or merely potential, of the imminent operation against the Soviet Union. As, presumably, the ally of the greatest geographic importance and the one whose anti-Soviet credentials could hardly be questioned by the Reich, the Finns were the first to be taken into Germany's confidence. Conversations between the General Staffs of the two states, which had been going on intermittently since December, 1940, culminated in the reception of the Finnish Chief of Staff, General Erik Heinrichs, by General Jodl of the O.K.W. in Salzburg on May 25.

Describing the Red Army buildup in western Russia as comprising about 180 divisions, Jodl asked of the Finns no more than a holding operation to tie down Soviet forces in the region of Lake Ladoga. After expressing his confidence in the swift relief of the Finns by the northern German Army Group advancing through all the Baltic States toward Leningrad, Jodl said, "I am no optimist and I don't expect the war to be over in a few weeks, but neither do I believe it will last many months." The next day in Berlin, however, Heinrichs met with General Halder, who gave vent to the more pessimistic view of the O.K.H. that the Finns must attack as opportunity offered on either side of Lake Ladoga within a fortnight of the commencement of *Barbarossa.*

Unfortunately, in accepting Halder's desire for a Finnish offensive, the Finns also agreed to function under the poorly

[60] *F.C.G.N., 1941,* 50–52, 99–101; *Hitler's Table Talk,* 23–24; *N.C.A.,* Vol. II, 861, Vol. VI, 978–1000.

organized proposed German command-structure. It will be recalled that this had left General Nikolaus von Falkenhorst's Army of Norway, reporting to the O.K.W., in charge of what Halder now termed the latter's impractical "expedition" against the Murmansk railroad in northern Finland. The principal Finnish forces remained under their own commander, the legendary Field Marshal Carl von Mannerheim, while the German Army Group moving up from the south through the Baltic States stayed under Brauchitsch's and Halder's Army High Command (O.K.H.). Since the campaign was expected to be a success in 1941, the difficulties of coordinating three separate headquarters in unified operations evidently were not expected to be insuperable. In any event, the Finns agreed to order a full mobilization of their Army reserves in stages between June 9 and 17.[61]

As an advocate of action against the Soviet Union, at least until he had become embroiled with Great Britain, Mussolini may have been the next privileged to receive definite word from Germany concerning *Barbarossa*, although Count Ciano, whom the Germans distrusted with reason, was carefully excluded from this information. Already well informed through Italian Army Intelligence, Il Duce by the beginning of June was looking forward to seeing the Reich lose many feathers in a conflict with the well-armed Russians. Like his Germanophobe son-in-law and Foreign Minister, Mussolini needed compensations for his ignominious rescue in the Balkans by the so far invariably successful German Army.

Consequently, with the inveterate ambivalence which characterized his whole policy toward the Reich, at the end of May Mussolini had ordered the Chief of Staff of the Italian Army to prepare a motorized corps of three divisions for service in Russia. In return, Hitler did not accept this perhaps

[61] Halder, *War Diary*, Vol. VI, 115; Ziemke, *op. cit.*, 130–36; cf. Goerlitz, *Paulus*, 122–23; *G.D.*, Vol. XII, 787–1023; Halder, *Hitler als Feldherr*, 14; Greiner, *op. cit.*, 387–88; Warlimont, *op. cit.*, 142–46; Mannerheim, *op. cit.*, 406–11.

undesired Italian requital until the *Barbarossa* assault was about to be launched. Compensations in prestige with the currently triumphant Fuehrer were difficult to achieve, but it is untrue, as so often alleged, that on this occasion the Duce was taken completely by surprise over Hitler's action in Russia.[62]

Next in line for the news of Hitler's great decision were the distant and distrustful Japanese. As early as the middle of May the German General Staff had tipped off the Japanese Military Attaché concerning *Barbarossa*, and on June 6 Hitler personally informed the Japanese Ambassador, General Oshima, of his intention to destroy Russia in a campaign of not more than two or three months' duration. With Oshima, as with his other potential allies, at first Hitler did not give the precise date of *Barbarossa*, and this may have enabled the embarrassed Japanese Foreign Minister, Yosuke Matsuoka, to persuade his colleagues that the chances were still against the breaking-out of a Russo-German war. Such a conflict would further discredit the already unpopular author of the Russian Neutrality Pact with the rest of the Japanese Cabinet, since the Foreign Minister's instant readiness to dishonor his own pact and join Germany in the war against Russia had led his more conventional colleagues to conclude that Matsuoka's erratic personality was unstable almost to the point of insanity.[63]

On June 11, in a long-awaited conversation with Hitler, General Ion Antonescu of Rumania eagerly offered to join the Reich in an offensive war against Russia from the very first day on which Germany was engaged. Within a week the cooperative Rumanians were informed of the precise target date for *Barbarossa* in order to permit a last-minute mobiliza-

---

[62] *G.D.*, Vol. XII, 924–40; *Germany and Her Allies in World War II*, 32–33; *The Ciano Diaries*, 351–67; *Les Lettres Secrètes*, 127; Schmidt, *op. cit.*, 233; Ugo Cavallero, *Commando supremo: Diaro 1940–1943 del capo di S.M.G.* (Bologna, 1948), 112–13.

[63] *I.M.T.F.E.*, Exhibits 1068, 1084, 2735*A*, Part 19, 3989–92; Toshikazu Kase, *Journey to the Missouri* (New Haven, 1950), 160; Robert Butow, *Tojo and the Coming of the War* (Princeton, 1961), 208–12; *G.D.*, Vol. XII, 725, 809, 970.

tion of their extremely exposed forces. Not to be outdone in enthusiasm by the hated Rumanians, when definitely informed of *Barbarossa* on June 21, just before the campaign actually commenced, Admiral Miklós Horthy of Hungary told the German Minister that he had longed for this day for twenty-two years. Centuries later, Horthy went on to say, humanity would still be thanking the Fuehrer for his liberation of the Russian people from the yoke of Communism. It goes without saying that Horthy's exhilaration concerning the chivalric deed contemplated by Hitler in Russia in no way interfered with the static posture of the Magyar divisions in the parts of Transylvania recently acquired from Rumania. For Hitler's expedition in Russia, second-string Hungarian troops would suffice. At the last minute the Swedes, Spaniards, and Slovaks also came through with transit rights or volunteers for the great crusade against Bolshevik Russia; more judiciously, the Turks contented themselves with transports of joy.[64]

Like the British and Spaniards, the Turks had good cause for relief over the seeming deflection of the course of Nazi aggression toward the Soviet Union, for on June 11, in War Directive No. 32, the Fuehrer made clear that Turkish neutrality was scheduled to endure only as long as the Red Army —so feared by the Turks—itself held out. Similarly the British, spared from heavy air raids by the Luftwaffe since the night of May 10/11, were to be faced with the consequences of long-overdue top priorities for the German Air Force and Navy when these services could again return to their preferred task of strangling England, following the victorious Army campaign in Russia in 1941. And the Spaniards were finally to learn the dangers of interminable procrastination with the new overlord of the European Continent, once the Fuehrer was freed from the incubus in the East.

To hold down the anticipated German conquests in Euro-

---

[64] *G.D.*, Vol. XII, 1005–81; Goerlitz, *Paulus*, 125–26; *Germany and Her Allies in World War II*, 32–33; Greiner, *op. cit.*, 389; Hillgruber, *op. cit.*, 118, 133.

pean Russia at the end of 1941, Hitler asserted in War Directive No. 32 that sixty German divisions, in addition to satellite troops, would prove adequate. The bulk of the German Army would thereby be released for offensives from Libya against Suez, from Bulgaria through Turkey, and, if possible, from the Caucasus through Iran to the currently almost defenseless oil fields of Iraq and the Persian Gulf.[65]

German preparations for *Barbarossa* drew to their close at a general assembly of the military commanders concerned which was held in Berlin on June 14. Hitler again described the eastern campaign as inevitable, and preferable at the present time to one later when the Red Army would be better trained and equipped and the Germans might be engaged elsewhere. After June 14, Russian submarines near the German coasts might be attacked upon detection, the departure of German ships for Soviet ports having already been halted under various pretexts. On the seventeenth, the date for *Barbarossa* was confirmed for June 22, and commencing June 18 concealment for the ultimate stage of *Barbarossa* was no longer required.[66] Short of an ultimatum, Stalin could have had no more warning, but it is questionable whether even such a classic anachronism would have markedly altered Soviet policy at this juncture.

On the eve of *Barbarossa*, the German Order of Battle available for the first day of the whole Russian theater of war, including Finland, comprised 154½ German, 18 Finnish, and 14 Rumanian divisions. Italian, Hungarian, Slovak, and Spanish increments were scheduled to arrive after June 21. The German forces included 19 armored divisions of 3,350 tanks, or approximately 75 per cent of the tank strength per division employed in the French campaign, plus 13 motorized divisions and a cavalry division. Apart from the Finnish divisions,

---

[65] *G.D.*, Vol. XII, 1012–16; Blau, *Russia*, 3–37; Warlimont, *op. cit.*, 132; *Hitler's War Directives*, 78–79; Richards, *op. cit.*, Vol. I, 217–40; Greiner, *op. cit.*, 391–92, asserts that War Directive No. 32 never actually reached Hitler's or even Jodl's hands, as it was only a tentative planning study.

[66] *N.C.A.*, Vol. VI, 909–11, 1000–1001; *T.M.W.C.*, Vol. IV, 4007, Vol. XI, 16; Greiner, *op. cit.*, 389–90; Warlimont, *op. cit.*, 147.

the separate Finnish front, reporting to the O.K.W., embraced only 4½ German divisions, mostly in the far North as part of the Army in Norway commanded by General Nikolaus von Falkenhorst.

The 150 German divisions on the main Soviet front under the authority of the O.K.H. were organized in three Army Groups as well as in O.K.H. reserves for *Barbarossa*. Apart from the eventually very numerous forces of her allies, the German Army in the East alone amounted to 3,300,000 men at the start of the campaign. Army Group North, of 30 divisions, commanded by Field Marshal Wilhelm von Leeb, comprised the Sixteenth and Eighteenth Armies and included the Fourth Panzer Group with 3 armored divisions. Army Group Center, of 51 divisions, commanded by Field Marshal Fedor von Bock, included the Fourth and Ninth Armies as well as the Second and Third Panzer Groups with 9 armored divisions. Army Group South, of 43 German and 14 Rumanian divisions was commanded by Field Marshal Gerd von Rundstedt and comprised the Sixth, Eleventh, and Seventeenth German Armies, including the First Panzer Group of 5 armored divisions, as well as the Third Rumanian Army.

Figures on the Soviet Order of Battle before June 21, 1941, are, of course, much less precise, but appear to include as available in the area of European Russia alone about 235 divisions, plus some 85 armored and motorized brigades. Organized in 18 armies or separate mechanized corps, this vast force approximated 4,500,000 men available to meet the Germans and their allies.

Roughly parallel in organization, as in numbers, to the Axis armies was the composition of the Soviet "Fronts," as they would come to be known in Red Army parlance when hostilities commenced. The Baltic and Leningrad Fronts were each comprised of 3 armies; in White Russia, General D. G. Pavlov's West Front included another 3 armies as well as 4 tank or mechanized corps, while in the Ukraine, the Kiev, Southwest and Odessa Fronts maintained 6 armies and 4 more mechanized corps. These last corps were undergoing the difficult process of conversion from corps and brigade organizations into armored divisions in accordance with the seemingly successful earlier German practice, and they still lacked training, organic transport, and even adequate supplies of fuel.

Apart from immensely variable estimates of Soviet armored strength ranging from 17,000 to 24,000 tanks, of which only 1,500 were modern, the Red Air Force was supposed to have about 6,000 first-line combat planes in Europe against the 2,000 initially available for the Luftwaffe in Russia. Like the Russian tanks, the Soviet planes were correctly believed to be largely obsolete and their pilots still poorly trained. Another 60 German divisions were left guarding the western and southern European periphery against the British, a more than ample number, which, like the 35 Red Army divisions still guarding Central Asia and the Far East, provided gradually available reserves against crises for either belligerent in the principal theater of war.[67]

Hitler and his Army General Staff had imbued each other with new confidence since the recently successful campaign in the Balkans, but Hitler's political judgment in anticipating a popular revolt against Stalin in the event of serious Soviet defeats even found support in otherwise most unsympathetic sources. For example, only two weeks before Hitler struck in Russia, United States Ambassador Laurence Steinhardt reported from Moscow that peasant and Ukrainian dissatisfaction was so intense that no more than the simple arrival of the German Army might topple the Soviet regime. Of course, underestimation of Soviet popularity and capabilities had been a failing of all Western societies since 1917, and the

---

[67] *The Great Patriotic War*, Vol. I, 415 ff., 486, Vol. II, 11; *N.C.A.*, Vol. VI, 857–67; Blau, *Russia*, 38–43; Sherwood, *op. cit.*, 333–35; Edgar Howell, *The Soviet Partisan Movement* (Washington: Dept. of the Army, August, 1956), 24–25; Assmann, "The Battle for Moscow," 310–11, and his *Deutsche Schicksal Jahre* (Wiesbaden, 1950), 258; General Wladyslav Anders, *Hitler's Defeat in Russia* (Chicago, 1953), 16–19; Guderian, *Panzer Leader*, 150–51; Gallagher, *Soviet History*, 159–61; Hart, *The Other Side of the Hill*, 190; Kilmarx, *op. cit.*, 127 ff.; Erickson, *op. cit.*, 580–92, 768, and *loc. cit.*, 181–82; Paul Carell, *Hitler's War on Russia* (London, 1964), 16–59; Greiner, *op. cit.*, 386; Philippi and Heim, *op. cit.*, 36–37.

blame for such an erroneous assessment can hardly be laid to Adolf Hitler alone.[68]

The alternative and weaker argument that Hitler attacked Russia because he distrusted her growing strength and especially feared a Soviet assault in the autumn of 1941 is as meaningless as it is suspect, since Hitler had always intended, and still intended, to invade the Soviet Union at the earliest possible moment regardless of any differences in estimates of Soviet prowess. Illustrative of this determination is Hitler's remark in January, 1942, when his invasion had already gone astray, to the effect that although he had not believed in June, 1941, that the Russians possessed 10,000 tanks, in the event that they had, this was all the more reason for attacking them as quickly as possible. It should be noted, moreover, that German war production hardly rose at all in the year which the Germans spent preparing for *Barbarossa*, and, in fact, as far as the Army was concerned, was soon to be cut back in the autumn of 1941.

Only in the long-range sense can Hitler's excuse of Soviet strength be taken seriously as a cause for the Nazi assault. Even in retrospect, June, 1941, constituted Hitler's first real chance to attack Russia, as it constituted his last. Probably by 1942 and unquestionably by 1943, both Soviet and Anglo-American war production and mobilization of their vast military potential would have reached a point when German victory would become dubious. Good timing was always Hitler's rather feline forte, and if his consistently easy victories so far had obviously gone to his head, at least the Fuehrer's sense of the proper timing for *Barbarossa* cannot be criticized to this day.[69]

From the beginning of June the British Chiefs of Staff had

---

[68] *Foreign Relations of the United States, 1941*, Vol. I, 620–21; Hart, *The Other Side of the Hill*, 186–87; Goerlitz, *The German General Staff*, 392–93; Halder, *Hitler als Feldherr*, 39; Lossberg, *op. cit.*, 108.

[69] *Hitler's Table Talk*, 182; Raymond Goldsmith, "The Power of Victory," *Military Affairs* (Washington), Spring, 1946, 71–75; *N.C.A.*, Vol. VI, 890–91, Vol. VII, 926–27; Gilbert, *op. cit.*, 88–89; Schellenberg, *op. cit.*, 194–95; Guderian, *Panzer Leader*, 138–51.

become convinced of Hitler's firm intention to venture all in Russia, and on June 10 Foreign Secretary Anthony Eden assured the Soviet Ambassador that in the event of a Russo-German conflict, Britain would do everything within her power to distract the Germans in the West with air assaults. To this, Ambassador Ivan Maisky made no comment beyond informing Mr. Eden that the Soviet Government was not planning to negotiate a military alliance with the Reich. On June 13 Eden went further with Maisky, offering a British military mission and economic aid in the event of the now almost certain German attack. In return Maisky asked for more information concerning German preparations.

Two days later, on June 15, Churchill followed up these overtures to the taciturn Soviets with a direct warning to President Roosevelt of the expectations of the British Government regarding Hitler's proposed course of action. By June 20, Roosevelt had replied, agreeing to support publicly "any announcement that the Prime Minister might make welcoming Russia as an ally." More privately, however, the British Chiefs of Staff had resurrected an old idea of Churchill's and a still older fantasy of the French before him, namely, to threaten the Soviet oil fields in the Caucasus with British bombings as a method of putting pressure on Stalin not to reach a new accord with Hitler. Even under the imminent overture of *Barbarossa*, Anglo-Soviet relations had hardly reached a state of friendship, and, for that matter, never would.

On June 18, Maisky evidently informed Moscow that at last the previously skeptical British Ambassador to the Soviet Union, Sir Stafford Cripps, now also expected an attack on Russia at any moment by a German force of 147 divisions, an accurate enough estimate. Presumably the opinions of a Labor sympathizer of the Soviet Union, such as Cripps, might be thought to carry more weight with Moscow than those of Winston Churchill, but Left as he might be, Cripps himself does not seem to have given the Soviets credit for much chance of holding out against the Germans more than three or four weeks. And when the German attack actually appeared on June 22, Field Marshal Sir John Dill, the Chief of the Imperial General Staff, expressed the prevailing opinion of Western military staffs when he told the Prime Minister that he supposed the Red Army would shortly "be rounded up in hordes."[70] Given such a climate of opinion, neither Hitler's current euphoria nor Stalin's last-minute gestures at appeasement of the Germans seems in any way odd or unreasonable.

Postwar Soviet testimony regarding Russia's unreadiness to resist invasion in 1941 has become so detailed and all-embracing that the German belief that their qualitative superiority would outweigh any Soviet quantitative lead in manpower or matériel seems amply justified. Leading Soviet figures, from Stalin down through Marshal Timoshenko and the Chief of the Red Army General Staff since February, 1941, General Grigory Zhukov, have been involved in these recent Soviet charges and countercharges of responsibility for the inadequate preparations for war. For example, apart from the plethora of warnings from abroad, General M. P. Kirponos, in command of the key Kiev Military District, begged Stalin shortly before the German attack to permit evacuation of the civilian population of border areas in order to expedite the construction of fortifications. Stalin forbade either such action in the frontier districts on the grounds that they might provoke a German attack. Like the Americans in Washington and at Pearl Harbor six months later, the Soviet ruler forgot that inadequate defense measures can evoke attacks quite as much as appeasement may delay them.

Soviet deliveries of vital German imports of Far Eastern rubber,[71] Russian grain, oil, etc., might continue to the last day across the border, but the poor training, largely obsolete

---

[70] Churchill, *The Grand Alliance*, 34, 369–70; cf. Khrushchev, *op. cit.*, 537; *Foreign Relations of the United States, 1941*, Vol. I, 168–73; Woodward, *op. cit.*, 149–50; Butler, *op. cit.*, Vol. II, 542–44; Estorick, *op. cit.*, 268–70; John Winant, *A Letter from Grosvenor Square* (London, 1947), 145–46; Richards, *op. cit.*, 342; Gwyer, *op. cit.*, 83–84; Eden, *op. cit.*, 308–12.

[71] So vital were the imports of Far Eastern rubber to the *Barbarossa* campaign that Soviet interdiction of this item alone could have seriously interfered with the campaign against them; see Greiner, *op. cit.*, 384–85.

equipment, and unfilled cadres of advanced Red Army units had not escaped prying German eyes. The continued movement of green Red Army conscripts beyond the Stalin Line fortifications of the Dnieper River into the recently acquired territories of the West suggested that no integrated strategic plan for defense existed, as was, indeed, the situation. Moreover, the current reorganization and re-equipment of Soviet forces had stripped many Soviet units of still useful old matériel without having provided much new equipment in more up-to-date weapons for the forward units. For example, the 1,500 available modern tanks were sent to the frontier areas in the spring of 1941, but the great majority of the older tanks were no longer maintained in working order. Thus, in spite of stepped-up defensive measures in the west as a result of the state of readiness proclaimed on April 10, including the movement to the Ukraine of most of two new armies from the North Caucasus and Siberia, in many essentials the Red Army was still unprepared to meet the German assault in June.[72]

Following Stalin's ostentatious departure from Moscow for a vacation at the Black Sea, on June 14, Tass, the official Soviet news agency, had issued a blanket denial of the veracity of what it called the obviously absurd rumors of an imminent German attack. Tass likewise maintained that German troop movements toward the East involved no aggressive intentions, while the recent Soviet call-up of reserves was dismissed as nothing more than the usual summer training maneuvers of the Red Army. When this Russian trial balloon elicited nothing more than a resounding silence from Berlin, on June 21 the Soviet Ambassador to Germany, V. G. Dekanozov, inquired why no reply had yet been received to earlier Russian

---

[72] Khrushchev, *loc. cit.*, 538–39; Garthoff, *Doctrine*, 435–38; Markoff, *op. cit.*, 175 ff.; *G.D.*, Vol. XII, 981–82; Erickson, *op. cit.*, 574–77, and *loc. cit.*, 181; *N.C.A.*, Vol. I, 828–30; Gallagher, *Soviet History*, 158–61; Gorbatov, *op. cit.*, 151–54; *The Great Patriotic War*, Vol. I, 486, Vol. II, 12–13; Theodore Shabad, "Soviet Military Experts Upgrade Stalin and Make Khrushchev an Unperson," *New York Times* (New York), April 18, 1965, 20.

complaints regarding the increasing number of German reconnaissance flights over Soviet territory. At the same time, in Moscow, Foreign Commissar Molotov anxiously asked Ambassador Schulenburg whether the German Government was seriously offended with the Soviets.[73]

At four o'clock on the morning of the next day, June 22, Stalin's subservient intimate, V. G. Dekanozov, received the German reply from Foreign Minister Ribbentrop. In a state of high excitement, perhaps to compensate for what he acknowledged constituted the smashing of all his hopes for a renewal of Soviet-Nazi collaboration, Ribbentrop officially blamed the German invasion of Russia upon the hostility of Soviet policy, especially over Yugoslavia, as well as upon the Soviet buildup in the West. But as the Soviet Ambassador was departing, Ribbentrop evidently followed him to the door to whisper that he had opposed the Fuehrer's decision. Upon receipt of the official German explanation from Ambassador Schulenburg in Moscow, Foreign Minister Molotov could not forbear to reply and ask whether the equally dismayed Schulenburg believed that the Soviets had deserved such German treatment. Like Ribbentrop, Molotov's reputation was irredeemably tied to the now exploded non-aggression pact with the Third Reich.[74]

Mussolini was, likewise, the recipient of a dawn Nazi epistle, a lengthy apologia for his action from Hitler which stressed the need for a German attack before the Soviet, British, and American war economies were fully mobilized. Since German action against the United States was impossible, instead Hitler was attacking Russia, which, in turn, would increase the Japanese threat against the United States. Hitler asserted that should he be obliged to leave sixty or seventy

---

[73] *G.D.*, Vol. XII, 1027–72; *N.S.R.*, 345–56; Beloff, *op. cit.*, Vol. II, 381, n. 2; Hilger and Meyer, *op. cit.*, 335–36; *The Great Patriotic War*, Vol. II, 13.

[74] *G.D.*, Vol. XII, 1063–75; *N.S.R.*, 355–57; Schmidt, *op. cit.*, 234–35; Hilger and Meyer, *op. cit.*, 336; Erickson, *op. cit.*, 577; D. Dallin, *op. cit.*, 132–33; Victor Berezhkov, "On the Eve of Hitler's Invasion," *Atlas* (New York), January 1964, 13–15.

divisions in Russia at the end of a successful campaign there this year, they would be only a fraction of his current buildup in the East.

In conclusion Hitler wrote that as a consequence of his struggle through to his great decision for *Barbarossa*, he finally felt "spiritually free." Hitler added that in spite of what he insisted were his sincere efforts to conciliate the Soviets, his partnership with them was "often very irksome to me, for in some way or other it seemed to me to be a break with my whole origin, my concepts, and my former obligations. I am happy now to be relieved of those mental agonies."[75]

Despite the disloyalty of certain of his generals, the seductive diversions of his Air Force, Navy, and Foreign Ministry, the implacable hostility of Winston Churchill's Britain, and the frantic last-minute blandishments of Joseph Stalin, nothing had deflected Hitler from his deadly purpose in the East. For two years the German Navy had been engaged in a bitter struggle with the vastly superior British Navy; for a full year now the Luftwaffe had already met its match in the Royal Air Force. At last for the first time in the Second World War the vaunted German Army was to meet an opponent who, however unready for the initial German attack, in the long run was to prove worthy of Hitler's steel.

---

[75] *G.D.*, Vol. XII, 1066–69; *N.S.R.*, 349–53; *Les Lettres Secrètes*, 121–31.

"Russia is a country which is very easy to invade, but very difficult to conquer."[1] LLOYD GEORGE, April, 1919

"We've all studied in our military academies the lessons to be drawn from our military disasters in August, 1914. We've all made fun of Samsonov, and now we've wetted ourselves just like him."[2]

REPRESENTATIVE RED ARMY OFFICER, June 30, 1941

"Only the traitor renounces attack; only the simpleton reduces all strategy to attack."[3] TROTSKY, on military doctrine

"We must take possession of it [Smolensk], so that we may move on the two capitals simultaneously. In Moscow, we'll destroy everything; in St. Petersburg we'll keep everything."[4]

NAPOLEON, 1812

[1] *B.D.*, Vol. III, *1919*, 309.

[2] Konstantin Simonov, *Victims and Heroes* (London, 1963), 42–43.

[3] Deutscher, *The Prophet Armed*, 484; cf. Edward M. Meade's article on Trotsky's military pragmatism compared to the revolutionary distaste for the defensive promulgated by Stalin's appointees: *Makers of Modern Strategy* (Princeton, 1948), 342–46.

[4] Count Philippe Paul de Ségur, *Napoleon's Russian Campaign* (London, 1959) 34.

CHAPTER V

The Soap Bubble

June 22–September 20, 1941

As a consequence of a final flurry of intelligence warnings, at midnight of June 21/22 the Red Army and Navy sent out orders for a state of combat alertness against an imminent German attack. At 3:30 A.M. on June 22, the German assault commenced, only two days earlier in June than Napoleon's ill-fated invasion in the year 1812, when he also was at the height of his power. Many Red Army and Air Force units had not yet even received the midnight warning, let alone acted upon it by concentrating or occupying their combat positions. At least Admiral Nikolai Kuznetsov, commanding the Soviet Navy, on his own authority ordered immediate resistance to German attacks despite his inability to obtain orders from Stalin for more than a week.

The first Red Army reactions to Hitler's offensive were those of confusion. German Army Group Center promptly intercepted the now notorious wireless query from a subordinate Red Army unit to a higher headquarters: "We are being fired upon. What shall we do?" The senior Red Army headquarters reply topped any of the American reactions at Pearl Harbor six months later in saying: "You must be insane. And why is your signal not in code?" In the somewhat more effectively alerted Lemberg region opposite the German Army Group South, Soviet artillery did not at first answer to the German shellfire, its captured commander eventually explaining that he thought the German barrage was only a mistake.

Moreover, Soviet artillery units, especially on the frontier, lacked control of the distribution of their own munitions. This also was a reflection of Stalin's policy of avoiding provocation of the Germans at any cost.

The first known operational order issued to the Red Army four hours after the German attack was about on the same level of unprovocative passivity; it forbade any crossing of the German frontier by the already chaotic Soviet land forces.[5] While individual units of the Red Army immediately began to fight with a courage unprecedented so far in the German experience of the Second World War, especially at the border fortress of Brest-Litovsk, General Halder's conclusion on the second day of the campaign can hardly be denied, namely, that the Red Army command had lost control of the situation in White Russia and was both fighting desperately along the border and retreating blindly without plan. Moreover, the inexperience and misuse of the numerous Soviet tank formations during these opening days bordered upon the incredible.

The Third Panzer Group (or Army) of Bock's central Army Group had already punched a hole eighty miles wide between the Russian Northwest and West Fronts, while in Leeb's northern Army group the vital bridges across the Dvina River almost two hundred miles from the German border were captured intact by June 26, owing to Soviet confusion and the speed and determination of General Erich von Manstein's VIth Panzer Corps. But there is no doubt that the Red Army was already suffering from the grave shortage of

---

[5] General Guenther Blumentritt, "Moscow," in *The Fatal Decisions*, 56; cf. *The Great Patriotic War*, Vol. II, 11–19; Erickson, *op. cit.*, 586–87; and *loc. cit.*, 182; Carell, *op. cit.*, 23–29; Khrushchev, *loc. cit.*, 539; Poole, *loc. cit.*, 151; Werth, *op. cit.*, chap. ii. For Marshal Rodion Malinovsky's assertion in 1958 that the Soviet Supreme Military Command had not been caught unawares by the German attack, see Matthew Gallagher, "Trends in Soviet Historiography of the Second World War," in *Contemporary History in the Soviet Mirror*, edited by J. Keep and L. Brisby (New York, 1964), 226–27. For similar assertions by the Commander of the Soviet Navy, see "Stalin's Absence as Nazis Attacked Recalled," *New York Times* (New York), November 4 and 7, 1965, 19.

trained officers liquidated or still imprisoned by Stalin's terrible purges.[6]

In the air, matters were no better for the Russians. As a consequence of the excessively forward posture of the Red Air Force, a poor warning system, incomplete dispersion and inadequate camouflage, the all-out Luftwaffe attack on the dot of 3:15 A.M. on June 22 brought about the destruction, mostly on the ground, of an estimated two thousand Soviet planes within the first forty-eight hours of the campaign. Prolonged, high-level, and unopposed Luftwaffe reconnaissance, going back to Hitler's top-secret authorization in October, 1940, was paying off to such an extent that at first Hermann Goering did not credit the glowing reports of his pilots. For most practical purposes, during the next three or four tragic months the Red Army would fight without the immense, if sometimes overestimated, benefits of air cover.[7]

To the great disappointment of Adolf Hitler, who nevertheless continued to feel that a durable friendship with Britain would be achieved by the end of the war, on June 22 Winston Churchill publicly welcomed the Soviet Union as a partner in the struggle against Nazi Germany. Mincing no words concerning his previous antipathy to the Bolsheviks, Churchill declared once again that he would never parley with Hitler "or any of his gang." Churchill did warn, however, not merely in open, but also in secret session of the House of Commons, that the German attack upon Russia was no more than a prelude to an ensuing all-out invasion of the British Isles. Perhaps the German cover plans for *Barbarossa* had proved effective in deceiving the British, since the Russophile Sir Stafford Cripps likewise expected a German invasion of Brit-

---

[6] Erickson, *op. cit.*, 593–95; Gorbatov, *op. cit.*, 157 ff.; *G.D.*, Vol. XIII, 55–59; *The Great Patriotic War*, Vol. I, 520, Vol. II, 19–34; Seth, *Barbarossa*, 57–65, 102–3; Halder, *War Diary*, Vol. VI, 161 ff.; Garthoff, *Doctrine*, 226; Markoff, *loc. cit.*, 176; Carell, *op. cit.*, 29 ff., 66–79.

[7] Kilmarx, *op. cit.*, 181; Kesselring, *op. cit.*, 90; Halder, *War Diary*, Vol. VI, 161–90; Khrushchev, *loc. cit.*, 539; Erickson, *op. cit.*, 593 n., 600; *The Great Patriotic War*, Vol. II, 20–21, 476–77; Carell, *op. cit.*, 60–62.

ain in September, 1941, in the anticipated event of a Soviet collapse during the summer.[8]

The next day, a British military mission to the U.S.S.R. was appointed with an appreciation from the pessimistic British Army to the effect that Great Britain could not afford to lose even so poor a chance as that afforded by the Red Army for the sake of distracting the Germans in the East for a short time. Consequently, encouragement to the Russians to hold out in Siberia as long as possible, and in any case to destroy the oil fields of the Caucasus before a German occupation, bulked large in the initial instructions of the British mission.

In Moscow the British mission was received coldly, at first being "tolerated," in the words of American Ambassador, Laurence Steinhardt, rather than utilized or informed. Steinhardt busied himself with planning the evacuation of the United States Embassy in expectation of the fall of the Soviet capital within a month or so. At the same time, the British Chiefs of Staff turned down Churchill's suggestion of a large naval raid on the Channel ports of France in order to divert German attention from Russia. British resources were too limited in view of the anticipated German victory in the East.[9]

Another political personage planning to take advantage of the German attack on Russia was Yosuke Matsuoka, Foreign Minister of Japan. Immediately upon receipt of the news of the start of the German invasion, Matsuoka gained an audience with the Japanese Emperor and, without consulting the Cabinet, advocated assaulting the Soviet Union at once. Already much upset by what he called Hitler's "perfidious act" in attacking Russia, Prime Minister Fumimaro Konoye of Japan resisted Matsuoka's plans, a resistance rendered effective

[8] Churchill, *The Grand Alliance*, 371–73; and his *Secret Session Speeches* (New York, 1946), 140; *Hitler's Table Talk*, 12–13; Maisky, *op. cit.*, 55–58; Hesse, *op. cit.*, 134–38; *Foreign Relations of the United States, 1941*, Vol. I, 176–77; Eden, *op. cit.*, 312; James Leasor, *War at the Top: The Experiences of General Sir Leslie Hollis* (London, 1959), 154–57.

[9] *Foreign Relations of the United States, 1941*, Vol. I, 175–77; cf. Woodward, *op. cit.*, 151; J. Kennedy, *op. cit.*, 147–49; Gwyer, *op. cit.*, 94–95; *G.D.*, Vol. XIII, 176–177; Eden, *op. cit.*, 312.

by the Japanese Navy's opposition to a new campaign on the Asian continent on top of the Army's heavy existing involvement in China.[10]

At last, in response to the frantic inquiry of the German Ambassador in Tokyo, on July 1 Ribbentrop cabled that "the approaching collapse of the military power of Russia" offered Japan a "unique opportunity" to "get possession of Vladivostok and push as far as possible toward the West" in order to shake hands with the advancing Germans "at the half-way mark"in the Soviet Union before the advent of cold weather. What had precipitated this remarkable reversal of Hitler's policy while German confidence in an easy victory in Russia still reigned supreme remains obscure, although in the past Rudolf Hess had long advocated such a course with Hitler as one of the fundamental tenets of Karl von Haushofer's geopolitical doctrines.[11]

At a meeting of the Japanese Imperial Council on July 2, it was decided that, although military preparations for attacking the Soviet Union should be accentuated, nevertheless Japan should wait upon the development of the Russo-German war before deciding upon any action for the time being. The prospect of war with both the Soviet Union and the West had deterred a majority of the Council, notwithstanding the strenuous efforts of Foreign Minister Matsuoka on Germany's behalf.

Eventually and correctly informed of this decision by its own espionage, if not by the United States State Department, the Soviet Government continued its steady transfer of its Far Eastern forces to the newly active front in the West, a transfer which, in fact, had commenced in March, 1941, well

---

[10] "The Memoirs of Prince Konoye," *The Asahi Shimbun* (Tokyo), December 20–30, 1945, 3 ff.; cf. *Pearl Harbor Attack,* Parts 19–20, 3993; *Japanese Special Studies on Manchuria* (Washington: Office of the Chief of Military History, undated), Vol. I, 142–46; Butow, *op. cit.*, 212 ff.; *G.D.*, Vol. XIII, 1–2.

[11] *U.S. Dept. of State Bulletin* (Washington), July 16, 1946, 1040 ff.; *G.D.*, Vol. XIII, 36–41, 61–63; cf. *I.M.T.F.E.*, Exhibit 1096; Ernst Hanfstaengl, *Unheard Witness* (New York, 1957), 127.

before the April Neutrality Pact with Japan.[12] Not surprisingly, however, the doubling of the Japanese garrison in Manchuria in late 1941 greatly alarmed the United States Government, an alarm in no way alleviated by its misinterpretation of the meaning of the deciphered—but still misleading—Japanese messages to Berlin. But American questions to, and pressure on, Tokyo would still reflect nothing of the mortification of Ribbentrop's ensuing correspondence with the Japanese. For example, on July 10 the German Foreign Minister cabled that since Russia was about to collapse, it was "simply impossible that Japan does not solve the question of Vladivostok and the Siberian areas as soon as her military preparations" were completed.

The only response in Tokyo to Ribbentrop's appeal was the dismissal from the Japanese Foreign Ministry of Germany's good friend Yosuke Matsuoka. From Matsuoka's fall and the final setting of Japan's course in the direction of an initially easy southern expansion came about the eventual Japanese defeat at the hands of the one power she could not hope to conquer, the United States. Winston Churchill himself has recognized that in Matsuoka's seemingly reckless policy of thoroughgoing collaboration with Nazi Germany lay Japan's best and, in all probability, her only real chance of realizing victory in the Second World War. The excuses justifying their inaction at this time given by the Japanese to Germany—namely, their lack of armor and general unreadiness in Manchuria—also reflected Tokyo's recent unhappy experiences with the Red Army in 1938/39.[13]

During these diplomatic exchanges, although the central

---

[12] *Pearl Harbor Attack*, Parts 19–20, 4019; Willoughby, *op. cit.*, 105–6; *Foreign Relations of the United States, 1941*, Vol. I, 146, 787; *I.M.T.F.E.*, Exhibit 588; *G.D.*, Vol. XIII, 73–76; Johnson, *op. cit.*, *157–58*.

[13] *N.C.A.*, Vol. V, 564–65; cf. Churchill, *The Grand Alliance*, 194–95; Roberta Wohlstetter, *Pearl Harbor: Warning and Decision* (Stamford, 1962), 126–55; Takushiro Hattori, *A Complete History of the Greater East Asia War* (Tokyo, 1953), Vol. I, 149–51; Feis, *The Road to Pearl Harbor*, chaps. xxvii and xxviii; *Pearl Harbor Attack*, Parts 19–20, 3993–4004; *G.D.*, Vol. XIII, 110–13, 131–41, 158–60, 186–88.

German Army Group had continued its rapid advance, on the northern and southern flanks of the front the shape of a rather less promising future for *Barbarossa* was beginning to emerge. To be sure, Sweden had allowed passage of the German 163rd Infantry Division from Norway across her territory to Finland, but the logistic difficulties of the Far North, as well as the need for a belated concentration of German forces in northern Finland to avoid alerting the Russians, had resulted in the delay of the first German assault on Murmansk until June 29. Without the advantages of surprise or of a superiority in strength, in difficult terrain the two attacking German mountain divisions under General Eduard Dietl soon bogged down in the face of bitter Russian resistance thirty miles short of the Soviet Arctic port.

Two more German divisions with the aid of Finns proved almost as unsuccessful in another weak attempt to cut the Murmansk railway at Kandalaksha in the course of the next month, and it was left to the main Finnish Army under Field Marshal Mannerheim to reconquer Eastern Karelia in the middle of July. Profiting from better terrain, training, communications, and a temporary superiority in strength due to the weakening of the Twenty-third Soviet Army for the sake of opposing the rapid German advance in the Baltic, by the end of August the Finns had regained almost all of their former frontiers with the Soviet Union.[14]

In the flat and easily traversed Ukrainian sector of Field Marshal Gerd von Rundstedt's Army Group South, much the same circumstances had occurred, although here it was the First German Panzer Group that made modest advances while, according to plan, the mixed German-Rumanian forces comprising Rundstedt's right flank hardly progressed at all. Lemberg was captured on June 29, to the delight of its large Ukrainian Nationalist population, but the more alert nature of Lieutenant General Kirponos' Southwest Front, coupled

[14] Mannerheim, *op. cit.*, 415–26; Ziemke, *op. cit.*, 137–94; *The Great Patriotic War*, Vol. II, 50; *G.D.*, Vol. XIII, 21–22; Carell, *op. cit.*, 413–24.

with his fourfold superiority in tanks (2,400 to 600), prevented an effective German exploitation of this victory. As a result, approximately twenty-five Red Army divisions in the Carpathians, whose attack the pessimistic Rundstedt had feared on his right flank, were able to escape and retire to the east in good order. Repeated Red Army incursions from the cover of the Pripet Marshes against the Sixth German Army on Rundstedt's left flank did, however, slow down this elite unit from the onset.

A strong opponent of the campaign in the East as a whole, and inclined in any case to prefer a limited strategic advance along the Baltic upon Leningrad rather than an indefinitely expanding campaign in the Ukraine, Rundstedt quickly concluded that everything which he had previously read concerning Russia had been "nonsense." Even the German maps beyond the old Polish frontier turned out to be "all wrong." Major highways became mere tracks, and vice versa, railroads vanished mysteriously, and whole "American-type towns," complete with factories, suddenly materialized out of the blank spots on the German maps.[15]

Meanwhile, in Bock's decisive central German Army Group the rapid German advance continued. Although the Second and Third Panzer Groups had joined up at Minsk as early as June 28, the inability of German infantry marching on foot to keep up with the armored units gave the Russians a great many opportunities to escape from the resultant pocket around Bialystok. Nevertheless, a second German trap was sprung beyond Minsk during the first week of July, eventually capturing over 300,000 Soviet prisoners, comprising most of twenty divisions, along with such unmistakable hallmarks of victory as 2,500 tanks and 1,400 guns. Satisfaction mounted in the higher German headquarters, and even the cautious Army Chief of Staff, General Franz Halder, recorded on

[15] Shulman, *op. cit.*, 66; cf. A. Dallin, *German Rule*, 64–65, 119 ff.; Hart, *The Other Side of the Hill*, 185–90; Armstrong, *op. cit.*, 76 ff.; Blumentritt, *The Fatal Decisions*, 49–51, and his *Von Rundstedt: The Soldier and the Man* (London, 1952), 103–9; *The Great Patriotic War*, Vol. II, 116 ff.; Carell, *op. cit.*, 37–40.

July 3 that it was "probably no overstatement to say that the Russian campaign has been won in a space of two weeks." Manstein's LVIth Corps was finally released from its bridgeheads along the Dvina River in the direction of Leningrad, while in the center the equally impatient Panzer Group of General Guderian was now allowed to drive on across the formidable obstacles of the Berezina and Dnieper river lines before the Red Army had gained time to reoccupy in strength the old Stalin Line fortifications guarding Russia's heart.[16]

On July 4, Hitler himself declared: "For all practical purposes the enemy has lost this campaign. It is a good thing that we have destroyed the Russian armored and air forces right at the beginning. The Russians will be unable to replace them." More accurately, as it turned out, the Fuehrer conceded that his current hesitations regarding whether to favor the Leningrad or Moscow thrusts would probably prove "the most difficult decision of the entire campaign." Perhaps to postpone this already overdue decision still longer, Hitler decided, as noted by Halder on July 8, to wipe out by bombing both Leningrad, whose architecture the artist in Hitler had so much admired, and Moscow, the Fuehrer's particular antipathy as the center of Russian nationalism and of Bolshevik ideology. The ostensible grounds for this German inauguration of aerial genocide was to avoid the necessity for feeding the populations of these Russian political and cultural centers during the next winter, a rationalization which could hardly occur to the Western advocates of such horrors for the German cities over the course of the next few years.[17]

To his intimates, on the night of July 11/12, Hitler expressed himself on that "most extraordinary . . . clerk" Joseph Stalin,

---

[16] Halder, *War Diary*, Vol. VI, 196–97; cf. Guderian, *Panzer Leader*, 160 ff.; Hart, *The Other Side of the Hill*, 195–96; Blumentritt, *The Fatal Decisions*, 57–59; *The Great Patriotic War*, Vol. II, 39–47; Carell, *op. cit.*, 36–37. On July 7 General Andrei Yeremenko, the deputy commander to the West Front, appealed personally to Stalin for more tank replacements after describing their essential role in supporting Soviet infantry; see his *At the Beginning of the War* (Moscow, 1964), 104–5, 211.

[17] Blau, *Russia*, 45–48; cf. Halder, *War Diary*, Vol. VI, 212, and his *Hitler als Feldherr*, 40; *Hitler's Table Talk*, 40; Warlimont, *op. cit.*, 179–82.

who, dependent for power upon his subservient bureaucracy, was now apparently quite ready to abandon European Russia rather than lose everything. "Let nobody think," declared the Fuehrer, that "Stalin might reconquer Europe from the Urals!"[18] During the next week, instead of making the urgent strategic choice between Moscow or Leningrad as the center of gravity of the next German assault, Hitler busied himself with the more congenial task of planning the changeover of his combat forces in Russia into an occupation garrison during the autumn months. A directive which he issued on July 14 explained that the military domination of Europe after the defeat of Russia would enable the strength of the Army and the production of its equipment to be considerably reduced in the near future. Only the armored forces of the Army would be increased, as these were already wearing out under the heavy strain of carrying the principal offensive burden of the campaign in Russia; otherwise priorities would go to Goering's Air Force. At the same time Hitler's interventions in tactics impelled Halder to write: "This perpetual interference by the Fuehrer in matters the circumstances of which he does not understand is becoming a scourge which will eventually be intolerable."[19]

On July 16, Hitler was still engaged in the agreeable job of contemplating the glowing future rather than the more demanding present; on this occasion in the company of several Nazi Party colleagues, including Goering, Rosenberg, and Martin Bormann, the Fuehrer occupied himself with cutting up the skin of the Russian bear. Although, for propaganda purposes, the invading Germans were to stress their role as liberators from Communism, Hitler intended openly to annex to the Reich, first the Crimea (after expelling its indigenous population), the former Polish portions of the Ukraine, the Baltic States, the Baku oil fields, the German Volga colony, and the Kola Peninsula beyond Murmansk on the White Sea.

---

[18] *Hitler's Table Talk*, 8.

[19] Warlimont, *op. cit.*, 180–83; Halder, *War Diary*, Vol. VI, 212–34; cf. *N.C.A.*, Vol. II, 905–6; *T.M.W.C.*, Vol. XXXIV, 298–302; *Hitler's War Directives*, 82–85; Lossberg, *op. cit.*, 127.

The Finns were to receive eastern Karelia and the razed ruins of Leningrad. To the annoyance of Goering and Rosenberg, who wanted to exploit the hostility of the Ukrainians to Moscow, Odessa and other portions of the Ukraine were to go to Rumania or to the Reich itself.

Partisan war, went on the Fuehrer cheerfully, had certain advantages for the Germans, since it enabled them "to eradicate" more opponents. No Slavs should carry arms hereafter in any of the vast territories of the East, nor would any Soviet military power be permitted west of the Urals, "even if we have to wage war for a hundred years to attain this goal." Finally, in this new Nazi "Garden of Eden," any native who "looked sideways" at the Germans would be shot, evidently Hitler's guttersnipe conception of the British rule in India. Perhaps Ludendorff himself, whose program of June 9, 1918, for German imperial annexation in the East Hitler's present views so much resembled, would have disapproved of the Fuehrer's means of realizing them. In any event, as the more moderate Nazis themselves were well aware, there was little enough incentive in these policies of the Fuehrer to win over the numerous ethnic minorities of the Soviet Union, let alone the Great Russian nucleus of the U.S.S.R.[20]

Notwithstanding Hitler's indecision in strategy, with a heavy superiority in tank and plane strength his Panzer generals went on winning victories on the central Army Group front. Evading the restraints of his hostile immediate superior, Field Marshal Guenther von Kluge, Guderian, by the third week of July, had crossed the Dnieper and had captured Smolensk, almost two-thirds of the way to Moscow. When Guderian's Panzer Group met up with that of General Hermann Hoth coming from the north, notwithstanding bitter resistance, about 200,000 Russian prisoners from Timoshenko's West Front were eventually captured, along with vast quantities of matériel.

These impressive achievements, combined with the increas-

---

[20] *N.C.A.*, Vol. VII, 1086–93; cf. *G.D.*, Vol. XIII, 149–57; Freund, *op. cit.*, xviii.

ing exhaustion of the Panzer divisions and what Halder had already termed the catastrophic condition of the prolonged German supply lines, induced Hitler to issue War Directive No. 33 on July 19. Against the urgings of his tank commanders, including Manstein, a beneficiary of the order, the Fuehrer now directed that Army Group Center should mop up the many encircled Soviet units in its area and thereafter resume a slow advance on Moscow with its infantry divisions alone. The vital Panzer forces of Army Group Center were to be diverted, Panzer Group Three to the north to reinforce Leeb's bogged down drive to cut off Leningrad, and Panzer Group Two to the southeast to threaten the Soviet Fifth Army near Kiev from the rear, thus aiding Rundstedt's slow advance in the Ukraine. Within a few more days, in a supplement to Directive No. 33, the vainglorious Fuehrer added the Don, the Crimea, and the Caucasus to his southern targets for 1941, while Army Group North was directed to return most of its tanks to Germany, of all places, following the conquest and razing of Leningrad.

Hitler might assert in this period that to him Moscow was simply a place name, but his overconfidence at this time seems real enough in view of his cutback in production of Army weapons and ammunition, despite the rapid depletion of the German armored and motorized divisions to approximately half of their strength at the beginning of the campaign. Indeed, it was this serious depletion of the striking arm of the Army that may have evoked Brauchitsch's brief acceptance of what Halder called, on July 26, the abandonment of "our initial strategy of imaginative operations" in the center for the sake of purely tactical gains on the German flanks. Similarly, General Jodl's explanation at this same time that German supply difficulties justified a refusal to allow Russian civilians to flee from Leningrad represents another semiplausible excuse for another appalling error, if in this connection with respect to German policy rather than strategy. What the Red Army itself has considered its miracle of the Marne—the miracle which saved Moscow—was a direct result of Hitler's refusal to support the drive of Bock's Army Group Center, regardless of the consequences to less important operations elsewhere.[21]

Higher Soviet reactions to the great German attack became manifest as early as June 23, when the first version of the Stavka, or Army General Headquarters, was set up on the principles long before enunciated by one of the more important military survivors of Stalin's purges, Marshal B. M. Shaposhnikov. Drawing upon the resources of the General Staff of the Red Army, then headed by General Georgi Zhukov, the Stavka functioned directly under a new State Defense Committee, or Gko, created on June 30. The powers of the Gko were absolute, and as a *de facto* war cabinet, its membership initially included Stalin, Molotov, Voroshilov, G. M. Malenkov, and L. P. Beria.

On July 3, Stalin at last spoke to the Soviet people, and addressed them for the first time as brothers. In highly emotional Bolshevik language he warned of the supposed Nazi intentions to restore Czarism, of the German barons and the landlords, as well as of the need for ruthlessness in destroying resources abandoned to the enemy. In advocating guerrilla war, without adequate preparations having been made for it, Stalin was playing into Hitler's hands, since the Fuehrer sought for any excuse to decimate further the Russian population. Although he justified his pact with such "perfidious and monstrous" people as Hitler and Ribbentrop as a method of gaining time for preparations, Stalin did thank the British and American governments for their recent unsolicited offers of aid. In short, the Soviet dictator was extremely distraught and, according to Khrushchev's subsequent statement, had been induced to return to active political and military leadership at the beginning of July, following a temporary failure in

[21] Halder, *War Diary*, Vol. VI, 234–73; cf. his *Hitler als Feldherr*, 40–41; *Hitler's War Directives*, 85–90; *G.D.*, Vol. XIII, 181–83; Guderian, *Panzer Leader*, 183; Blau, *Russia*, 49–51; Assmann, *loc. cit.*, 315; Hart, *The Other Side of the Hill*, 196–99; Manstein, *Lost Victories*, 192–98; Warlimont, *op. cit.*, 181–84; Carell, *op. cit.*, 82–88; Leon Goure, *The Siege of Leningrad* (Stanford, 1962), 18; *The Great Patriotic War*, Vol. II, 54 ff., 90.

nerve, only at the behest of several members of the Politburo.[22]

From the first day of the German assault the full resources of revolutionary terror had been brought to bear against disloyal, defeatist, or merely incompetent Soviet citizens and soldiers alike. According to secret German reports, the Soviet Secret Police had butchered four thousand Ukrainian political prisoners in Lemberg alone in the week before its capture by the Germans on June 30. At the same time, on June 28, General D. G. Pavlov, in charge of the West Front in White Russia, was replaced by General Andrei Yeremenko, who had been hurriedly recalled from the Far East. Officially, at any rate, the unhappy armored expert Pavlov and several of his subordinates were shot as scapegoats for the initial Red Army disaster before Minsk. Marshal Timoshenko, as Defense Minister, endeavored to stave off incipient panic by threatening court-martial for anyone who even discussed retreat. A few days later the situation on the West Front had degenerated so far that on July 3 Marshal Timoshenko had to assume command himself, keeping Yeremenko as his Chief of Staff.

Similar such threats in Voroshilov's Northwest Front in mid-July were followed on July 16 by the reintroduction of the command responsibility of the political commissars, always a sign of alarm within the Communist Party over a possible loss of control over the Red Army. Stalin's secret order of July 16 went so far as to admit that the number of firm and steady Red Army commanders was not very great under the overwhelming impact of the surprise German assault against the Soviet center.

---

[22] Potemkin, *op. cit.*, Vol. III, 711–12; cf. Deutscher, *Stalin*, 462–64; Khrushchev, *loc. cit.*, 540; Erickson, *op. cit.*, 598; *Foreign Relations of the United States, 1941*, Vol. I, 628; Ilya Ehrenburg, Vol. V: *The War, 1941–1945* (London, 1964), 10–11; Werth, *op. cit.*, 162–67; "Stalin Hid as Nazi Attack Began, Ex-Envoy Recalls," *New York Times* (New York), January 7, 1965, 2; Carell, *op. cit.*, 51–52, 73; *The Great Patriotic War*, Vol. II, 74–80; "Stalin's Absence as Nazis Attacked in 1941 Recalled," *loc. cit.*, 19.

The return of Stalin to active leadership, signalized by his assumption of the Defense Commissariat on July 19, and his open role as Commander in Chief of the Soviet armed forces after August 9, does not appear to have improved matters much, since without any personal observation of conditions at the front, the Soviet ruler persisted in giving unrealistic orders for continuous attacks and against any retreats whatever. As a consequence of such political intervention into tactics, as with Hitler later in the war, far more Red Army troops were cut off and captured by the German Panzers at Smolensk and elsewhere than would otherwise have been the case. Even capture offered no refuge from Stalin's ferocity for the wretched Soviet prisoners of war, because Soviet doctrine damned all such inevitable victims of an untenable offensive strategy in 1941 as traitors to their country. Little wonder that, as Nikita Khrushchev, who was then serving as Political Commissar to Marshal Budënny in the Ukraine, remarked in 1964: "Anyone who loves Stalin can take him if they like the smell of corpses."[23]

Notwithstanding considerable doubts within the State Department, the vociferous opposition of the Isolationists, and a profound pessimism in the United States Army and Navy regarding the Russian chances of survival, American policy had followed British in welcoming the Soviet Union as an ally. But as early as July 6, certain elements of the British press, notably the newspapers of Lord Beaverbrook on the Right and of the Labour Party on the Left, had begun to demand more support for the Soviet Union, support even to the extent of opening an Allied second front in France in the near future. Always close to his old friend Beaverbrook, and spurred on by mounting public anxiety concerning the possibility of a

---

[23] "Khrushchev Calls Attack By Chinese Reds 'Crazy,'" *New York Times* (New York), April 6, 1964, 1; cf. Khrushchev, "The Crimes of the Stalin Era," 540; Garthoff, *op. cit.*, 250–52; Erickson, *op. cit.*, 600–5; Armstrong, *op. cit.*, 77; A. Dallin, *German Rule*, 64 n. 2; *Foreign Relations of the United States, 1941*, Vol. I, 630–31; Carell, *op. cit.*, 40–55; *The Great Patriotic War*, Vol. II, 57.

Russian collapse, on July 7 Winston Churchill took the initiative in resuming the long-interrupted Western dialogue with Moscow.

Congratulating "Monsieur Stalin" on the courage of the Red Army and the Russian people, the British Prime Minister declared that "the longer the war lasts, the more help we can give." Churchill emphasized that the aid the Royal Navy and Air Force were bringing would "gradually" increase, doubtless a cold consolation to the Soviet ruler currently facing the virtual collapse of his central front in White Russia. The next day, July 8, however, all Stalin asked British Ambassador Sir Stafford Cripps for was guarantees of mutual help and against a separate peace.

Churchill promptly agreed to these terms, for, as he explained to the First Lord of the Admiralty on July 10 in justifying the movement of a British squadron to the Arctic, such an action might raise Soviet morale and thus "spare a lot of English blood" in the long run. In this private message, Churchill went on to point out the "measureless" advantages to Britain of Russia's endurance "at any rate until the winter closes in," while on the other hand "a premature peace by Russia would be a terrible disappointment to great masses of people in our country." Churchill concluded his minute in terms still more unpalatable to the desperate Russians, had they heard of them, writing: "As long as they [the Soviets] go on, it does not matter so much where the front lies."[24]

Stalin finally replied to Churchill on July 18, to thank him for the recently concluded Anglo-Soviet accord along the lines he had previously suggested. After a brief justification of his 1939 pact with Hitler as gaining the Red Army a buffer zone of territory, Stalin launched the first of many appeals for the prompt establishment of a second front in France, or

---

[24] Churchill, *The Grand Alliance*, 380–82; cf. Woodward, *op. cit.*, 152–53; W. H. McNeill, *America, Britain and Russia: Their Cooperation and Conflict, 1941–1946* (New York, 1953), 50–51; *Foreign Relations of the United States, 1941*, Vol. I, 179–83, 766–67; Herbert Feis, *Churchill, Roosevelt, Stalin: The War They Waged and the Peace They Sought* (Princeton, 1957), 10 n. 9.

failing that, in the Arctic. Such a front would not merely relieve pressure in the U.S.S.R. at a "tense" moment, Stalin assured Churchill, it would also be popular with the population of "Southern England" as well as with the British Army. If these last incentives for action, proffered by the Soviet dictator to Churchill, remind one somewhat of a conversation conducted between two beings from different planets, Churchill's answer to Stalin on July 20—to the effect that there was no possibility of a serious British assault against the supposedly heavy fortifications of the French coast—was based upon the current belief of British military planners that because of shipping shortages the United Kingdom could not hope to mount a major invasion of the Continent. Naval support in the Arctic and the shipment of munitions from Britain's own scant supplies were the utmost the Prime Minister could offer the hard-pressed Soviets at this juncture.[25]

An indirect sacrifice which the British soon made for the Russians appeared shortly thereafter, when on July 25 President Roosevelt ordered the transfer of munitions already allocated to the British to the Soviet Union instead. At the same time, the President sent Harry Hopkins to Moscow as his personal representative, both to ascertain on the highest level Russia's real needs and chances and to bolster Soviet morale for the future.

Arriving in the Soviet capital on July 30, Hopkins saw Stalin in two long conferences which were to prove decisive for the future of effective Allied coalition warfare. Stalin immediately made clear his need for mobile antiaircraft guns to replace Soviet losses in fighter planes. Priority requests for aviation gas and aluminum for plane construction, as well as Anglo-American promises of fighter planes themselves, reflected the disaster to the Red Air Force of the opening days of the war. More ominously, Stalin also asked for a million

---

[25] Churchill, *The Grand Alliance*, 383–87; *Stalin's Correspondence with Churchill, Attlee, Roosevelt, and Truman, 1941–1945* (London, 1958), 12–15; Butler, *op. cit.*, Vol. II, 548–49.

or more rifles, although he said that he had plenty of ammunition. In the first divulgence of Soviet intelligence figures to the West, Stalin asserted that the campaign had commenced with approximately 175 German divisions against 180 Red Army divisions, the latter not fully mobilized or in position. At present, the Soviet ruler claimed, the Germans had sent 232 divisions to Russia in opposition to 260 Red Army divisions, twenty of which were in reserve and a third of which had not yet seen action. By the spring of 1942, Stalin anticipated having 350 divisions in service, evidently throughout the whole of the U.S.S.R. Stalin's figures are reasonably accurate for the German side, if allowance is made for his bland description of Axis divisions as purely German; for the Red Army, Stalin's figure of 180 divisions is confirmed by German sources, although the Soviet dictator did not admit to the heavy Russian losses in complete divisional units or to the rapid diminution in size and quality of the surviving Soviet divisions.

So far as tanks were concerned, Stalin exaggerated German resources almost tenfold, probably to a considerable extent being misled in this respect himself. He also defended the current Red Army practice of allocating fifty tanks to each Soviet infantry division on the grounds that this diverted the strong German Panzer divisions from their proper offensive functions in order to brace the tankless German infantry. Declaring that Soviet production of tanks amounted to one thousand a month (or three times the actual German production at this date), Stalin claimed still to have 24,000 tanks, including 4,000 of the fine new heavy Soviet categories so superior to their German counterparts.

For planes, the Soviet dictator admitted that the Luftwaffe was employing its obsolete aircraft in the Russian theater, but he asserted that the German plane production was 2,500 monthly as against his own of 1,800. Stalin stated that the German Army was already tired and that it would be held off from Kiev, Moscow, and Leningrad throughout the year.

Hopkins got the impression that if these three Soviet political centers and their peripheries fell to the Germans, approximately 75 per cent of Soviet industrial capacity would have been lost. Since Stalin had expressed the belief that the whole front would become solidified with the advent of the rainy season at the beginning of October, it was agreed that this would be a good date for an inter-Allied conference to decide upon more serious Western support for what by that time could be considered a viable front against the Third Reich.[26]

Meanwhile, in the German camp, Hitler was continuing to ignore the advice of both his Army and Navy chiefs, the latter more justifiably. On July 25, Grand Admiral Raeder, who had been nagging his Fuehrer since the beginning of the Russian campaign to take countermeasures against increasingly hostile American naval activities in the Atlantic, was "once again" informed by Hitler that an American declaration of war was to be avoided "while the Eastern campaign is still in progress, especially as the Army is still involved in heavy fighting." Subsequent to the completion of *Barbarossa*, Hitler reserved "the right to take severe action against the U.S.A. as well."[27] Even Hitler did not yet propose to repeat the folly of the German Navy in the First World War by provoking an American entry against Germany before he had at least terminated active major operations on the European Continent.

Correctly informed by its espionage net in Switzerland regarding the German concentration on the center, between June 27 and July 1 the Stavka or Soviet Grand Headquarters had sent five new armies to restore its shattered West Front guarding Smolensk and the main road to Moscow. Subsequently these replacement units would be reinforced by no less than thirteen additional Soviet armies in this sector alone. Thus there is no cause for surprise that on July 27 General

[26] Robert E. Sherwood, *Roosevelt and Hopkins: An Intimate History* (New York, 1948), 317–48; *Foreign Relations of the United States, 1941*, Vol. I, 797–815; E. R. Stettinius, Jr., *Lend-Lease: Weapon for Victory* (New York, 1944), 132–36; Blau, *Russia*, 60; Klein; *op. cit.*, 190.

[27] *F.C.G.N.*, *1941*, Part II, 1–13.

Jodl of the normally acquiescent O.K.W. asked the Fuehrer to reconsider his opposition to an early resumption of the drive on Moscow.

Appealing to Hitler in the language of the Fuehrer's purported mentor, Clausewitz, Jodl stressed that he favored the assault on Moscow, not because it was the Soviet capital, but simply because the Russians would employ their last reserves to defend it. Thus the Germans would be upholding Hitler's avowed aim in the U.S.S.R., namely, to destroy the Red Army rather than just to pursue the innumerable other political or economic acquisitions all too available in the vast territories of the East. Reverting to his original conception of a *Barbarossa* campaign with the offensive emphasis on the flanks, on July 28/29 Hitler replied to Jodl by saying that his new economic objective of crippling the Soviet armaments base in the eastern Ukraine was now more important than the destruction of the Red Army.[28]

Nevertheless, Hitler must have been impressed by the combined opposition of the O.K.H. and O.K.W., because on July 30 he retreated somewhat from his previous preference for the flanks. Army Group Center was to be permitted time for rest and rehabilitation of its tank forces before undertaking any further offensive toward Moscow, and for the moment it might preserve its existing strength intact except for the diversion of some Luftwaffe support to Army Group North. But on August 4, in a conference with Field Marshal von Bock and Panzer Generals Hoth and Guderian at the headquarters of Army Group Center, Hitler turned down the plans of all three of these officers for the resumption of the attack on Moscow in late August.

---

[28] In contrast to Alan Clark's argument that Hitler was really upholding Clausewitz against his generals' desire for the purportedly geographical objective of Moscow. Alan Clark, *Barbarossa: The Russo-German Conflict, 1941–1945* (New York, 1965), 77 ff.; Blau, *Russia,* 56–57; Warlimont, *op. cit.*, 184–85; Assmann, *loc. cit.*, 310; *Military Strategy: Soviet Doctrines and Concepts*, by Marshal V. D. Sokolovsky *et al.* and cited hereafter under his name (New York, 1963), 153; Carell, *op. cit.*, 57–58; *The Great Patriotic War,* Vol. II, 74 ff.

Hitler made his rejection all the more effective by refusing Guderian an adequate number of replacements for his worn-out tank engines, although he tried to conciliate his embittered Panzer commander with the statement: "If I had known that the figures for Russian tank strength which you gave in your book were in fact the true ones, I would not—I believe—ever have started this war." However questionable this last assertion, Hitler continued to speak of Leningrad as his primary objective and dwelt upon the importance of capturing Kharkov and the Donets industrial basin in the eastern Ukraine as well as upon the importance of neutralizing the Crimea, which he now described as "that Soviet aircraft carrier operating against the Rumanian oil fields." At this stage, of course, the Soviet Air Force was scarcely functioning on a tactical level, let alone as a serious long-range strategic threat to anything.[29]

At the same time, when the ever more anxious Army was pressing for a resumption of the attack on Moscow rather than for the premature acquisition of the political and economic booty so eagerly sought by the politician in Hitler, the O.K.H. also submitted a request to the Fuehrer for a public collection of winter clothing from the German civilian economy for the sake of the Army in Russia. The infuriated Nazi dictator rejected this suggestion on the grounds that he had promised the German people that their soldiers would be home for Christmas and that in any event there was not going to be a winter campaign in Russia.[30]

On August 6, meeting with his Army Group South commanders in the Ukraine, and notwithstanding Field Marshal von Rundstedt's disinterested advocacy of a Moscow thrust, Hitler repeated what Halder now called the Fuehrer's "old gramophone record" of Leningrad first, the Donets Basin second, with Moscow third "only as a last resort." In an

---

[29] Guderian, *Panzer Leader*, 189–190; cf. *Hitler's War Directives*, 91–92; Blau, *Russia*, 61–62; Hart, *The Other Side of the Hill*, 198–99; Goerlitz, *Paulus*, 36–37; Warlimont, *op. cit.*, 185–86; *G.D.*, Vol. XIII, 235–37.

[30] Halder, *Hitler als Feldherr*, 39–44, and his *War Diary*, Vol. VII, 7; Goerlitz, *Paulus*, 34–35.

unusual private discussion with Jodl on the next day, Halder thought that Leningrad and Moscow might be seized simultaneously, but the Chief of Staff's opposition to Hitler's attempt to pursue both major military and economic objectives at the same time remained unabated.

Halder, of course, had been raised in the school of Clausewitz. The great Prussian military theorist had written commending Napoleon's desperate thrust to Moscow in the following vein: "Has his heart failed him that he has not taken the enemy's capital, the defenceless Moscow . . . and thus left a nucleus round which new elements of resistance may gather themselves? He had singular luck to take this far-off and enormous colossus by surprise . . . and he makes no use of his good fortune, halts in the middle of his victorious career as if some evil spirit laid at his heels . . . ?"[31]

To be sure, Rundstedt's Army Group had at last begun to achieve successes comparable to those of Bock's center Group. Fleshed out with Italian, Hungarian, and Slovak reinforcements, in early August Army Group South had surmounted and destroyed a large proportion of some twenty-odd Russian divisions of the Soviet Sixth and Twelfth Armies at Uman in the central Ukraine. By the end of the month Rundstedt's group had arrived at the line of the Dnieper everywhere, except at Kiev, and had thrown firm bridgeheads across the great Russian river at several points. Hitler enthusiastically informed his intimates that the new German India in the East was finally secure and that the anticipated fall of Leningrad and Kharkov would be tantamount to a Soviet surrender.

With the last German reserves about to be committed to the campaign, Franz Halder, however, was reaching very different conclusions from those of his Fuehrer. In a famous notation entered in his war diary on August 11, Halder wrote:

The whole situation makes it increasingly plain that we have underestimated the Russian Colossus, who consistently prepared

---

[31] Karl von Clausewitz, *On War* (London, 1918), Vol. III, 160–61.

for war with that utterly ruthless determination so characteristic of totalitarian states. . . . At the outset of the war [i.e., of the campaign] we reckoned with about 200 enemy divisions. Now we have already counted 360. This conclusion applies as much to its organization as to its economic resources and its system of communication, but above all to its purely military efficiency. The time factor favors them, as they are near their own resources while we are moving farther and farther away from ours. And so our troops, sprawled over an enormous frontline, without any depth, are subjected to the incessant attacks of the enemy. Sometimes these are successful, because too many gaps must be left open in these enormous spaces.[32]

In the long-stalled Army Group North, too, matters began to improve for the Germans, thus enhancing Hitler's mounting eagerness to favor his flanks. Already, on August 7, the German Eighteenth Army had split the Soviet Eighth Army in northern Estonia into its two component corps, driving one Russian corps back upon the naval base at Tallinn, which it defended for another three weeks with the aid of Soviet naval forces, and the other Red Army corps to the Luga River line beyond Narva. For once exploiting a marked superiority in strength, on August 10 Field Marshal von Leeb's group launched a general offensive across the Luga aimed at cutting Leningrad off from the rest of the Soviet Union.

Despite an impressive display of personal courage, Marshal Klymenty Voroshilov, whom Trotsky had once said could command nothing larger than a regiment, was unable to rally his inferior forces along the Luga, particularly as many Soviet replacements were only raw militia and factory workers. Furthermore, Voroshilov and his Political Commissar, A. A. Zhdanov, annoyed Stalin by setting up a Military Soviet on August 20 for the emergency defense of Leningrad without prior authorization from the Soviet dictator. Although this somewhat defeatist Leningrad Military Soviet was soon

---

[32] Halder, *War Diary*, Vol. VII, 25–36; cf. Blau, *Russia*, 62–65; *Hitler's Table Talk*, 24–26; Blumentritt, *Von Rundstedt*, 106; Philippi and Heim, *op. cit.*, 69; *The Great Patriotic War*, Vol. II, 121–23; Clark, *op. cit.*, 132–36.

enough abolished, confusion in the command structure of Voroshilov's sector remained so great that reinforcements of two additional Soviet armies to establish a fresh defense line along the Volkhov River soon proved inadequate.

Despite a rather effective diversionary attack by the Red Army on Staraya Russa and the escape of some of the encircled units of the Soviet Eighth Army by sea from Estonia, by early September Leeb's group had penetrated the southern suburbs of Leningrad, and on September 8 the Germans captured the historic fortress of Schluesselburg on Lake Ladoga, thus servering Leningrad's last rail and land link from the rest of Russia. Less than 700,000 Soviet civilians had been evacuated from the city, leaving approximately 3,000,000 residents and refugees still in and about Russia's cultural capital to face the famine currently advocated for Leningrad by Hitler and Goering as a substitute for its more expensive occupation. It would seem, therefore, that Marshal Voroshilov's replacement in early September, General Zhukov, was successful in stabilizing this front in the southern suburbs of the city chiefly because of the diversion of German offensive strength to Moscow in mid-September rather than just because of his own high military abilities.[33]

Meanwhile, the great strategic debate between Hitler and the Army High Command regarding the strategic center of gravity of the campaign had continued to rage. On August 18, Brauchitsch and Halder returned to the fray with a memorandum which stressed that since two months would comprise the estimated minimum time required for the capture of Moscow, and this only if given priority in resources over all other enterprises, an immediate start was essential for the sake of completing the Moscow operation before the begin-

---

[33] Goure, *op. cit.*, 18–19, 53–99; Erickson, *op. cit.*, 604–7; G. A. Deborin, *Second World War* (Moscow, 1958), 80–82; *T.M.W.C.*, Vol. XXXVI, 109; Clark, *op. cit.*, 114–28; Vice Admiral Friedrich Ruge, *Der Seekrieg* (Annapolis, 1957), 201–3; Werth, *op. cit.*, 201, 307; Carell, *op. cit.*, 232–67. For the astonishing parallels between Andrei Zhdanov's demoralized Leningrad at this time and G. V. Zinoviev's defeatist Petrograd in 1919, see Trotsky, *My Life*, chap. xxxv.

ning of the autumn rains in October. In an accurate expression of Clausewitz' doctrine, the O.K.H. declared that economic benefits of the south would accrue automatically from a decisive military victory over the Red Army. Brigadier General Walter Warlimont of the O.K.W. Operations Staff endorsed the O.K.H. conclusions on this same day, pointing out that operations in the south could wait longer because of the greater likelihood of good weather in the Ukraine until later in the autumn season.[34]

On August 20, however, General Jodl, Warlimont's immediate superior on the Operations Staff of the O.K.W., replied to the O.K.H. on behalf of the Fuehrer, affirming that the chances of catching the Russians by surprise and of destroying a large portion of the Red Army in the deepening Kiev pocket were too good to be missed, while such an attack in the south was necessary anyway to protect the right flank of a subsequent advance of Army Group Center upon Moscow. In vain, Lieutenant General Adolf Heusinger, Chief of Operations for the O.K.H., pleaded that the capture of the nodal point of all Russian communications—Moscow—apart from the capital's immense intrinsic political and economic importance, would disrupt Red Army logistics far more than would any advance elsewhere.

On the other hand, aside from the crucial time factor, it can be conceded that Jodl's arguments were plausible enough, but it may well be, as Alan Clark and Andreas Dorpalen have argued, that privately Hitler had already decided with Halder that the Russian campaign would be a long one. From this painful hypothesis, perhaps secretly held in common with the O.K.H., Hitler, however, evidently drew the politically-minded conclusion that the Reich must therefore seize whatever economic resources she could while the going was still good in the south. According to this reasoning, Moscow could wait until later, since its capture in any event might have to wait upon an overall weakening of the Soviet military econ-

[34] Blau, *Russia*, 65–69; Lossberg, *op. cit.*, 130; Warlimont, *op. cit.*, 187–88; Clark, *op. cit.*, 107–10.

omy. In short, in this interpretation of Hitler's sentiments, Moscow was now recognized as being so strongly held that it could hardly be assaulted at all with much real hope of success before winter.[35]

Whatever his motives, on August 21 in War Directive No. 34, Hitler angrily rejected the Army memorandum of August 18. In Halder's record the Fuehrer said quite explicitly: "The principal object that must be achieved yet before the onset of winter is not the capture of Moscow but rather in the south the capture of the Crimea and the industrial and coal region of the Donets, together with the isolation of the Russian oil regions in the Caucasus, and in the north the encirclement of Leningrad and junction with the Finns." Hitler rubbed in his rejection on the next day with what Halder called the "unheard of" insult of describing the O.K.H. as filled with minds "fossilized" in obsolete theory.

Halder's indignant suggestion to Brauchitsch that they submit their joint resignations in protest against the Fuehrer's "zig-zag course" met with the passive rejoinder of the weak Commander in Chief of the Army to the effect that this would change nothing. So acquiescent, in fact, was Brauchitsch that when on August 23, at Halder's halfhearted suggestion, Guderian visited Hitler in a final effort to change his views, the Commander in Chief of the Army forbade Guderian to bring up the subject of a Moscow offensive with the Fuehrer at all. When Guderian did so anyway, Hitler loftily informed him that his generals knew nothing about the economic aspects of war. To top it all, in the aggressive

---

[35] Adolf Heusinger, *Hitler et l'OKH, 1923–1945* (Paris, 1952), 87–89; *The Great Patriotic War,* Vol. II, 89; Andreas Dorpalen, "Hitler, the Nazi Party, and the Wehrmacht in World War II," in *Total War and Cold War: Problems in Civilian Control of the Military* (Columbus, 1961), 75–76; Clark, *op. cit.*, 102; Hart, *The Other Side of the Hill,* 199–201. See, especially, the British official historians' emphasis upon the exhaustion of the German Army's reserves of oil as the cause for War Directive No. 34, and Gwyer, *op. cit.*, 102–4, and *G.D.*, Vol. XIII, 383–84, for Hitler's assertion to Mussolini on August 25 that German Intelligence had failed to ascertain either the fine equipment or fanatic fighting spirit of the Red Army.

Guderian's judgment, Halder, too, thereafter appeared to undergo a nervous collapse, a collapse replete with charges and countercharges between Halder and Guderian regarding the latter's sudden acquiescence in the Fuehrer's orders as long as his Panzer Group was kept intact.[36]

Faced with such military irresolution and disunity in the High Command, it is hardly a matter for surprise that once again Hitler got his way in spite of a warning on August 28 from the greatly disappointed commander of Army Group Center, Field Marshal von Bock, that given the loss of both of his Panzer Groups to the north and the south, he foresaw the inability of his Army Group even to resist the constant Soviet counterattacks, let alone to mount a new offensive with his depleted and exhausted infantry divisions alone. On this same day, however, in a memorandum on strategy issued to a select few with Hitler's approval, it was suggested that the original *Barbarossa* objective line of Archangel on the White Sea to Astrakhan on the Caspian Sea was unlikely to be accomplished in 1941. Thus for 1942 the Reich's first task would remain the defeat of the Soviet Union. To realize such a defeat, in accord with the Fuehrer's new-found pessimism, gains in the southern regions of the U.S.S.R. were particularly important for reasons of potential political dissidence in these areas as well as for the sake of economic goals. Moreover, in all other theaters nothing should be done to stretch further the already much overstrained resources of the Wehrmacht.[37]

Similarly, with respect to the prospect of Japanese aid against Russia, the Germans were becoming more realistic. Although in late August Hitler had consoled Grand Admiral Raeder for the repeated frustration of his desires with assurances that the Japanese would attack Vladivostok as soon as their current heavy military buildup in Manchuria was com-

---

[36] Halder, *War Diary*, Vol. VII, 59–62; cf. Guderian, *Panzer Leader*, 198–203; Manstein, *Lost Victories*, 75; Warlimont, *op. cit.*, 189–92; Carell, *op. cit.*, 98–103; *Hitler's War Directives*, 95–96.

[37] Assmann, *loc. cit.*, 317–18; Playfair, *op. cit.*, Vol. II, 261–62.

pleted, by September 10 Halder noted that Hitler did not want to press the Japanese any more so as to avoid giving them the impression that they were really needed in Russia, despite the fact that the Japanese Army had "cold feet" and would "probably do nothing for the time being."

At last the Fuehrer had been correctly informed regarding the intentions of his Far Eastern partner. As Richard Sorge had likewise told the Soviet Intelligence Service in September and October, under pressure from the Navy and Foreign Ministry the Japanese Army had decided that the German progress in Russia had been insufficient to justify any immediate action on the part of Japan. Intervention against the Soviet Union was thereby postponed until at least the spring of 1942, and then only in the event that the German Army had first reached the Volga, a prerequisite about which Hitler may well have learned.[38]

Perhaps as a result of the O.K.H. pressure, even before the pincers of the new German trap east of Kiev closed on the Red Army in mid-September, in War Directive No. 35 on September 6, Hitler had ordered a rebuilding of the Panzer strength of Bock's depleted Army Group Center. The Fuehrer's stated purpose was to launch a decisive offensive against Marshal Timoshenko's aggressive forces before Moscow "in the limited time which remains before the onset of winter weather." Hitler supplemented this ambitious directive, at first scheduled for inauguration within a mere fortnight, with pressure on the Finns for a new offensive to tie down as many Soviet divisions as possible north of Leningrad. He obviously hoped that a Finnish advance beyond the Svir River line to a junction with the German Army Group North would enable him to strip Leeb's weak Army group of its sole offensive striking force, the Fourth Panzer Group,

[38] Halder, *War Diary*, Vol. VII, 88–99; cf. *F.C.G.N.*, *1941*, Part II, 27; Butow, *op. cit.*, 220 n. 63; Willoughby, *op. cit.*, 207–28; *Germany and Her Allies*, chap. iv., Part II, 281–82; *G.D.*, Vol. XIII, 282, 351–79, 446–49, 466; Johnson, *op. cit.*, 157–59.

in favor of an overwhelming, if belated, concentration upon the German center.

As it turned out, unknown to the reluctant Finns, Leeb's Army Group North finally received orders to divert most of its armor and air strength to Bock during the second half of September.[39] The consequence of Hitler's inability to adhere to any consistent course of action long enough to achieve decisive results was that, like Yudenich's White Forces in the autumn of 1919, the weakened German Army Group North was forced to halt in the suburbs of Leningrad and rely solely upon starvation and lowered morale to conquer the great city on the Neva.

Following the fall of Kiev on September 19 and the capture —according to the Germans—of approximately 665,000 Red Army soldiers with 3,700 guns in late September, an exultant Fuehrer described this unprecedented bag of prisoners as the greatest battle and victory in the history of the world. To his intimates, Hitler could not forbear to observe that he had "had to throw all my authority into the scales to force it through. I note in passing that a great part of our successes have originated in 'mistakes' we've had the audacity to commit." The intoxicated Nazi chief went on to say that he would prefer another decade of war than to lose any of "the spoils of victory" in the East.

Some of the reasons for the unexpected size of this Fuehrer victory over both the O.K.H. and the Red Army may be found to be the consequence of a similar, if less successful, intervention on the part of Stalin. Furthermore, the price paid for the astonishing German tactical achievement in terms of subsequent strategic failure was not yet fully apparent, even to Franz Halder and his mortified colleagues among the professional pessimists of the Army General Staff. Victory

[39] *Hitler's War Directives*, 96–98; *G.D.*, Vol. XIII, 355–57, 395–99, 456–58; cf. Assmann, *loc. cit.*, 319; Halder, *War Diary*, Vol. VII, 83–84; Mannerheim, *op. cit.*, 427–32; Lossberg, *op. cit.*, 131–33; Deborin, *op. cit.*, 128–45; Philippi and Heim, *op. cit.*, 84.

is its own justification and now the O.K.H. was to be quickly silenced with the prospect of a renewal of the long-sought Moscow advance against a Red Army at last presumably about ready for the German *coup de grâce*.[40]

Apparently as another example of both his characteristic distrust of his own Intelligence Service and his undue faith in the likelihood of a logical (i.e., General Staff) enemy reaction, in late August Stalin had ordered the strengthening of the southern approaches to Moscow at the expense of Marshal Budënny's forces in the Ukraine. Thus, Guderian's abrupt passage of the Desna River to the south took the Red Army completely by surprise and rendered certain the success of the northern wing of the German *Kessel* (trap). As the German pincers were about to close on September 11, Budënny and his Political Commissar in the Ukraine, N. S. Khrushchev, asked Stalin for permission to withdraw the five Soviet armies threatened with encirclement. Ascribing the situation at Kiev to panic, on September 13 Stalin and the Chief of Staff of the Red Army, General B. M. Shaposhnikov, instead replaced Budënny with Marshal Timoshenko, until then commanding the crucial central region before Moscow. Presumably for political motives, Stalin was as reluctant to give up Kiev as Hitler, more curiously, was to seize it.

According to the recent and post-Khrushchevian account of Marshal I. K. Bagramyan, a participant in the disaster, it was Timoshenko who, presumably with Khrushchev, finally gave the orders for the retreat of the Soviet Southwest Front. Unfortunately, Timoshenko's orders came too late to save most of the Southwest Front, although General Andrei Vlasov's Thirty-seventh Army, for one, did manage to fight its way out of the German pocket. The commander of the

---

[40] *Hitler's Table Talk*, 32–35; cf. Lossberg, *op. cit.*, 131; Assmann, *loc. cit.*, 319; Hart, *The Other Side of the Hill*, 201–3. The Soviets claim that their losses at Kiev amounted to only one-third of those the Germans recorded; *The Great Patriotic War*, Vol. II, 130.

Soviet Fifth Army was less fortunate; as he explained to his captor, General Guderian, the countermanding by Stalin of his original orders to retreat after September 8 had rendered his Army's loss inevitable. The enormity of this Soviet disaster may be seen in the death of the commander of the whole Southwest Front, Lieutenant General M. P. Kirponos, killed in one of the uncoordinated and frantic attempts of his armies to escape.

At last either Stalin or those about him began to show some signs of profiting from Soviet mistakes—about time, with 75 per cent of the tremendous Red Army reserve in tank strength already lost in only three months of war. In any event, it was Stalin himself who had said in 1923: "When one side wants to save the cadres of its army and lead them out from under the blows of superior forces of the enemy . . . it gives up without fighting, whole cities and areas." The draining exhaustion of maintaining constant Russian attacks along the whole line was halted hereafter, tentative efforts toward differentiating between elite and mass formations commenced, and the first antitank guns began to reach Soviet formations in the field.[41]

At the same time, the ever more unconcealed manifestations of Nazi intentions toward the Eastern peoples began to work on behalf of Soviet interests. The vast majority of the 2,000,000 Soviet prisoners of war captured by the autumn of 1941 (or the more precise figure of 3,600,000 recorded by the end of the year) was in some cases being shot outright after a cursory investigation concerning their relative importance in the Soviet scheme of things or, if inoffensive enough to Nazi

[41] Leites, *op. cit.*, 495–502; cf. Shabad, *op. cit.*, 20; Erickson, *op. cit.*, 612–17; *The Great Patriotic War,* Vol. II, 126–30; *Hitler's War Directives*, 94; John Armstrong, "Recent Soviet Publications on World War II," *Slavic Review* (Seattle), September, 1962, 515–16; Garthoff, *Doctrine*, 161–63, 431; Carell, *op. cit.*, 121–28; Clark, *op. cit.*, 136–43; Guderian, *Panzer Leader*, 225–26; George Fischer, *Soviet Opposition to Stalin* (Cambridge, Mass., 1952), 173; Sokolovsky, *op. cit.*, 155; Gallagher, "Trends," 228–32.

ideology, were simply left to die of hunger, disease, or exposure in their pens in open fields during the approaching long, hard winter.

To be sure, much of the appalling death rate among the ordinary Soviet prisoners of war resulted from German Army indifference and lack of adequate preparations for such unexpected hordes of prisoners, but the systematic Nazi decrees designed to terrorize the whole population of the U.S.S.R. cannot be called incidental to this catastrophe. Moreover, the deliberate creation of famine conditions in the captured urban areas of the Ukraine, the evasive refusal to grant any recognition to Ukrainian independence movements, the haphazard mass roundups of civilians for forced labor within Germany, the abolition of nonvocational education above the fourth grade of grammar school, the well-publicized mass reprisals against casual civilian hostages, and the refusal to abolish or modify the hated Soviet collective farm system soon enough revealed, even to those elements of the population most hostile to the Communist regime, how much worse off they would be in the event of a Nazi triumph. Far more than Napoleon in 1812, Hitler was rapidly making clear to all that his crusade in Russia had not been undertaken for the sake of liberating serfs, and that, if victorious, the new Nazi overlords would disdain Russian popular assistance, except for the most manual and degraded functions.

In November, the enthusiasm of the Ukrainians in particular for liberation, Nazi-style, would receive another cruel check when Hitler ordered that prisoners of this nationality should no longer be released from the overburdened German Army camps, although 80 per cent of the first Ukrainian labor contingents to the Reich had consisted of volunteers, while continued imprisonment meant almost certain death for such potential labor. Characteristically, Goering was not beating about the bush when he smugly told Count Ciano at the end of November that "in the camps for Russian prisoners they have begun to eat each other. This year between twenty and thirty million persons will die of hunger in Russia. Perhaps it is well that it should be so, for certain nations must be decimated."[42]

So cocksure and arrogant had the Nazi leaders become that the Soviet soap bubble was about to burst for all time that their natural barbarism could now emerge in its fullest and most horrifying flower. But the first fruit of such unfeigned Nazi sadism was developing rapidly, flourishing in the charnel-house atmosphere of German imperial dreams.

---

[42] Ciano, *Diplomatic Papers*, 464–65; cf. *N.C.A.*, Vol. III, 837, Vol. IV, 57, Vol. VI, 961–62; *T.M.W.C.*, Vol. XV, 413, Vol. XXII, 72–75; *Hitler's Table Talk*, 34, 40, 54, 68–69, 207, 236, 319, 327, 401; A. Dallin, *German Rule*, 69 ff., 324, 427; Armstrong, *op. cit.*, 118–25; Carroll, *loc. cit.*, 82; *G.D.*, Vol. XIII, 6–7, 289–316, 596–97, 690, 893–94, 901; *Foreign Relations of the United States, 1941*, Vol. I, 1016–17.

"We are defending the fatherland against the imperialists. We defend, we shall conquer. . . . Of Russia nothing is left save Great Russia."[1]

LENIN, early 1918

"It was not Napoleon alone who had the nightmare feeling that the mighty arm was stricken powerless; all the generals, all the soldiers of the French Army . . . after all their experiences of previous battles (when after one tenth of the effort the enemy had always run), showed the feeling of horror before this foe, who, after losing *one half* of the army, still stood its ground as dauntless at the end as at the beginning of the battle. The moral force of the French, the attacking army, was exhausted."[2]

TOLSTOY

"Winter will come like a bombshell—and you cannot be too apprehensive, considering the present state of the army."[3]

CAULAINCOURT, to NAPOLEON,
October, 1812

"I've always detested snow, Bormann; you know, I've always hated it. Now I know why. It was a presentiment."[4]

HITLER, February 19, 1942

[1] Lenin, *Sochineniya,* Second Edition, Vol. XXII, 13–14.
[2] *War and Peace*, Part VII.
[3] Caulaincourt, *op. cit.*, 155.
[4] *Hitler's Table Talk*, 319; cf. Goebbels, *op. cit.*, 188.

CHAPTER VI

Winter Crises

August 25–December 31, 1941

AUGMENTING Western hopes for a Soviet survival, at least into 1942, led to a resumption of the Anglo-Soviet dialogue on a momentarily more auspicious note at the end of August. Employing the excuse that German intrigues in Persia threatened the oil wells in this linchpin of the Middle East, the British and Russians jointly occupied this Moslem country, commencing on August 25. As Churchill made clear to both Stalin and Roosevelt, the most important British motive for this abrupt intervention was to gain an invulnerable supply route from the West to the U.S.S.R.

Given the immense distances or dangers of the alternative supply routes to Russia through Vladivostok or Murmansk—routes which at any time might be severed through Axis action—even with the wretched condition of Persian roads and railways, this Middle Eastern route at least constituted a hedge against the darkening prospects for the Allies. As it turned out, after a thorough rebuilding and expansion of Persia's communications by the United States Army, this route eventually sustained the movement of the equivalent of sixty American divisions' worth of equipment for the Red Army.[5]

Concurrent with the problem of the safe conveyance of supplies to Russia was the question of diverting a proportion

[5] Churchill, *The Grand Alliance*, 454–84; T. H. Vail Motter, *United States Army in World War II: The Middle East Theater; The Persian Corridor and Aid to Russia* (Washington, 1952), 6 ff.; Langer and Gleason, *op. cit.*, Vol. II, 801–10.

of the still hopelessly inadequate war production of Great Britain and America to this same end. Flaying the unhappy British military services of their hard-won allocations of Anglo-American production, on August 30 the canny Prime Minister took some of the wind out of the Russophile sails of Lord Beaverbrook by appointing him chief of a mission to Moscow to negotiate a British offer of supplies for the Soviet Union. Beaverbrook was warned, however, not to bleed Britain "white in the process," regardless of the nature of the Soviet reception of his mission. Lest his ebullient disposition arouse undue Soviet hopes, Beaverbrook was also reminded that the bulk of Western supplies for the U.S.S.R. could not arrive until the latter part of 1942 or even in 1943, a bleak enough prospect for a state confronted with imminent destruction.

On September 4, Stalin's desperate acknowledgment of Churchill's offer of more fighter planes was personally delivered by Soviet Ambassador Maisky to the Prime Minister. Stalin wrote that British fighter planes were no longer enough to save the Soviet Union from being reduced to military impotence or defeat. In view of the recent arrival of what the Soviet ruler described as thirty to thirty-four fresh German divisions, purportedly released by the lack of any British threat in western Europe, Stalin now urgently requested a British second front in France or the Balkans capable of pulling those new German forces away from Russia. At the same time Stalin asked for a minimum monthly supply of 400 planes, 500 tanks, and 2,500 tons of aluminum commencing in October to compensate for her admitted losses of over 4,000 planes and 5,000 tanks so far in the campaign.

Maisky reinforced his master's plea with a poignant reference to the gravity of the moment, but, sensing an underlying reproach or even menace in Maisky's manner, Mr. Churchill became angry and referred to the Soviet support of Germany prior to June, 1941. In his turn, Maisky, who had long known and admired the Prime Minister, told Mr. Churchill to calm down; yet it was clear that the first official Soviet broaching of the basic issue of a second front had returned Anglo-Soviet relations to their customary level of mutual distrust and recrimination.

The Prime Minister replied to Stalin at once, explaining that there was "no possibility of any British action in the West, except air action, which would draw the German forces from the East before winter sets in." Mr. Churchill further explained that a British return to the Balkans was dependent upon Turkish aid, while the possibility of a British invasion of France in 1942 depended, as it always would hereafter in Churchill's judgment, upon "unforeseeable events." Only in Norway or Libya could the Prime Minister and his Chiefs of Staff offer Stalin any possibility of a British action on land.[6]

It was probably fortunate for the emergence and growth of Churchill's long-sought Grand Alliance with Russia and America that Stalin had not heard of the conclusions of the British and American Chiefs of Staff at the Atlantic Conference five weeks earlier. Here Admiral Sir Dudley Pound, the First Sea Lord, had informed the United States Joint Chiefs of Staff that the British did "not foresee vast armies of infantry as in 1914–1918." Elite British armored forces would suffice as a catalyst to arouse the conquered populations of Europe. While in eventual disagreement with this British opinion, the United States Chiefs themselves opposed any employment of American troops on the European Continent in the near future in what, at this juncture, would necessarily involve a commitment in "a premature and indecisive" fashion "against a superior enemy under unfavorable logistic conditions."[7] In land warfare, still more than in the matter of sup-

---

[6] Churchill, *The Grand Alliance*, 452–59; *Stalin's Correspondence*, Vol. I, 18–22; cf. Eden, *op. cit.*, 317–20.

[7] Maurice Matloff and Edwin M. Snell, *United States Army in World War II: The War Department*, Vol. I: *Strategic Planning for Coalition Warfare, 1941–1942* (Washington: Dept. of the Army, 1953), 55 ff.; cf. Churchill, *The Grand Alliance*, 850–53; Sherwood, *op. cit.*, 413–17.

plies, the Soviets were beginning to appreciate that they were going to have to fend very largely for themselves over the decisive forthcoming year.

After warning President Roosevelt that the Soviets might start again thinking of separate terms with the Reich, Churchill on September 5 cabled his again Russophile Ambassador in Moscow, Sir Stafford Cripps, a detailed explanation of his reasons for inaction across the Channel. The Prime Minister said that any British lodgment in France would have no chance of success owing to heavy German fortifications and probable superiority in land strength over the British. In an explanation to his Chiefs of Staff a fortnight later, however, Mr. Churchill stressed the more serious problem of the shipping shortage, which could render impossible any major land operations on the Continent. Only in retrospect has Mr. Churchill dwelt upon the crucial absence, at this stage of the war, of landing craft for the sake of mounting a large-scale invasion across the Channel. It would seem, then, that in this period others besides the desperate Russians did not understand what Churchill has called; "the nature of the amphibious operation necessary to disembark and maintain a great army upon a well-defended hostile coast."

However diverse the explanations for the British opposition to a second front over the next thirty months, one very real reason for British difficulties in this respect, not vouchsafed to Stalin, may be found in the one million men being assigned to the Royal Air Force along with top priorities to the production of heavy bombers. Whether he appreciated it or not, Stalin was going to get British support principally in the air until the last ten months of the war—no longer in Winston Churchill's Britain were infantry casualties on the Soviet or First World War scales being contemplated under any circumstances.[8]

---

[8] Churchill, *The Grand Alliance*, 379–80, 460–62, 851–53; Gwyer, *op. cit.*, 198–99.

On September 7, Cripps reported that he had found Stalin very depressed and tired, and inclined to return to his former attitudes of suspicion and distrust. Stalin did, however, offer assurances against a separate Soviet peace with Germany, but made no promises that the Soviets could continue active operations in the event they were driven beyond the Volga with the resultant loss of two-thirds of their war industry. With the closing of the colossal German trap on his armies in the Ukraine, on September 13 Stalin further appealed for the transfer of twenty-five to thirty British divisions to the Russian front by way of either Archangel or Persia. As Churchill has justly remarked of this logistic fantasy, "It seemed hopeless to argue with a man thinking in terms of utter unreality." The Red Army commanders at Kiev and Bialystok had already learned the appalling veracity of this Churchill conclusion during this tragic period of Stalin's military ignorance and despair.[9]

After considerable haggling during the second half of September, the British and American governments agreed between themselves to provide the U.S.S.R. jointly with four hundred planes and five hundred tanks monthly over the next nine months. Lord Beaverbrook and Mr. W. Averell Harriman, the latter representing the United States, were sent to Russia at the end of the month to negotiate the First Russian Protocol for military aid to the Soviet Union. Beaverbrook's letter of introduction from Churchill to Stalin included the following explanation to be delivered along with the British assurances of aid:

"You will understand," wrote the Prime Minister, "that our Army . . . is perhaps only one-fifth or one-sixth as large as yours or Germany's. Our first duty and need is to keep open the seas, and our second duty is to obtain decisive superiority in the air. These have the first claims upon the manpower of

[9] Churchill, *The Grand Alliance*, 462–65; cf. *Stalin's Correspondence*, 24–25, for the correct date of emission; Woodward, *op. cit.*, 154–55.

our forty-four million in the British Islands. We can never hope to have an army or army munitions industries comparable to those of the great Continental military powers."

While the last assertion of the Prime Minister had certainly not been so during the First World War, nor was it true as far as munitions production was concerned during the Second World War either, nevertheless Stalin had received another warning not to count upon the British Army expending its blood after 1941 as relentlessly as it had in 1916 or 1917 in what again appeared to be a futile endeavor to save the Russians. Mr. Churchill had, however, previously written Stalin that another goal of British policy was to gain "the great prize" of what, hereafter, he would enjoy calling the "powerful" Turkish Army. As Churchill had good reason to know, this now determinedly neutral Army had been effective enough against the British in the First World War after benefiting from a modicum of German aid and leadership.[10]

Arriving in Moscow on September 28 for a three-day discussion with Stalin, Beaverbrook and Harriman found the Soviet dictator nervous and under intense strain. In his opening statement Stalin indirectly admitted to the destruction of the bulk of the Soviet tank forces in referring to a supposed German tank superiority of three or four to one over the Red Army, as opposed to a fictitious German initial advantage of five to four at the beginning of the campaign. In divisional units, Stalin boldly claimed the figures were now 320 Axis divisions to 280 of the Red Army. Although the Soviet Government still showed no interest in opening strategic discussions with Major General Sir Hastings Ismay, who had accompanied Lord Beaverbrook for this purpose, Stalin did reply to a British suggestion of forwarding part of their small

---

[10] Churchill, *The Grand Alliance*, 464–67; cf. Leighton and Coakley, *op. cit.*, 97–101; *The United States Strategic Bombing Survey*, Overall Economic Effects Division (Washington, 1945), 6–9; Trumbull Higgins, *Winston Churchill and the Second Front* (New York, 1957), 73–77, 143; Klein, *op. cit.*, 97–100.

Persian garrison to the Caucasus to relieve Soviet divisions for active service. Evidencing a typical Old Bolshevik distrust of British motives in these regions, Stalin said briefly that there was no war in the Caucasus, but that he could always employ British troops in active operations in the Ukraine. It is possible that the Soviet ruler replied to Beaverbrook's suggestion of a British relief force in Archangel by dryly remarking that at least Churchill knew the way to that particular point.

Considering Russia's condition on this occasion, Stalin showed a remarkable interest in making arrangements with the British for a postwar extension of the Anglo-Soviet Alliance as well as for a discussion of the terms of a possible peace treaty. Skirting such delicate topics as too dangerous for discussion at this time, the British were also the recipients of Stalin's advice that "if the British Empire is to survive, it must become a land power as well as a sea power." It is not surprising that so unsympathetic an observer as General Ismay resented the hectoring that the British put up with at Soviet hands on this occasion.[11]

His personal enthusiasm for aiding the Soviet Union in no way abated by the British reception in Moscow, Lord Beaverbrook returned to England more determined than ever to advocate the Soviet cause. Both in his newspapers and in private, the Beaver pleaded the need for a second front against the desires of the British Government and military. Degrading the British movement into Persia as trivial, in a memorandum of which he took care to let Harry Hopkins see a copy, Beaverbrook wrote that the overall British conception of the war had become "completely obsolete on the day when Russia was attacked." The British chiefs of staff, he charged, "would have us wait until the last button has been sewn on the last gaiter before we launch an attack [evidently in

[11] William Standley and Arthur Ageton, *Admiral Ambassador to Russia* (Chicago, 1955), 65–75, cited hereafter as Standley; cf. Sherwood, *op. cit.*, 387–91; Woodward, *op. cit.*, 156; *The Memoirs of General Lord Ismay* (New York, 1960), 231–34; Leasor, *War at the Top*, 158.

France]." Less controversially, Beaverbrook concluded that, failing immediate British help, Russia might well collapse.

Among the Americans, too, United States Army Colonel Philip Faymonville, sent back by Harry Hopkins to Moscow to handle the question of supplying the U.S.S.R., was similarly soon subject to much criticism on the part of his more pessimistic Army colleagues for persistently reporting that the Red Army would pull through the winter. Of course this common conclusion of Hopkins and Beaverbrook was a *sine qua non* of an effective aid program for Russia, and at times, Soviet propaganda on this subject aside, it is difficult to ascertain how much the hostility to Communist Russia, *per se*, contributed to Western military pessimism, since these two Western attitudes naturally marched hand in hand.[12]

By no means unresponsive to the desperate pressure of Soviet needs—accentuated by the mounting clamor in England for a second front—the Prime Minister eagerly sought for some action within his limited means to aid the Russians beyond supplies. Raids on the Continent were discussed—and promptly discarded—by the British Chiefs of Staff, driving Churchill to complain in mid-October that his generals did not want to fight the Germans. A more serious operation against Trondheim in Norway for the sake of guarding the convoys to Russia was also opposed by his military advisors; as Beaverbrook had lamented, the Continent was now considered out of bounds by British services, quite disillusioned with half-baked landings followed by costly and humiliating ejections at the hands of the still ever-victorious Germans.

Indeed, expecting the worst in Russia, the Chief of the Imperial General Staff, Field Marshal Sir John Dill, opposed stripping the United Kingdom of tanks for the U.S.S.R., while the Royal Air Force desperately needed planes in the Far

---

[12] Sherwood, *op. cit.*, 393–96; cf. Standley, *op. cit.*, 75; Werth, *op. cit.*, 290; Motter, *op. cit.*, 25 n. 41; *Foreign Relations of the United States, 1941*, Vol. I, 846; Leasor, *War at the Top*, 161–75.

East against the waxing Japanese threat and the Royal Navy was already vastly overburdened under the additional strain of the perilous convoys to the Soviet Arctic. For that matter the War Plans Division of the United States Army was no more optimistic and had already proposed an army of 200-odd American divisions to replace the anticipated collapse of the Red Army by early 1942. Under these circumstances, Hitler can hardly be blamed for overconfidence.[13]

Having failed to spur his own military into action, the unhappy Prime Minister, perforce, returned to his dismal correspondence with Stalin. On the day of the rejection of his Trondheim plan, October 12, Mr. Churchill wrote Stalin renewing his offer to replace Soviet divisions in the Caucasus with Anglo-Indian divisions from Persia, thus freeing Red Army divisions for active service. Although Sir Stafford Cripps soon would suggest that the British Government had seriously blundered in refusing to commit two of its own divisions to Rostov or Murmansk, Churchill's fear of their loss "as a symbolic sacrifice," as well as the adverse effect their conveyance would have upon the already clogged Persian supply lines to Russia, prevented any such action.

Nevertheless, the British refusal to undertake symbolic sacrifices for Russia after making them for Norway and Greece, especially when coupled with Churchill's tendency to recriminate with Cripps over Stalin's earlier dealings with Hitler, leads to the surmise that the Prime Minister was not in any event unduly fond of his new Soviet ally. The Russians, too, had some cause for bitterness and a demoralizing sense of isolation in this, their terrible moment of truth and defeat.[14]

---

[13] Bryant, *op. cit.*, Vol. I, 256–76; J. Kennedy, *op. cit.*, 162–70; Ismay, *op. cit.*, 235; Mark Watson, *United States Army in World War II: The War Department; Chief of Staff, Prewar Plans and Preparations* (Washington, 1950), 355–57.

[14] Churchill, *The Grand Alliance*, 472–85, 525, 548; cf. *Foreign Relations of the United States, 1942*, Vol. III, 655–57; Gwyer, *op. cit.*, 206 ff.

by the necessity for bringing Guderian's Second
oup four hundred miles back from the Ukraine,
eration *Typhoon* only took off against Moscow
r 30, or much later than originally envisaged by
Fuehrer, let alone by the Army High Command. At last concentrating three whole Panzer Groups for *Typhoon*, including the Third Panzer Group from Leningrad, Field Marshal von Bock commanded sixty-nine divisions, of which fourteen were armored and seven motorized. But almost all his divisions were worn down and seriously understrength, and Hitler was most reluctant to assign adequate replacements from Germany's small production for the vital tank divisions in Russia.

Disbelieving that the Germans would launch an all-out drive against Moscow so late in the year, the overly logical Soviet High Command was again caught by surprise at this tremendous new German assault. On October 3, Guderian's advancing Panzers burst into the city of Orel so rapidly that the streetcars were running in this industrial center south of Moscow, and factory equipment still in the process of evacuation to the Urals was captured intact.

General Yeremenko, in command of the Briansk Front southwest of Moscow, now begged for permission to retire three threatened Soviet armies before they were trapped. At the Stavka, on October 5, General Shaposhnikov put Yeremenko off. The next day the town of Briansk itself fell and Guderian's great thrust had scooped up most of the Third, Thirteenth, and Fifteenth Soviet Armies. At the same time, unfortunately for the Germans, Guderian first encountered the vast superiority in mud of the easily maneuverable Soviet T-34 tank over his own Mark IV's, while the first rains and sleet of the autumn season soon rendered the already wretched Russian roads impassable for all except tracked vehicles.

Although General Zhukov was appointed on October 10 to replace Marshal Timoshenko as commander of the Soviet

West Front with no less than 40 per cent of the whole of the Red Army in European Russia at his disposal, Bock's Army Group had already successfully sprung another gigantic trap at Vyazma which, with that at Briansk, eventually claimed about 660,000 Red Army prisoners from seven Soviet armies, along with some 5,500 guns and 1,200 tanks. Once again the rash decisions of Adolf Hitler appeared to be vindicated by events, and even the cautious Halder conceded on October 8 that "with reasonably good direction and moderately good weather, we cannot but succeed in encircling Moscow."[15]

Expecting the fall of Moscow within two or three weeks, Hitler had publicly proclaimed as early as October 3 that the Red Army had been "struck down" to "never rise again," a statement reiterated by the Nazi Propaganda Ministry on October 9, to the great disgust of its shrewd chief, Dr. Paul Joseph Goebbels. Prior orders to reduce the size of the German Army and to cut back its already inadequate munitions production were now confirmed, and on October 7 the triumphant Fuehrer again enjoined that the capitulation of Moscow, like that of Leningrad, was not to be accepted. The flight of the inhabitants of these two cities was to be encouraged, so as to spare the Germans the feeding of their populations and to enhance the chaos and burden of their support behind the Soviet lines.

The Rumanians were less reluctant to accept the fall of Odessa, which their Fourth Army finally captured on October 16 after a long and costly siege. As with their other naval bases on the Black Sea, owing to a continued naval dominance of these waters, the Russians were able first to supply and finally to evacuate most of their large forces from Odessa to the now threatened Crimea, although almost all of their

---

[15] Halder, *War Diary*, Vol. VII, 147; cf. Guderian, *Panzer Leader*, 228–38; Lossberg, *op. cit.*, 135; *The Great Patriotic War*, Vol. II, 245 ff., 281–86; Blau, *Russia*, 76–81; Blumentritt, *The Fatal Decisions*, 62–67; Seth, *Barbarossa*, 144–84; Erickson, *op. cit.*, 617–18; Carell, *op. cit.*, 134–42; Clark, *op. cit.*, 148 ff.; Yeremenko, *At the Beginning of the War*, 369.

matériel had to be left behind for the greedy and under-equipped Rumanians.[16]

The Germans were not alone in their faith that Moscow was about to fall, for after all, few—if any—armies have ever risen again after a loss of several million prisoners as well as the bulk of their equipment. The chaos and demoralization of the subordinate commands on the Soviet West Front were now communicating themselves to the Russian capital. Accentuated by abruptly ominous exhortations from the Soviet Government on October 13 and 14, the sudden transfer of the diplomatic corps to Kuibyshev on October 15 and the advance of the Germans to within only sixty miles of Moscow at Mozhaisk by the eighteenth, precipitated a sense of panic in the city.

The more than half million civilians who had been systematically evacuated from the city before this date were now joined by a flood of Government officials, Party members, and many of the Secret Police, in a frequently unauthorized flight by all possible means to the East. Looting, the burning of official papers, and by October 19, even the cessation of orders from the Moscow espionage center to the numerous and essential Soviet agents in foreign countries, all signalized the Russian expectation of the imminent fall of the great Soviet nerve center.

Whether Stalin actually left the city briefly or not, his proclamation of a state of siege on October 19/20, as well as the bogging down of the German Panzers in mud, allowed a rapid restoration of conditions in Moscow to their more customary state of apathy. Half a million civilians were hurriedly set to work building defense lines within the capital, in addition to strengthening the fortifications already con-

---

[16] *Voelkischer Beobachter* (Munich), October 4, 1941, 1; cf. Otto Dietrich, *Hitler* (Chicago, 1955), 86–88; *N.C.A.*, Vol. VI, 931–32; *T.M.W.C.*, Vol. XXIV, 426; *G.D.*, Vol. XIII, 384, 623–24, 696, 853–54; Halder, *Hitler als Feldherr*, 43; Klein, *op. cit.*, 190–95; Blau, *Russia*, 81–82; *The Great Patriotic War*, Vol. II, 141; Carell, *op. cit.*, 284–86.

structed in August and September outside of it. Two leading Communists, General Zhukov and Georgi Dimitrov, although no particular admirers of Stalin, have testified to their admiration for the Soviet leader's courage during this overwhelming crisis.

By November 7, when Stalin publicly reviewed and addressed a large military parade in Red Square celebrating the October Revolution (Old Time), the Soviet regime had weathered the gravest threat to its political control during the Second World War. Significantly, in another speech, on November 6, Stalin had hailed the "great Russian nation" which the Germans had the "effrontery" to attempt to exterminate. At the same time, he held out the promise of the imminent overture of a second front in the West as a certain form of relief for the hard-pressed Red Army.[17]

Nevertheless, at the beginning of November, if the difficulties of further operations in the approaching winter of 1941 were becoming steadily more apparent, the Germans had cause for hope of defeating the Russians during 1942. By November/December, 1941, the gross production of the areas still within control of the Soviet Government was less than one-half that of June, 1941. Forty per cent of the population of the U.S.S.R. had already been lost to the enemy along with two-thirds of the Soviet production of coal and pig iron, 38 per cent of her grain fields, and 41 per cent of her rail lines. Owing to the disruption of production caused by moving factories to the East, Soviet steel output dropped by two-thirds, while the manufacture of ball bearings, indispensable to the functioning of all machinery, was less than 3 per cent of normal. In the previous two months alone the production of combat planes fell to less than a quarter of its

[17] Werth, *op. cit.*, 232–50; cf. Erickson, *op. cit.*, 622–23; Leon Goure and Herbert Dinerstein, *Moscow in Crisis* (Glencoe, 1955), 177–219; Garthoff, *Doctrine*, 216; Foote, *op. cit.*, 126; Milovan Djilas, *Conversations with Stalin* (London, 1962), 38–39; *Foreign Relations of the United States, 1941,* Vol. I, 651–52; Ehrenburg, *op. cit.*, Vol. V, 14, 44.

output in September; only in ammunition was there an increase (unlike that for the German Army), although an increase still insufficient for the needs of the desperate Red Army.

No wonder Churchill had written at the end of October that, through the loss of her munitions production, Russia would shortly be reduced to "a second-rate military power," even if Moscow and Leningrad should hold out against the Germans. Like Hitler, Churchill naturally anticipated that the German Army would soon be free to send most of its forces against Britain, the Mediterranean, or the Middle East.[18]

During October the immense German victories before Moscow had led to an acceptance by the O.K.W. of the largely passive situation on the Finnish front, but on October 26 Leeb's Army Group North opened a final drive to establish a land connection with the Finns now on the Svir River beyond Lake Ladoga and thus to cut off Leningrad from even her last trickle of supplies, currently water-borne across Lake Ladoga. Without the aid of the now immobile Finns or of his own armor, at present engaged in the encirclement of Moscow from the north, Leeb's drive bogged down at Tikvin in early November still seventy-odd miles short of a junction with Germany's most sovereign Scandinavian ally. But an unexpected fringe benefit of this abortive operation for the Reich was found in the new dispute which this German threat precipitated between the British and the Russians.

On November 8, replying to a Churchill message seeking alternative solutions to a British declaration of war upon Finland and Germany's other Continental allies, Stalin bitterly called this British inaction an "intolerable" public demonstration of the lack of inter-Allied unity. Wisely, Churchill made no immediate attempt to answer this Soviet cry of rage, nor did the British make any effort to aid the Poles when this

---

[18] Churchill, *The Grand Alliance,* 548; cf. Erickson, *op. cit.,* 628; N. A. Voznensky, *The Economy of the U.S.S.R. During World War II* (Washington, 1948), 24 ff.; *G.D.*, Vol. XIII, 687–92, 901.

unfortunate Ally discovered in mid-November that most of their officer prisoners, formerly in the Soviet Union, had long since disappeared without a trace.[19]

Simultaneous with the renewal of the German drive on Moscow had come fantastic orders from Hitler to exploit the Kiev victory in the Ukraine by advancing before winter some four hundred miles further in the southeast to the Stalingrad-Maikop line. To garrison these huge domains, Hitler gladly accepted an unsolicited offer of six more divisions from Mussolini, divisions which the Fuehrer indicated would eventually be employed in a new Italian Lebensraum beyond the Caucasus in the warmer regions of Georgia and Armenia.

Following the capture of Kharkov and the Donets industrial basin in late October, Hitler imposed still another divergent advance upon Rundstedt's overstrained Army group, namely, to break through the Perekop Isthmus and occupy the Crimean Peninsula. Panzer General Erich von Manstein, now placed in charge of the Eleventh (Infantry) Army in this ideal tank country, managed to pierce the weak defenses of the isthmus by early November and take possession of most of the Crimea, with 100,000 prisoners from the Soviet Fifty-first Army. At this time, however, Manstein lacked the reserves to assault the fanatically defended Soviet naval base at Sevastopol on the tip of the Crimean Peninsula. As a consequence, for long hereafter the German Eleventh Army would be tied down to Hitler's favorite aircraft carrier (the Crimea) and thus not be available for carrying out the Fuehrer's more overweaning ambitions further east. At least by this time Hitler had come to realize that the seizure of the Caucasian oil fields had to be postponed until the spring of 1942.

Incredulous regarding the Fuehrer's order for a preliminary

---

[19] Churchill, *The Grand Alliance*, 527 ff.; cf. Goure, *op. cit.*, 145–47; *G.D.*, Vol. XIII, 634–37; Mannerheim, *op. cit.*, 432 ff.; Ziemke, *op. cit.*, 178, 201–2; Stanislaw Kot, *Conversations with the Kremlin and Dispatches from Russia* (London, 1963), 44, 113 ff.; *Foreign Relations of the United States, 1942*, Vol. III, 506.

movement toward the Volga and the Caucasus that autumn in any event, Rundstedt, on November 9, advocated a general cessation of the German advance in Russia, including that of Bock's Army Group Center. Rejected even by the O.K.H. on this suggestion, by November 21 Rundstedt had reluctantly sent his armored and motorized forces ahead as far as Rostov, the gate to the Caucasus, merely in order to destroy the important bridges there across the Don.

Unfortunately, thereupon committed to hang on in this untenable position both by Hitler's orders and Goebbels' excessive propaganda, Rundstedt was unable to order his Panzers to retreat for the winter to prepared defensive positions on the river Mius. Already suffering from a bad heart, Rundstedt submitted his resignation to the Fuehrer on November 30. It was immediately accepted, but his successor and old Nazi favorite, Field Marshal Walther von Reichenau, was permitted to make the necessary retirement of the III Panzer Corps upon the Mius just the same only a day later.[20] Marshal Timoshenko's recapture of Rostov at the end of November was the first major Soviet offensive success since the beginning of the war and constituted an ominous omen for the weak and exhausted German Army at last about to encounter the full impact of a Russian winter.

By early November the arrival of frost in the Moscow region as well as the exhaustion of the bogged-down German forces nearing Moscow had precipitated second thoughts regarding any further advances within several German headquarters. Count Ciano was now informed that the German Army in Russia was wearing out under the folly of Hitler's leadership and the Fuehrer himself conceded in a most un-

---

[20] Blumentritt, *Rundstedt*, 111–15; Heusinger, *op. cit.*, 93–95; Hart, *The Other Side of the Hill*, 204–6; Halder, *War Diary*, Vol. VII, 156, 170, 184–96; Lossberg, *op. cit.*, 143–44; Goerlitz, *Paulus*, 44–45, 145; Warlimont, *op. cit.*, 194; Shulman, *op. cit.*, 68–69; *The Ciano Diaries*, 396; Blau, *Russia*, 86–91, 110–13; Elizabeth Wiskemann, *The Rome-Berlin Axis* (New York, 1949), 286; Erickson, *op. cit.*, 641–47; Carell, *op. cit.*, 286–90, 302–7; *The Great Patriotic War*, 263–73.

wonted fashion on November 9 that "the recognition" that neither Germany nor Russia could "annihilate the other will lead to a compromise peace." The next day the Commander in Chief of the Army, Field Marshal von Brauchitsch suffered from a heart attack, but continued to agree with Halder and Bock that Russian resistance must be on the verge of collapse.

On November 13, at a conference held at Orsha in White Russia with the Chiefs of Staff of the three German Army Groups, Halder talked these dubious chiefs into a resumption of the offensive on Moscow by stressing to the more sympathetic Army Group Center the danger of waiting for the anticipated arrival of fresh Siberian reserves in the Soviet capital. Taking off on the at last frozen roads on November 15, Bock's understrength and poorly clad Army Group Center was given as its wildly ambitious initial objective the severing of the many railways leading into Moscow from the east. Within another two days, in below-zero weather, the Germans had already met Zhukov's new Siberian reinforcements, and at the suggestion of Field Marshal von Kluge, the O.K.H. was forced to modify its unrealistic plans for cutting off the Moscow railways to the east of the city.

Now it would be enough for the ever more exhausted Army Group Center simply to fight its way into the Soviet capital before winter on any terms. The Fuehrer consoled himself for this disappointment by ordering that the Kremlin be blown up upon capture to signalize the overthrow of Bolshevism.

Although by November 19 Hitler had accepted the postponement of operations beyond Moscow and Rostov until the spring of 1942, arguing from the famous analogy of the Battle of the Marne, on November 22 Field Marshal von Bock urged a final effort against the Soviet capital upon his distraught subordinates. The next day Guderian himself was unable to persuade the O.K.H. to call a halt to the attack, evidently because of direct pressure from Hitler. Crushed by his responsibilities, with already panicky troops and the grimmest forebodings himself, Guderian was ordered to continue his advance, by-passing the old munitions center of Tula against growing forces of fresh and warmly-clad Siberians. Perhaps it was just as well that at his most advanced headquarters in Tolstoy's famous home at Yasnaya Polyana, Guderian did not know that in the past Tula had saved Moscow from both the Tartars and White generals alike.[21]

Although the Red Army in Europe had been reduced to a little over two million frequently untrained and demoralized men, while the tanks at his disposal in the West Front did not number more than seven hundred, with the approval of the Stavka on November 30 General Zhukov submitted to Stalin a plan for unleashing a Soviet counteroffensive before the very gates of Moscow. Notwithstanding the unusual German quantitative superiority both in armor and artillery, the grave depletion of the Wehrmacht, the freezing of much unwinterized German equipment and locomotives, the tremendous Soviet logistic advantages in the great Moscow railroad nexus just behind their lines, and a partial recovery of Soviet air superiority (due to the cold weather and the diversion of some Luftwaffe strength to the Mediterranean), all offered the Red Army an exceptional opportunity to strike.

Only with the German artillery on Moscow's doorstep did Stalin reluctantly consent to the Stavka plan for an offensive and, learning from his former mistakes, apparently at last confined his intervention to a simple acceptance of the Red Army proposal. German infantry units, over 50 per cent short of manpower, were to be matched in strength by approximately twenty fresh Soviet divisions arriving in the Moscow area in a steady stream from the Far East and Central Asia. More than the winter and the terrain, Japan's fatal inertia

---

[21] Assmann, *loc. cit.*, 321–22; cf. Hart, *The Other Side of the Hill*, 207–8; Blau, *Russia*, 83–90; Halder, *War Diary*, Vol. VII, 168–91; Blumentritt, *The Fatal Decisions*, 68–70; Guderian, *Panzer Leader*, 246–52; Ciano, *Diplomatic Papers*, 456; *The Ciano Diaries*, 402; Lossberg, *op. cit.*, 136–39; Kesselring, *op. cit.*, 96; Carell, *op. cit.*, 157–73, 191; Clark, *op. cit.*, 167 ff.

along the Amur was to prove Russia's salvation. Had the Siberian divisions arrived earlier in the West during the period of Stalin's full and devastating control of Soviet strategy, these fine units would have soon disappeared down the maw of the then still efficient German Army.[22]

By December 1, even that proponent of an all-out offensive against Moscow, Field Marshal von Bock, reported to his superiors that it was possible henceforth to make only minor advances, and over the next two days a final thrust of the German Fourth Panzer Army within five miles of the northwestern suburbs of Moscow was halted by Red Army tanks and factory militia without exposing the reserves for the impending Soviet counteroffensive. Accompanied by a drop in the temperature to thirty degrees below zero Fahrenheit, on December 5 General I. S. Koniev's Kalinin Front opened its attack against part of the out-thrust German pincers north of Moscow, followed on December 6 by Soviet forces of Zhukov's West Front against Guderian's already retreating Second Panzer Army to the south of the Soviet capital. Aided by complete surprise and a general freeze-up of the few German tanks which had survived the grueling autumn campaign, the Soviet counteroffensive immediately precipitated a new row within the German High Command.[23]

Notwithstanding Halder's, Jodl's, and even Keitel's belated

---

[22] Erickson, *op. cit.*, 631–67, 768; *G.D.*, Vol. XIII, 438–39; Marshal Vasili Chuikov, *The Beginning of the Road* (London, 1963), 365–67; *Pearl Harbor Attack*, Part 14, Exhibit 33, 1335–66; Michael Cherniavsky, "Corporal Hitler, General Winter, and the Russian Peasant," *Yale Review* (New Haven), Summer, 1962, 551–56; *The Great Patriotic War*, Vol. II, 260; Blau, *Russia*, 86–90; Halder, *War Diary*, Vol. VII, 192–93; Ehrenburg, *op. cit.*, Vol. V, 37, 45; Lee, *op. cit.*, 111–19; Kilmarx, *op. cit.*, 175–83; Eden, *op. cit.*, 339–41; *Hitler's Table Talk*, 200, 339; Carell, *op. cit.*, 309–13; *The German Army High Command O.K.H. Synopsis* (Washington: Office of the Chief of Military History, December, 1949), 53; Philippi and Heim, *op. cit.*, 90–91; Yeremenko, *At the Beginning of the War*, 340, 396–97.

[23] Guderian, *Panzer Leader*, 257–60; Lossberg, *op. cit.*, 145; *Effects of Climate on Combat in European Russia* (Washington: Dept. of the Army, February, 1952), 4–6; Shulman, *op. cit.*, 67; Erickson, *op. cit.*, 650 ff.; Hart, *The Other Side of the Hill*, 208–9; Carell, *op. cit.*, 175–95, 314–20; *The Great Patriotic War*, Vol. II, 310–34; Clark, *op. cit.*, 180–81.

recognition that a halt and retirement to a more defensible line was necessary in Russia, Hitler's initial reaction was to call his faithful toady, Keitel, a moron and to refuse to accept the need for resting and rehabilitating the Army in Russia before undertaking further offensive operations. On December 7, the desperate Halder wrote that his by-passed superior, Brauchitsch, had been reduced to little more than messenger boy, with Hitler dealing directly with the Army Groups over his head. Although "pretty angry" himself over the possibility of his own replacement now being bruited about, as usual Jodl played the successful moderator and soon talked Keitel out of a rather nominal threat of suicide.

In his turn, by December 8 in War Directive No. 39, Hitler recognized that he had gone too far with his armies, if not with his generals. Blaming the "surprisingly early" winter weather, the Fuehrer now admitted to the necessity of the Army going on the defensive all along the line, except for the capture of Sevastopol in the Crimea. The reason adduced for this step was, however, no more than to gain an opportunity to bring the depleted Panzer and infantry divisions up to strength with replacements from the Reich, France, and the Balkans. At the same time, already being made the scapegoat for the unexpected failure in Russia, Field Marshal von Brauchitsch submitted his resignation as Commander in Chief of the Army on the more than valid grounds of poor health.[24]

The Fuehrer's recognition of the need for a halt all along the line in Russia was just as well, since on December 9 the exposed German salient at Tikvin near Lake Ladoga in the north fell to a sudden Soviet attack and the German northern Army Group was soon forced to retire upon the strong line

---

[24] *Kriegstagebuch des Oberkommandos der Wehrmacht,* edited by Percy Schramm, *et al.* (Frankfurt am Main, 1963), Year 1942, Vol. II, Book 1, 707; cf. Warlimont, *op. cit.,* 205–6; Goerlitz, *The German General Staff,* 403–5; Blau, *Russia,* 91–93; *G.D.,* Vol. XIII, 984–87; Assmann, *loc. cit.,* 323; *Hitler's War Directives,* 107–10; Lossberg, *op. cit.,* 146; Halder, *War Diary,* Vol. VII, 206.

of the Volkhov River, no longer able fully to interdict Soviet supply lines across frozen Lake Ladoga to the rapidly starving city of Leningrad. By December 16, however, the crude Soviet frontal attacks against the German pincers north and south of Moscow having achieved considerable results, Hitler angrily remarked that, just because the enemy had made a few deep penetrations into the German front, it was "fantastic" to think of building up lines in the rear.[25]

At last, on December 17, fed up with being by-passed by Hitler's orders directly to the commanders of the Army Groups in Russia, Field Marshal von Brauchitsch submitted his resignation as Commander in Chief of the Army once again. Already recognizing his immense political need for a military scapegoat for the waxing catastrophe in Russia, Hitler accepted Brauchitsch's resignation on December 19. After some hesitation concerning a replacement for Brauchitsch, the Fuehrer had now decided upon choosing himself for the role of Feldherr, thus carrying to a disastrous conclusion the fatal process begun as early as the Weimar Constitution of degrading the Army High Command to a level of practical impotence.

In no manner concerned over the military consequences of placing a politically-minded amateur at the head of the Army, alone of the three German military services, Hitler explained to the ambivalent Halder—who had decided to hang on as Chief of Staff in the hope of limiting the damage as much as possible—that "the trifles" of the operational leadership of the Army was a task "anybody" could perform. More important in the Fuehrer's view, it was the job of the supreme commander of the Army "to educate the Army in National Social-

[25] Assmann, *loc. cit.*, 324; cf. Halder, *War Diary*, Vol. VII, 209–27; *The Great Patriotic War*, Vol. II, 260–62; Erickson, *op. cit.*, 652–56; Blau, *Russia*, 98–99; Werth, *op. cit.*, 297–362; Goure, *op. cit.*, 147–66; Ziemke, *op. cit.*, 202–3; Mannerheim, *op. cit.*, 436–41; Guderian, *Panzer Leader*, 262–63; Khrushchev, as usual, blames Stalin for insisting upon the costly Soviet frontal attacks: Khrushchev, "The Crimes of the Stalin Era," 542.

ist principles." Since Hitler knew of no general who could properly carry out this peculiar conception of operational command, he had decided to exercise it himself.[26] Under these circumstances it is hardly surprising that Lieutenant General Heusinger, operations chief of the O.K.H., would soon be groaning that "the chaos" at the head of affairs in the High Command was "becoming greater every moment."[27]

The next day, December 20, amid chastened public Nazi appeals for winter clothing for the Army in Russia, General Guderian chose to visit Hitler at his gloomy headquarters—appropriately code-named "Wolf's Lair"—at Rastenburg in East Prussia in a futile attempt to brief the Fuehrer on the utter exhaustion and overexposure of his troops at the front. Hitler assured his Panzer general that he had been "too deeply impressed" by the suffering of his soldiers. "Believe me, things appear clearer when examined at longer range," explained the Fuehrer.

Guderian only succeeded in infuriating Hitler with his blunt additional suggestion that Hitler should replace his own staff with men who had had some experience in the field of the conditions actually prevailing in Russia. Termed a coward by the Fuehrer for his temerity, Guderian was to be retired from command of his Second Panzer Army within a week as a result of a new retreat without the permission of his jealous superior, Field Marshal Guenther von Kluge. Thus the creator of the German tank arm, who, as Walter Goerlitz has written, was feared by the Russians more than any other tank leader, returned to the Reich a discredited and powerless victim of the first German defeat on land in the Second World War.[28]

---

[26] Halder, *Hitler als Feldherr*, 15, 45; cf. Lossberg, *op. cit.*, 149 ff.; Halder, *War Diary*, Vol. VII, 233; Warlimont, *op. cit.*, 219; *N.C.A.*, Vol. VIII, 733–35; *T.M.W.C.*, Vol. XX, 586–87; Goebbels, *op. cit.*, 135–36.

[27] Heusinger, *op. cit.*, 98–101; cf. Warlimont, *op. cit.*, 215–22.

[28] Guderian, *Panzer Leader*, 263–70; cf. Goerlitz, *The German General Staff*, 406; *The Ciano Diaries*, 421–22.

After accepting the retirement of the Army Group Center Commander, Field Marshal von Bock, for reasons of ill health, on this same December 20 Hitler issued an order to the whole Army Group, widely scattered in the open countryside before Moscow. The central Group must "not retire a single step. Every man must fight where he stands." Like Reichenau in the Ukraine, the new Army Group commander, Field Marshal von Kluge, was soon forced to retreat anyway, but Kluge still forced another of his subordinates, Panzer General Erich Hoepner, to face dismissal from the Army for disobeying the Fuehrer's order on his own volition.[29] No wonder that Halder would shortly complain that the troops simply could not hold out in thirty-degree-below-zero weather and would note resignedly in the next month that "this sort of command will lead to the destruction of the Army."[30]

An argument has been made justifying Hitler's orders to the Army in Russia to hold the most advanced lines at all costs, apart from the Fuehrer's own convenient rationalization that "generals must be tough, pitiless men, . . . such as I have in the Party. Those are the sort of soldiers who impose their will on such a situation."[31] General Kurt von Tippelskirsch has declared that Hitler's order to hold Russian towns like hedgehogs even when completely cut off by Soviet encirclement was the Fuehrer's "one great achievement. At that critical moment the troops were remembering what they had heard about Napoleon's retreat from Moscow, and living under the shadow of it. If they had once begun a retreat it might have turned into a panic flight."

In sharp contrast to Tippelskirsch's, however, is Runstedt's opinion that "it was Hitler's decision for a rigid resistance that caused the danger in the first place. It would not have

---

[29] Hart, *The Other Side of the Hill,* 210 ff.; cf. Halder, *War Diary,* Vol. VII, 235; Carell, *op. cit.,* 340–41.

[30] Halder, *War Diary,* Vol. VII, 247 ff.; Assmann, *loc. cit.,* 324; cf. Heusinger, *op. cit.,* 106.

[31] *Hitler's Table Talk,* 220; cf. Heusinger, *op. cit.,* 108–9.

arisen if he had permitted a timely withdrawal." For that matter Tippelskirsch himself has admitted that the holding-out policy during this winter "ruined the Luftwaffe," which was used up, in an ominous anticipation of Stalingrad, flying supplies under appalling conditions to the encircled Army hedgehogs. Moreover, Hitler's rigid stand-fast order was costly in German casualties even when the hedgehogs held out. But Hitler would convince himself, at least, that his fateful adoption of the Soviet policy of allowing no general retreat, at a time when Stalin at last was close to abandoning it, had been validated by the survival of the German Army during this terrible first winter in Russia.[32]

It will be recalled that Hitler's order on December 8 for a halt in the advance in Russia had excluded the besieged Soviet naval base of Sevastopol in the Crimea. Consequently, in spite of the retirement of the German Army in central Russia, on December 17, some three weeks behind schedule, the Eleventh German Army opened its assault upon Sevastopol. The Stavka promptly ordered new reserves to be transported to the naval base by sea from the Caucasus, and in late December followed this stopgap action by landing two whole armies at weak points on the Kerch Peninsula of the Crimea in order to divert German pressure from Sevastopol. Although with much difficulty Manstein's small Eleventh Army managed to seal off these threats on the Kerch Peninsula, the bold Soviet amphibious operations at least succeeded in weakening the German attack on Sevastopol, and by the end of December the realistic Manstein had recognized his failure to capture the historic Russian fortress for the time being.[33]

The decisive arrival and full commitment of the twenty or more Siberian divisions involved in the Soviet winter counter-

---

[32] Hart, *The Other Side of the Hill*, 209–13; cf. Halder, *Hitler als Feldherr*, 48; *Operations of Encircled Forces: German Experiences in Russia* (Washington: Dept. of the Army, January, 1952), 3–6; Carell, *op. cit.*, 333 ff.; Clark, *op. cit.*, 182–83.

[33] Erickson, *op. cit.*, 656–58; Manstein, *Lost Victories*, 222–28; Ruge, *op. cit.*, 208; Carell, *op. cit.*, 292–302.

offensive had resulted, of course, from the growing realization of the Soviet Government that, despite the ominous buildup of the Japanese Army in Manchuria, the actual aspirations of the Japanese now lay in another direction. Well informed by its superb agent in Tokyo, Richard Sorge, the Soviet Government cut almost in half its effective strength in the Far East between March, 1941, and the spring of 1942, when it expected a Japanese attack following the completion of Tokyo's ambitious projects in the Pacific. By the time of Sorge's discovery and arrest in Tokyo in October, 1941, Moscow seemed to have become fairly well convinced of Japanese dissatisfaction over the course of the German campaign in Russia.

In fact, in early October, General Hideki Tojo, soon to become the Japanese Premier, had already informed the Germans that *Barbarossa* was a mistake and had suggested a diversion of the German offensive from Russia to Japan's proposed target, the British Empire. In mid-November the Japanese were warned by the German Military Attaché in Tokyo not to count upon the success of *Barbarossa*. In his turn, the German Attaché was questioned by the Japanese Army General Staff concerning the likelihood of German armed support in the event of a Japanese-American war.[34] The Japanese received an affirmative answer from Foreign Minister Ribbentrop on November 29 to their requests for full German military support against America in the event of war, although at the same time, Ribbentrop admitted that the German campaign in Russia might not yet be concluded in 1942. The next day Tokyo warned Berlin that a break with the United States was imminent and coupled this grim prospect with promises

---

[34] *Japanese Special Studies on Manchuria*, Vol. XIII, 60–68; *Germany and Her Allies in World War II*, Part I, 39, Part II, 285–87; *Pearl Harbor Attack*, Part 12, Exhibit 1, 48, 165; Part 14, Exhibit 33, 1083, 1360–66; Part 15, 1825; *U.S. Dept. of State Bulletin* (Washington), September 29, 1946, 482; *G.D.*, Vol. XIII, 608–11, 745, 798–800; Butow, *op. cit.*, 220 n. 63; *I.M.T.F.E.*, Exhibits 601–603*A*, 835, 2670–76; Willoughby, *op. cit.*, 106–7; *N.C.A.*, Vol. I, 866 ff., Vol. V, 566 ff.

that any now highly unlikely Soviet attack in the Far East would meet with Japan's full-fledged resistance. That Japanese intentions in the Far East remained exclusively defensive toward Russia was again borne on the Germans on December 6, when Tokyo explained that it would not even seize Soviet ships carrying American Lend-Lease supplies to Vladivostok.[35]

Notwithstanding so many Japanese warnings, warnings abetted in any case by the foolish German promises of formal support against the United States, the Japanese attack on Pearl Harbor on December 7 still came as something of a shock to Berlin. Whether from reasons of long-festering resentment or simply from relief over having gained an ally in the Pacific with whom to divert the Americans from the Atlantic, by December 11 Hitler had acceded completely to Tokyo's continued insistence upon a German declaration of war upon the United States. Washington learned on the same day that the Soviet Union had no intention of indulging in the similar folly of engaging in an unnecessary offensive war against another peaceful and distant nonbelligerent; until his campaign against Germany was won, nothing would induce a more cautious Stalin to add to Russia's already appalling military burdens. Hitler would have been far better advised to have followed the canny Georgian's example.

And with her decision to attack the United States instead of Russia, as Winston Churchill has remarked, "Japan certainly missed the best chance—for what it was ever worth—of realizing her dreams."[36] *East Wind Rain*—the basic Japanese plan for war against the United States—had replaced

---

[35] *N.C.A.*, Vol. II, 506, Vol. VI, 308–12, Vol. VII, 160–63; *Pearl Harbor Attack*, Part 9, 4200, Part 12, Exhibit 1, 201–29; *G.D.*, Vol. XIII, 868–70, 943 n. 6, 958–59.

[36] Churchill, *The Grand Alliance*, 195; cf. Hull, *op. cit.*, Vol. II, 1111; *N.C.A.*, Vol. II, 507, Vol. V, 603, "Supplement B," 1199–1200; *T.M.W.C.*, Vol. X, 297, Vol. XV, 39; *G.D.*, Vol. XIII, 991 n. 4; Ribbentrop, *op. cit.*, 159; Schmidt, *op. cit.*, 237; *Hitler's Table Talk*, 181–88; Weizsaecker, *op. cit.*, 263; Hesse, *op. cit.*, 146; Lossberg, *op. cit.*, 148; Trumbull Higgins, "East Wind Rain," *United States Naval Academy Proceedings* (Annapolis), November, 1955, 1198–1203.

North Wind Rain—the Japanese plan for war against Russia; and in due course the fundamental Axis error in World War II, embodied in *East Wind Rain*, would bring into effect *Rainbow No. 5*, the basic American war plan to intervene decisively in Europe regardless of what the Japanese might do hereafter.

"No leading statesman need be angry with those who set up far-reaching goals which may go beyond what can be realized at the time. . . . It is desirable to strive for the impossible."[1]

GUSTAV STRESEMANN, January, 1916

"If, on the contrary, my plan envisages a preliminary retreat, if the plan is clear to the senior commanding staffs, . . . if their confidence does not founder on the prejudice that one ought invariably be the first to attack—then I have every chance of regaining tempo and winning."[2] TROTSKY

"A large portion of intelligent Britons say: 'We are waging this war by bluff and it's the only way we can wage it.' "[3]

HITLER, August 1, 1942

"You should know that my conscience is a good girl I always come to terms with."[4] CHURCHILL, to DE GAULLE, August 7, 1942

[1] Marvin Edwards, *Stresemann and the Greater Germany* (New York, 1963), 72–73.

[2] Deutscher, *The Prophet Armed*, 485.

[3] *Hitler's Table Talk*, 604.

[4] Charles De Gaulle, *War Memoirs*, Vol. II: *Unity, 1942–1944* (New York, 1959), 17.

CHAPTER VII

The Last Chance

January 1–August 19, 1942

FOLLOWING the unexpected Japanese attack on Pearl Harbor, Adolf Hitler had been faced with his perennial choice between a renewed emphasis upon the destruction of his Soviet bugbear or upon the alternative again pressed by some of his military and naval advisors, that is, to suspend any further offensive operations in the East in favor of building up a more adequate defensive against Britain and the United States in the West and the Mediterranean. At the same time, Foreign Minister Ribbentrop may have made the first of many subsequent suggestions in behalf of opening peace negotiations with the U.S.S.R. Like Goering, the German Navy, and Japan, Ribbentrop had always preferred a German war against the West in any event.

Notwithstanding accurate information from the United States regarding the American intention of putting its weight in the war against Germany rather than Japan, after some hesitation Hitler decided to remain faithful to his crusade against Bolshevism. It is probable that in spite of growing anxieties concerning an Allied landing in Norway, Hitler preferred to rely upon the assurances of an O.K.W. memorandum of December 14, 1941,[5] to the effect that the Reich

[5] Hans-Adolf Jacobsen, *1939–1945: Der Zweite Weltkrieg in Chronik und Dokumenten* (Darmstadt, 1959), 282–93; cf. Ribbentrop, *op. cit.*, 167–68; Captain T. B. Kittredge, "A Military Danger," *United States Naval Proceedings* (Annapolis), July, 1955, 734 ff.; Playfair, *op. cit.*, Vol. III, 132; *F.C.G.N.*, *1941*, Vol. II, 79–80; *1942*, Vol. I, 6–18, 126; Ziemke, *op. cit.*, 213–17; Warlimont, *op. cit.*, 208–10.

still had at least a year in which to dispose of Russia before the Western Allies could launch a serious attack from the Atlantic or Mediterranean. It is also very possible that the Fuehrer believed in Ribbentrop's additional hope that Japan would attack the Soviet Union in May, 1942, following her conquest of Southeast Asia. Moreover, suspending the war in Russia without a decisive defeat of the Red Army was hardly a practical possibility for the Reich, whatever Grand Admiral Raeder might assert to the contrary over the forthcoming year.

Hitler's momentary dalliance with the Mediterranean could also have received no encouragement from the strident note of Soviet overconfidence which greeted the first major German retreat in Russia; the Fuehrer's pride was hurt, and when on January 15 he finally accepted the necessity for a large-scale withdrawal of Army Group Center, he insisted that it be conducted by his frozen and weary warriors in "a form worthy of the German Army." Doubtless dignity on the part of the retreating German Army was most desirable at a time when Hitler himself confessed to feeling groggy from the sudden winter upset and actually admitted to despair regarding the chances for the survival of his embattled troops. Since the losses of German Panzer vehicles had been five times as great between October and December, 1941, as in the summer months of June through September, Hitler's action was inevitable in any event; there were now almost no German tanks left in operating condition in Russia and the Army in the East had dropped too far short of its assigned infantry strength.

At the same time, Field Marshal Wilhelm Ritter von Leeb, who commanded Army Group North, resigned because of Hitler's refusal to allow the German Xth Army Corps to retire before being encircled at Demyansk, south of Lake Ilmen. Furthermore, with several of his fellow commanders in Russia, Leeb advocated a general retreat to Poland, a strategic desire considerably enhanced by his disgust with the horrors of Nazi policy in the Soviet Union. With a disastrous transport crisis facing the overburdened German railways in Russia simultaneously on hand, more drastic action was needed than simply forbidding the circulation of Caulaincourt's prophetic memoir regarding the disintegration of Napoleon's Grand Army in Russia during the winter of 1812.[6]

On January 23, 1942, Hitler belatedly accepted the need of doubling German tank production from its present pitiful rate of three hundred monthly, as well as of introducing new models such as the Tiger, to compete successfully with the Soviet T-34 and KV. Since German tank production had not increased at all in the previous six months and—even with the great advantage of the current vast disorganization of the Russian war economy—confronted a Soviet production two or three times its own (not to mention a total Allied tank production already more than five times that of the Reich), this new German production program inaugurated under Albert Speer in the spring of 1942 was urgently needed, if not, in fact, hopelessly overdue.

Nevertheless, in spite of higher priorities, German tank production did not appreciatively increase until the end of 1942, a static disaster for the German Army paralleled by that of fighter production for the Luftwaffe. Of the armament categories most vital for the campaign in the East, only the doubling of artillery ammunition production in 1942 was achieved, an achievement which at least afforded the German Army an increased defensive, although inadequate offensive, capacity over the next decisive year.[7] Equally distressing was the desperate shortage of oil supplies, a shortage already crippling the operations of the German and Italian navies, and about to be

[6] *Kriegstagebuch des Oberkommandos der Wehrmacht, 1942,* Vol. II, Book 1, 41; cf. *Hitler's Table Talk*, 135, 221; Halder, *War Diary*, Vol. VII, 254 ff., Vol. VIII, 26; Blau, *Russia*, 104–5, 135; Hart, *The Other Side of the Hill*, 216; *Foreign Relations of the United States, 1941*, Vol. I, 665; Goebbels, *op. cit.*, 131–32; Philippi and Heim, *op. cit.*, 112–13.

[7] *The United States Strategic Bombing Survey*, 75, 165–68, 278–83; *G.D.*, Vol. XIII, 680–81; Guderian, *Panzer Leader*, 276 ff.; Blau, *Russia*, 113–14; Clark, *op. cit.*, 188–95.

accentuated by the practical cessation of Rumanian oil deliveries.

During the latter part of January, Hitler faced a new crisis when Soviet forces broke through the German lines on the Donets River south of Kharkov, threatening the Donbas industrial region, whose production the Nazis had in any event almost wiped out through a policy of artificially created starvation. When a month later elements of the Sixteenth German Army were encircled at Demyansk south of Lake Ilmen, significantly for the future they had to be supplied entirely by the Luftwaffe until relieved by a German force in the spring.

By late March, 1942, however, a combination of frequent thaws and the stringent Soviet shortage of trucks, tanks, planes, and even food for their poorly coordinated offensives had enabled the Germans to establish firm positions along most of the front, albeit too far back from Moscow to menace the Soviet capital any longer with imminent capture. Despite numerous cases of frostbite, overall German casualties were diminishing in the defensive warfare of the winter and by the end of February, 1942, had still amounted to no more than 258,000 men dead or missing from the beginning of the campaign in June, 1941. Out of an army of 3,200,000 men engaged in Russia, not counting the millions of Germans stationed elsewhere in Europe, such casualties were by no means prohibitive, especially when compared with the Red Army losses by this time of approximately 4,000,000 prisoners of war alone.[8]

Concerning the approximately one million wretched survivors of German mistreatment from among the Red Army prisoners of war, the more intelligent Nazis themselves were coming to have second thoughts. The growing labor shortage in Germany itself in February, 1942, also now led to protests

---

[8] Blau, *Russia*, 105–8; Halder, *Hitler als Feldherr*, 47, and his *War Diary*, Vol. VII, 69, 279; *The Great Patriotic War*, Vol. II, 402; Assmann, *loc. cit.*, 325–26; Sokolovsky, *op. cit.*, 144; Lee, *op. cit.*, 119; *Effects of Climate on Combat in European Russia*, chap. i. See Chapter IX, for Demyansk.

among German officials against a policy of such rapid extermination of millions of potential slave laborers. Furthermore, as an erstwhile Nazi Leftist, Propaganda Minister Goebbels soon realized the Bolsheviks were effectively exploiting this particular Nazi barbarity in order to discourage desertions from the Red Army. It is striking hereafter how Soviet losses in captured manpower would drop dramatically in 1942, notwithstanding another demoralizing summer of rapid retreat.[9]

Nevertheless, in spite of the higher morale of the Red Army noted by a British military mission in Moscow in February, 1942, Stalin still expected—or said he expected—a Japanese attack upon the Soviet Union before spring. As for the Germans, the Soviet dictator anticipated a new assault in the spring with what he still claimed was a greatly superior number of tanks. Caught between pressure from his pessimistic Chief of the Imperial General Staff, General Sir Alan Brooke, not to send so many tanks and aircraft to Russia, and the contrary cries of Lord Beaverbrook for an immediate second front, Churchill attempted to compromise by upholding existing supply promises to Russia. In his words, the fulfillment of such promises represented the West's only way at this time of weaving "the mighty Russian effort into the general texture of the war." That this overall war would still remain a British conception, however, may be seen in his simultaneous injunction to the effect that no "vast American Army of ten millions" should be created for eventual employment on the European Continent. In 1942, in Mr. Churchill's view, far smaller numbers of British and American infantry would do for the limited type of land war he had in mind in the future.[10]

As early as January and February, even before the halting of the Soviet winter offensive, Hitler had reverted to his desire

---

[9] *N.C.A.*, Vol. III, 126–30; Goebbels, *op. cit.*, 182–85; Igor Kamenetsky, *Secret Nazi Plans for Eastern Europe* (New York, 1961), 145–55; Carell, *op. cit.*, 82; A. Dallin, *German Rule in Russia*, chap. vii.

[10] Churchill, *The Grand Alliance*, 646–55; cf. Bryant, *op. cit.*, Vol. I, 376; Leasor, *War at the Top*, 176–82; Sherwood, *op. cit.*, 495–96; Leighton and Coakley, *op. cit.*, 552–59.

of the autumn of 1941 for a German campaign directed at the Caucasus. Both his own psychic need for attack—in spite of Halder's new warnings concerning Soviet tank superiority—and the pressing shortage of oil for the Axis impelled Hitler to resume his advance at a date again considerably delayed as a consequence of the heavy German losses during the winter. On February 12, an O.K.H. directive enunciated plans for the re-equipment of the German Panzer arm, at present reduced to 140 operational tanks on the whole Eastern Front. Army Groups Center and North were to be stripped of most of their tanks in behalf of Army Group South, while 500,000 infantry replacements were scheduled to reach the Russian theater before the beginning of May. For the sake of misleading the Soviet High Command—which the O.K.H. thought intended to forestall the anticipated German movement in the south with a spoiling attack of its own—Field Marshal Keitel ordered that false information concerning a supposed resumption of the German offensive toward Moscow be bruited about.

Since this was a logical enough German action—in fact, in the opinion of many critics, one far wiser than Hitler's premature offensive in the south before a decisive defeat of the Red Army—such a cover plan was well calculated to deceive the Russians, for whom the defense of Moscow was essential. In any event, both the Luftwaffe and Panzer arms would be too weak to sustain more than a single major offensive in a limited sector of the Eastern Front for any length of time, and a successful campaign in the Caucasus might precipitate the longed-for entry of Turkey and Japan as active allies against the Soviet Union.[11]

To interdict the augmenting shipments of Allied supplies

---

[11] Blau, *Russia*, 114–20; Hart, *The Other Side of the Hill*, 215–16; Halder, *Hitler als Feldherr*, 48–54; Heusinger, *op. cit.*, 112–17; Lee, *op. cit.*, 122–23; Werth, *op. cit.*, 369–72; Warlimont, *op. cit.*, 226–29; *G.D.*, Vol. XIII, 424–31; Goerlitz, *Paulus*, 51, 146–49.

to Murmansk, on March 14 Hitler ordered the strengthening of both the German offensive and defensive postures in Norway, an action the consequences of which would be felt severely by Allied convoys during the next summer. And on March 23, in War Directive No. 40, Hitler instructed that a normally unified command be set up in Western Europe to resist any Allied landings on the coasts of France or the Low Countries. To head this new organization, Field Marshal von Rundstedt was recalled to active service.[12]

Finally, on April 5, in War Directive No. 41, confusingly rewritten by himself, Hitler spelled out his operational plans for the eastern campaign in 1942. Code-named *Blau* (and subsequently *Braunschweig*), this operational plan envisaged the principal German thrust in the south of Russia with the aim of destroying the opposing Soviet forces before reaching the Don River. Thereafter the object was to penetrate the Caucasus and seize its oil fields. Although at this stage Stalingrad remained no more than a name on the map for the German staff planners, Hitler's orders did enjoin reaching the city, if at all possible, in order to eliminate it as a major communications and production center for the Soviet Army and war economy. When additional German forces became available later on, the complete encirclement of Leningrad by means of a juncture with the Finns was to be achieved (Operation *Nordlicht*). For the time being, as the Germans well knew, the death by starvation of over a million of its inhabitants in the previous four months alone, the evacuation of a half million of its survivors, and the almost complete cessation of the city's industrial production, appeared to be serving Hitler's purposes in this region adequately.

In preparation for *Blau*, the whole front in the south was to be consolidated and, in particular, the Soviet winter incursions across the Donets and on the Crimea were to be liqui-

---

[12] Blau, *Russia*, 119; Warlimont, *op. cit.*, 199, 235; *Hitler's War Directives*, 111–16; Shulman, *op. cit.*, 88; Blumentritt, *op. cit.*, 123–29.

dated as soon as possible. Then Manstein's Eleventh Army was to complete the capture of Sevastopol, a questionable action which would cause further unnecessary delay in the overture of Operation *Blau*. To the great distress of General Halder, twenty-one new Italian, Hungarian, and Rumanian divisions, now organized at the insistence of their governments in four complete armies, were to be sent to guard the ever more prolonged German left flank along the Don as part of the proposed new German Army Group B. Less dependent upon this dangerous reliance on the more than fifty poorly armed and led divisions of Germany's Allies (excluding the Finns) now in Russia was Army Group A, commanded by Field Marshal Wilhelm List. This group, composed of the First Panzer German Army, the Eleventh and Seventeenth German Infantry Armies as well as the Fourth Rumanian Army, at this stage was conceived to be acting as the principal German thrust, a thrust intended to cross the lower Don and occupy the Caucasus in 1942.[13]

As Manstein's swiftly successful attack against the Kerch Peninsula of the Crimea opened on May 8, second thoughts regarding the revival of Soviet strength began to assail the German High Command. On May 10, General Jodl of the O.K.W. expressed his fear of Russian attacks in the north against the German forces now stripped of their tanks and infantry replacements on behalf of the proposed offensive in the south. Two days later, Halder reflected the influence of new information when he estimated that while the German tank strength in Russia by July, 1942, would have returned to the 3,300 level of June, 1941, the shortage and poor training of the infantry replacements, the paucity of vehicles and horses lost in the costly winter fighting, and the inadequacy of Army ammunition production until late 1942 might well

[13] *Hitler's War Directives*, 116–21; Goerlitz, *Paulus*, 53, 156; Blau, *Russia*, 121–33; Warlimont, *op. cit.*, 231–32; Hart, *The Other Side of the Hill*, 218–19; Goebbels, *op. cit.*, 178–79; Goure, *op. cit.*, 166, 218, 239; Churchill, *The Hinge of Fate*, 343; Clark, *op. cit.*, 190–92; Cavallero, *op. cit.*, 250; Jacobsen, *op. cit.*, 297–300.

cripple any prolonged or difficult offensive in 1942. On the other hand, in overall size as well as in equipment available, the Red Army was at its lowest ebb during the Second World War. As Hitler may well have surmised, if the Germans could not defeat it in 1942, in all probability there would never be another chance.

Upon being exposed to these doubts, which inwardly he may have shared himself, Hitler flew into a rage and denied outright Halder's figures on the Red Army's manpower and tank strength. Moreover, Halder had not referred at all to the recovery of the Soviet Air Force, whose fighter superiority in numbers over the Luftwaffe fighters available for Russia was already becoming noticeable. Fortunately for the early stages of Operation *Blau*, the bulk of the Soviet Air Force still remained in the north against the anticipated renewal of the German attack on Moscow.[14]

To be sure, Manstein's rapid conquest of the poorly situated Soviet forces on the Kerch Peninsula by May 18 reassured the doubters in the O.K.H. and O.K.W. Over 170,000 Red Army troops and vast quantities of equipment were trapped and captured from the numerically superior Forty-fourth and Fifty-first Soviet Armies by Manstein's seven German and Rumanian divisions. Moreover, Manstein himself has justified the decision of Hitler and the O.K.H. (to assign him next to the savage and prolonged siege of Sevastopol rather than to support an earlier takeoff in Operation *Blau*) on the grounds that otherwise half of his Eleventh Army would in any event have had to remain in the Crimea because of the necessity of containing the powerful garrison of the great Russian naval base.[15] But the price for Sevastopol in terms of warm weather for the principal operation, *Blau*, may have been as high as

---

[14] Blau, *Russia*, 134–39; Halder, *Hitler als Feldherr*, 57; Shulman, *op. cit.*, 70; Kilmarx, *op. cit.*, 184–85; *The Ciano Diaries*, 464, 494; Heusinger, *op. cit.*, 117–212; Philippi and Heim, *op. cit.*, 109.

[15] Manstein, *Lost Victories*, 233–39; Marshal A. I. Yeremenko, *Stalingrad, Notes du Commandant-en-Chef* (Paris, 1963), 58; *The Great Patriotic War*, Vol. II, 405–6; Carell, *op. cit.*, 448–54; Heusinger, *op. cit.*, 121–22.

that realized by Hitler's divergent Balkan campaign in the spring of the previous year against the major German operation in Russia that summer.

Another factor in May, 1942, militating against an early jumping-off date for *Blau* was the abortive attempt on the part of the Red Army to encircle and capture the vital German depot and logistics center of Kharkov. Launched on May 12 by Marshal Timoshenko with approximately forty divisions, this heavy Soviet effort was fully anticipated by General Halder and by the current German Commander in Chief in the Ukraine, at this juncture the former commander of Army Group Center, Field Marshal Fedor von Bock. Thus, the first Soviet employment of massed tank formations was promptly countered on May 17 by a long-planned German riposte against the Izyum salient, known as *Fridericus*. After several anxious days, the Sixth German Army in Kharkov was relieved, but not before its inexperienced new commander, General Friedrich Paulus, had decided that the distant O.K.W. and O.K.H. had gauged the tense situation there better than he had himself on the spot.

By the end of May, as a result of the speedy German countermeasures, poor Soviet strategic coordination, and Stalin's customary refusal to allow a Soviet retreat in time, the bulk of Timoshenko's Sixth and Fifty-seventh Armies had been encircled and largely destroyed, with the loss of 240,000 prisoners and most of the relatively few Soviet tanks in the Ukraine, at a cost to the Germans of only 20,000 men. Well might Nazi confidence swell again with the return of warm weather and victories in the southern regions of the Soviet Union. Nevertheless, as a consequence of Timoshenko's unsuccessful attack, Operation *Blau* had again been delayed for approximately a month, while hereafter Stalin evidently allowed rapid Soviet retreats in the face of the forthcoming German offensive. This belated Soviet return to the politically unpopular, but militarily effective, strategy of retreat of Kutuzov in 1812 would prevent the Germans from capturing any more shattering bags of Soviet prisoners in the course of their southern offensive in 1942.[16]

Nikita Khrushchev has given us a vivid, but presumably somewhat embroidered, picture of Stalin's evasive refusal to permit the timely escape of Soviet forces below Kharkov. In this account, Stalin would not personally reply to a telephoned appeal from Khrushchev for a retreat, instead insisting through Khrushchev's subsequent rival, Georgi Malenkov, that nothing should be changed at the front. As Khrushchev concluded savagely in 1956, such was "Stalin's military genius."[17]

Hitler, too, has been subject to much *ex post facto* criticism for operations in 1942, in this case for attacking at all in Russia during this year. Actually, of course, the Fuehrer had little choice, since this was Germany's last chance to achieve even a draw against the potentially vastly superior Allied coalition. The only real argument which can be put against Hitler's offensive operations in 1942 was that they were misdirected toward political and economic goals in the U.S.S.R. rather than directed toward resuming his attack on Moscow, an attack which in all probability would have been met by the bulk of the Red Army. Whether from fear of the consequences of such an encounter or from a bona fide anxiety over the Reich's serious shortage of oil, Hitler instead chose the Caucasus. He told the officers of Army Group South on June 1 that "if we don't get Maikop and Grozny [the Caucasian oil fields], I shall have to liquidate the war [perhaps as a whole]."[18]

These were limited enough objectives for a whole year's

---

[16] *Kriegstagebuch des Oberkommandos der Wehrmacht, 1942*, Vol. II, Book 1, 391; Philippi and Heim, *op. cit.*, 123–35; Blau, *Russia*, 139–40; Goerlitz, *Paulus*, 151–52, 159–61, 181–83; Halder, *War Diary*, Vol. VII, 309; Foote, *op. cit.*, 206; Yeremenko, *Stalingrad*, 55–57; Sokolovsky, *op. cit.*, 144; Warlimont, *op. cit.*, 242–43; Carell, *op. cit.*, 455–63; Clark, *op. cit.*, 197–203.

[17] Khrushchev, "The Crimes of the Stalin Era," S41; cf. *The Great Patriotic War*, Vol. II, 404–15.

[18] Goerlitz, *Paulus*, 155–56; cf. Heusinger, *op. cit.*, 118; Warlimont, *op. cit.*, 239–40; Blau, *Russia*, 128–38.

campaign, but apart from its fuel shortage the German Army in Russia was still severely in need of tank and infantry replacements, while a reoccurrence of the ammunition crisis of the last winter was to be anticipated again by August at latest. In short, by 1942 the always modest margins on which the Wehrmacht traditionally operated were rapidly becoming desperate; despite gradually increasing war production, there were no longer adequate reserves against mistakes.

Meanwhile, the Western Allies, too, were contemplating the prospects for the Russian front in 1942, and not enjoying what they saw. In February, the British Joint Planners began to consider the possibility of crossing the Channel in the spring of 1943, or still earlier in the event of a crumbling German opposition. At the same time, the United States Joint Strategic Committee had come to emphasize the importance of supporting the Soviet Union as the only power actively and aggressively operating against Germany. United States Army war planner, Brigadier General Dwight D. Eisenhower, now wrote that "*Russia's problem is to sustain herself during the coming summer*, and she must not be permitted to reach such a precarious position that she will accept a negotiated peace."[19]

By mid-April, notwithstanding grave doubts among the British planners concerning the lack of landing craft and air cover available for a major cross-Channel operation, under the urgent spur of President Roosevelt and Harry Hopkins, the British had agreed to a large-scale invasion of northern France in the spring of 1943, an invasion involving no less than forty-eight Anglo-American divisions. Code-named *Roundup,* this ambitious concept was to be supplemented by another smaller-scale essentially sacrificial operation across

---

[19] Gordon Harrison, *United States Army in World War II: Cross-Channel Attack* (Washington, 1951), 11 ff.; cf. J. R. M. Butler, *History of the Second World War: Grand Strategy* (London, 1964), Vol. III, 512–13, 568 ff.; Matloff and Snell, *op. cit.*, Vol. I, 178 ff.

the Channel in the autumn of 1942. This latter operation, termed *Sledgehammer*, was to be launched only in the event of a threatened Soviet collapse, a significant American reversal of the earlier British requirement of an imminent German collapse as the vital prerequisite for any cross-Channel operation in 1942.

The President and Mr. Churchill to some extent had arrived at this bold decision as part of their common desire to fob off strong Soviet pressure for recognition of its 1939/40 territorial acquisitions by giving in to the Russians on strategy. As a consequence of this influence, of mounting military anxiety over Russia's chances in 1942, and of a strong personal concern with the common Allied coalition interest, President Roosevelt lost no time in inviting Soviet Foreign Minister Molotov to Washington to discuss the creation of a second front in a manner calculated to relieve German pressure from the overstrained Soviet forces.

Stopping off in London on May 22, on his way to Washington, Molotov was informed of the many British doubts concerning his hopes of drawing off at least forty German divisions from the Soviet Union by means of a second front. Nevertheless, as he had in London, in Washington a week later Molotov warned that a Soviet collapse in 1942 would simply make the problem of a cross-Channel assault in 1943 all the more difficult. Eventually, to quiet his persistent interlocutor, and notwithstanding the grave doubts of Army Chief of Staff General George Marshall concerning the early date, President Roosevelt authorized Molotov to inform Stalin that the Western Allies expected to initiate a second front in 1942.

Before any public statement was released on this subject, however, on his return through London in early June, Molotov was handed an *aide-mémoire* which stressed the British refusal to give any promise to cross the Channel under circumstances of what they believed might involve a disaster. As Winston Churchill has written in his war memoirs with relative candor, that while baffling the enemy on the question of a second front was desirable, misleading his Soviet Ally could not similarly be deemed so. Moreover, by this date the British Army seems to have become somewhat more optimistic than were the Americans regarding Soviet chances of survival in 1942.[20]

Perhaps in order to extort a British commitment, and certainly as a method of revivifying sagging Soviet public morale, following Molotov's return to Moscow in mid-June the Soviet Government gave immense publicity to what it now called the Allied promise of a second front in 1942. Both the British and the American ambassadors in Russia warned their governments of the resultant popular expectation in the Soviet Union on this delicate issue and the bitterness and sense of betrayal which would inevitably ensue when the apparent deception became evident to the Russian people. At least the lack of Allied action in the West in 1942 would afford the Soviet Government a plausible explanation at home for the new and unexpected defeats shortly to be sustained by the Red Army at the hands of the Germans.[21]

Delayed by rain and prolonged preliminary operations around the German *point d'appui* at Kharkov, Operation *Blau* did not finally commence until June 28. Despite the accidental Soviet capture of certain of the German plans for the offensive a few days before the attack, the serious dissipation of Marshal Timoshenko's reserves in the early battles before Kharkov and the promised release of the Eleventh German Army, which had at last captured Sevastopol with 90,000 prisoners on July 4, augured well for *Blau*. In accordance

---

[20] Sherwood, *op. cit.*, 528–78; Churchill, *The Hinge of Fate*, 332–42; Woodward, *op. cit.*, 192–97; Feis, *Churchill, Roosevelt, Stalin*, 57–69; J. Kennedy, *op. cit.*, 234–38; *Foreign Relations of the United States, 1942*, Vol. III, 577–83.

[21] *Foreign Relations of the United States, 1942*, Vol. III, 608–9; Standley, *op. cit.*, 203–4; Woodward, *op. cit.*, 196–97; Werth, *op. cit.*, 381–86; Ehrenburg, *op. cit.*, Vol. V, 77–79.

with the basic concept of an advance first by Army Group B in the northern Ukraine, the Fourth German Panzer Army moved rapidly toward the Don at Voronezh. This offered the twin advantages of not merely misleading the Red Army regarding the eventual direction of the German thrust as long as possible, but also of building a strong German defensive posture along the famous Russian river.

The establishment of such a secure German left flank was particularly important since from the beginning *Blau* had envisaged the bulk of the ever extending Don River line eventually being held by the weak new armies of Germany's allies, that is, by the Second Hungarian, Eighth Italian, and Rumanian Third Armies respectively. Furthermore, with the gradual concentration of Soviet reserves in the region of Tambov beyond the Don, equally well positioned for a movement north to Moscow or south to Stalingrad, the rapid creation of a strong Axis defensive posture on its exposed Don flank was rather more than amply desirable.[22]

Although Army Group B unexpectedly met with heavy Soviet resistance within the city of Voronezh, just across the Don, so confident had the Fuehrer become of an easy victory in the south of Russia that by July 6 he ordered the diversion of two Panzer divisions from *Blau* to western Europe. Hitler had convinced himself that as a result of the public Soviet cries for help the British would shortly have to open a second front in France. On July 9, Hitler promised that in the event of such an Allied landing in the West, he would personally assume the direction of operations there, a fate which happily the Fuehrer's commanders in France were to be spared.

At the same time Hitler told the Japanese that they should attack Russia only if they were eager and ready for such an operation. Although the Japanese were returning divisions to

---

[22] Blau, *Russia*, 141–43; Goerlitz, *Paulus*, 183–89; Hart, *The Other Side of the Hill*, 218–20; Goerlitz, *The German General Staff*, 414–15; Manstein, *Lost Victories*, 238–59; Carell, *op. cit.*, 464–85.

Manchuria following the completion of their offensive in Southeast Asia, the Red Army nevertheless withdrew another six trained infantry divisions from the Far East, replacing them only with recruits. For Russia, at least, the Caucasus still came first, and for Japan the war against America could no longer be abandoned on behalf of her long-contemplated *OTSU* plan for the conquest of the Soviet Far East in 1942.[23]

Alleging that Field Marshal von Bock had allowed an unnecessary delay of the Fourth Panzer Army contrary to prior plans during the fierce fighting in Voronezh, on July 13 Hitler relieved this dour opponent of his total control over *Blau* with expressions of professed rage and indignation. In reality, German Intelligence failures, leaks, the rapid Soviet retreat and a marked superiority in Soviet manpower had enabled the Red Army to halt the German advance into Voronezh. Of course, Operation *Blau* no longer envisaged a serious German thrust north of the Don to Saratov on the Volga, as Stalin would assert for many years during and after the war. Far from intending to flank Moscow with a drive up the Volga from the south in 1942, the German aim was essentially directed toward the seizure of the oil fields in the Caucasus, as recent official Soviet accounts, less concerned with concealing Stalin's miscalculations, have freely admitted.[24]

Moving his headquarters, as well as that of the Army High Command, from East Prussia to Vinnitsa in the Ukraine, on July 16 Hitler ordered the Fourth Panzer Army, already short of gasoline, sent south to aid Army Group A's rapid

---

[23] *Hitler's War Directives*, 123; Erfurth, *op. cit.*, 293; Halder, *Hitler als Feldherr*, 50, and his *War Diary*, Vol. VII, 343; Warlimont, *op. cit.*, 247; *N.C.A.*, Vol. V, 580; *Japanese Special Studies on Manchuria*, Vol. XIII, 67–69; *I.M.T.F.E.*, "Record," 8095–8132.

[24] Blau, *Russia*, 145; Warlimont, *op. cit.*, 246; Kilmarx, *op. cit.*, 230, 184–85; Yeremenko, *op. cit.*, 60–61; Carell, *op. cit.*, 487–94; Gallagher, *Soviet History*, 162–63; *Collection of Materials for the Study of War Experiences*, No. 6, Office of the Chief of Military History, Dept. of the Army (Washington, undated), 14; Hart, *The Other Side of the Hill*, 219; Philippi and Heim, *op. cit.*, 133–35.

and easy advance upon Rostov and the Don River crossings to the Caucasus. Although, as Halder had warned, this simply resulted in an excess of unnecessary German armor cluttering up the approaches to Rostov, Hitler compounded his error by sending off two more Panzer divisions from his gravely weakened Army Group B to Army Group Center in the north. Here these vital armored divisions were no longer particularly required, since the Fourth and Ninth German Armies before Moscow had just completed an entirely successful liquidation operation against large-scale Soviet partisan and Red Army thrusts to their rear areas. As a consequence of Hitler's reckless dissipation of the strength of his Panzer striking arm, Paulus' Sixth Army was left almost alone in a very briefly unopposed advance upon Stalingrad.[25]

By July 23, the newly fleshed-out Army Group A had penetrated Rostov and the mouth of the Don against rapidly disintegrating Soviet resistance. To be sure, the bulk of the Soviet infantry escaped across the Don, and not many prisoners were netted by the vast German concentration of armor around Rostov, but the speed of the advance convinced the Fuehrer that his judgment had once again been vindicated over that of the Army General Staff. Consequently, in the most fateful of all his war directives, No. 45, issued on July 23, Hitler ordered a simultaneous advance on divergent axes of his two southern Army groups. Group B, now commanded by General Maximilian von Weichs, was to move on Stalingrad with its Sixth Army again reinforced with two armored divisions taken from Group A. This latter group, led by Field Marshal Wilhelm List, was to be further weakened by Hitler's concurrent decision to reassign most of the Eleventh Army in the Crimea to the siege of Leningrad, a perennial

[25] Blau, *Russia*, 147–51; *Military Improvisations During the Russian Campaign*, (Washington: Dept. of the Army, August, 1951), 12–16; Warlimont, *op. cit.*, 248–49; Gerhard Weinberg, "The Yelyna-Dorogobuzh Area," in *Soviet Partisans in World War II*, edited by John Armstrong (Madison, 1964), chap. vii.

objective which Hitler currently proposed to capture by September.

Thus, at the moment of his greatest need for armor on the flat, easily traversed fields of the Kuban on the approaches to the Caucasus, List was to lose most of his Panzer units. His mission, it goes without saying, remained that of crossing both the lower Don and the Kerch Strait from the Crimea and advancing to the Caucasian oil centers with a striking force of not more than 435 tanks and very little fuel with which to sustain them. Once in the rugged terrain of the Caucasus, List, likewise, would find himself with only two German mountain divisions—the remainder of those valuable, specialized troops, as well as the Italian Alpine Corps, having been frittered away in ordinary infantry tasks elsewhere.[26]

For all these reasons there is no mystery why Hitler's foolhardy decision on behalf of two such shoestring offensives in divergent directions should have evoked a long-pent-up explosion on the part of General Halder that same evening of July 23—within, however, the comparative privacy of his war diary. The Chief of Staff of the Army wrote: "The chronic tendency to underrate enemy capabilities is gradually assuming grotesque proportions and develops into a positive danger. Serious work is becoming impossible here. This so-called leadership is characterized by a pathological reacting to the impressions of the moment and a total lack of any understanding of the command machinery and its possibilities." In his turn, Hitler the next day openly raged against the General Staff, blaming it and Halder for his own incompetence and confusion in operational command.[27]

Still more disastrous in the long run—as perhaps the ablest strategist in the German Army, Erich von Manstein, has ob-

---

[26] Blau, *Russia*, 150–55; *Hitler's War Directives*, 129–31; Carell, *op. cit.*, 505–7; Jacobsen, *op. cit.*, 338–40.

[27] Halder, *War Diary*, Vol. VII, 358; cf. his *Hitler als Feldherr*, 50–51; Heusinger, *op. cit.*, 124–26; Manstein, *Lost Victories*, 239–40, 260–62.

served—Hitler's squandering of his Eleventh Army on yet another offensive against Leningrad without obtaining the aid of the Finns had destroyed the possibility of organizing a central defensive reserve for the German armies in the south. Manstein, in particular, would have cause to regret this omission.

By July 29, Army Group A was pouring across the lower Don against very little Soviet resistance, and Hitler was already proposing cutbacks in German armaments production in favor of civilian goods. Because of the slowing down of the weak Sixth Army drive toward Stalingrad—at this stage more from supply difficulties and fuel shortages than from enemy resistance—on July 30, Hitler reverted to Halder's original conception that "the fate of the Caucasus would be decided at Stalingrad." General Jodl of the O.K.W. thereupon announced that the whole Fourth Panzer Army, plus a Rumanian Corps, would be transferred back to the right flank of Army Group B to spur the advance on Stalingrad. With the direct Soviet rail line to the Caucasus severed, cutting the principal warm-weather Russian oil supply route of the Volga River became a major aim of the essentially economic war Hitler was waging in Russia. If the capture of distant Baku may have been beginning to seem less and less likely in 1942 for Field Marshal List's enervated forces, at least by occupying Stalingrad on the Volga, the Germans might hope to stop the Soviets from receiving petroleum from their principal producing region.[28]

The covertly defensive nature of Hitler's grand strategy this year had also been expressed in his war directive on July 21, ordering a new offensive to cut the Murmansk railway in the White Sea. Both the Stalingrad and White Sea offensives would serve to interdict Western supplies to the Soviet Union, a point of great importance to the Fuehrer in

---

[28] Halder, *War Diary*, Vol. VII, 363; cf. Warlimont, *op. cit.*, 249–50; Klein, *op. cit.*, 199 ff.

view of his disbelief in the recovery of Soviet armaments production in the new Russian bases beyond the Volga.

On the other hand, underestimation of the Soviet Union again lay at the root of Hitler's continued determination to withdraw still another elite unit, the Grossdeutschland Motorized Infantry Division, from Field Marshal List's already emasculated Army Group A in mid-August, in order to strengthen the German Army in France against an anticipated British attack. As Hitler rhetorically asked Halder: "What is the use of victories in Russia, if I lose Western Europe?" Hitler also refused to construct fortifications in the East against a Red Army he considered defeated, holding instead that the west coast of Europe constituted an ideal posture for a defensive wall.[29] Surprisingly, however, Hitler had now come to respect the high quality of Soviet war matériel. And Stalin similarly commanded the Fuehrer's "unconditional respect." In his own way, Hitler explained, Stalin was "a hell of a fellow," who, failing German intervention, would have made Russia the strongest state in the world in another ten or fifteen years.[30]

Hitler's *idée fixe* that a Soviet recovery was impossible, of course, had some basis in fact at the end of July, 1942. The Red Army was so short of equipment in the Caucasus that truck-borne mortars had to serve in lieu of artillery; the Soviet Air Force was still concentrated in the north, and recent Soviet accounts have made no effort to deny the existence of frequently panicky flights which affected much of the Red Army in the operational area of the south during this period. Stalin's order at the end of July—calling for iron discipline, summary punishments, and no retreats without orders—reflected the realization of the Soviet Government that much

---

[29] Blau, *Russia*, 156–57; cf. Klein, *op. cit.*, 211; *Hitler's War Directives*, 127–28; General Heinz Guderian, *Interrelationship of Eastern and Western Fronts*, U.S. Army MS T-42, The National Archives (Washington, undated), 3.

[30] *Hitler's Table Talk*, 587; cf. *ibid.*, 624, 657, 661.

of its highly trained and stubborn manpower of the previous year had gone the way of its former quantitative superiority in equipment, i.e., down the German drain. Less realistic was the Soviet dictator's splitting of the Stalingrad Front on August 2 into two Front Headquarters, although the two headquarters were established together in Stalingrad, with one commander for both of them.[31]

That amateur political interference with professional military doctrine was not confined to the Germans or Russians in the summer of 1942 may be seen in the Western camp. In mid-June the Anglo-American discussion regarding a second front to aid Russia was resumed. Admiral Lord Louis Mountbatten, the Chief of Combined Operations, informed President Roosevelt for the British planners that no sacrifice landing in France by the Allies would draw away any German troops from Russia, on the grounds that there were already adequate German forces in the West. The President replied that he did not wish to send a million soldiers to England and then find that a complete collapse of Russia had made a frontal attack across the Channel impossible in 1942. The President's pessimism regarding Russia's chances was no more ill-conceived than Mountbatten's underestimation of Hitler's fear of a second front.

Arriving in Washington a few days later to exploit such dubious bases for a cross-Channel operation, Winston Churchill immediately broached his old idea of a landing in French Northwest Africa as a safer and more practical alternative to an invasion of France that year. The unexpected fall of Tobruk on June 21, with heavy losses to the British Army in Libya, greatly helped the Prime Minister's endeavors to interest the more than susceptible President in his African

---

[31] Werth, *op. cit.*, 414–20; Goerlitz, *Paulus*, 173; Yeremenko, *op. cit.*, 44–49; Ehrenburg, *op. cit.*, Vol. V, 73; Gallagher, "Trends," 229–30; Alexander Dallin, "The North Caucasus," in *Soviet Partisans*, 569–70; B. H. Liddell Hart, *Defense of the West* (New York, 1950), 30.

venture. Only the resistance of the British and American navies made it possible for General Marshall to stall a little longer on an adverse decision by the statesmen on the United States Army's passionate desire to cross the Channel. Of course, Marshall's motive in stressing a sacrifice cross-Channel invasion in 1942 was chiefly induced by his need to stave off any threatening alternatives to the creation of a far more probable and realistic second front in 1943, a point which the Russians and British, through ignorance at the time, or from motives of subsequent self-interest, have continued to neglect.[32]

Churchill returned to England to face the most savage criticism of his ministry during his conduct of the war. Successfully weathering the Parliamentary debate on July 1/2, the Prime Minister resisted both the Tory attempts to limit his control of strategy and the Labour efforts to induce him to open a second front. Nevertheless, Mr. Churchill's position was weakened by the defeat at Tobruk, following so soon upon the loss of Burma and Malaya, and he was now menaced with a possible loss of control over the War Cabinet itself. Consequently, on July 8, with the approval of the British Chiefs of Staff, the Prime Minister informed the United States Joint Chiefs that there was no possibility any more of crossing the Channel in 1942 and that any effort to do so would "merely ruin all prospects" for invading France in 1943.[33]

The reaction of the American Chiefs of Staff to Churchill's concomitant assurances to the President that his "true second front of 1942" was to be found in North Africa was explosive. With the inevitable approval of the United States Navy,

---

[32] Sherwood, *op. cit.*, 582–94; Churchill, *The Hinge of Fate*, 371–90; Matloff and Snell, *op. cit.*, Vol. I, 235–44; Henry L. Stimson and McGeorge Bundy, *On Active Service in Peace and War* (New York, 1948), 419–24; General Dwight Eisenhower, *Crusade in Europe* (New York, 1948), 70.

[33] Harrison, *op. cit.*, 27; cf. Churchill, *The Hinge of Fate*, 391–401; Bryant, *op. cit.*, Vol. I, 417–25; J. Kennedy, *op. cit.*, 249–50; *House of Commons Debates*, Fifth Series, Vol. 381, 237–576; Butler, *op. cit.*, Vol. III, 629–32.

General Marshall suggested foregoing the British peripheral strategy in the Mediterranean in favor of a principal American emphasis upon the war against Japan. To thwart any such essentially Isolationist reaction, President Roosevelt promptly ordered his Chief of Staff, accompanied by his own political intimate, Harry Hopkins, in the office of chaperon, to go to London to settle finally upon the fundamental coalition strategy for 1942.[34] As Adolf Hitler had already remarked happily, apropos of the Allied strategic hurly-burly: "To harness to a common purpose, a coalition composed of Great Britain, the United States, Russia, and China demands little short of a miracle."[35]

Underlying the whole Anglo-American debate over a second front, of course, were somewhat divergent views concerning Russia's chances of survival. But should the Red Army really be expected to collapse in 1942, it is significant that the Chief of the Imperial General Staff, General Sir Alan Brooke, and Major General Dwight D. Eisenhower, the new American commander in Britain, found themselves in implicit agreement that the Allies should enter French North Africa as soon as possible, while the going was still good.

Of course, this honest and excellent argument on behalf of his African operation could not be employed by Mr. Churchill in forthcoming conversations with Moscow, nor would the Pacific alternative advocated by the disappointed United States Chiefs of Staff have materially helped the Red Army either. In short, the loss of emphasis upon crossing the Channel accepted by the Western Allies in July, 1942, was postulated upon the willingness to face a Russian defeat regardless of the eventual consequences to the West.[36] If for purportedly military reasons the Soviets had abandoned the West in

---

[34] Churchill, *The Hinge of Fate*, 432–34; cf. Stimson and Bundy, *op. cit.*, 424–25; Sherwood, *op. cit.*, 600–1.

[35] *Hitler's Table Talk*, 538–39.

[36] Harrison, *op. cit.*, 28–30; Bryant, *op. cit.*, Vol. I, 422–23.

August, 1939, similar military rationalizations could be easily adduced by the Anglo-Americans to let the East face most of the active forces of the German Army from 1941 to 1944.

Before the arrival of the United States Joint Chiefs of Staff in London, Winston Churchill, with the concurrence of the President, had been forced to write Stalin concerning another painful subject, the temporary cessation of the Allied convoys to Archangel during the long summer days of 1942, as a consequence of high losses caused by German sea and air forces in Norway. Churchill carefully explained to the Soviet ruler that further such losses of Allied shipping would render impossible the building up of a really strong second front in 1943. There were also possibilities of an amphibious Allied operation to aid the Soviets in northern Norway or Finland, a particular fancy of Churchill's which fortunately the British Chiefs of Staff were able to postpone indefinitely.

Faced with such a strong hint concerning the immediate prospect for a cross-Channel operation, Stalin replied on July 23 that his naval experts found the British Admiralty's convoy policy "puzzling and inexplicable." As for a second front, Stalin stated "most emphatically" that the Soviet Government could "not tolerate" its postponement until 1943.

Wisely, Churchill did not attempt to answer what he has called this bitter message from Stalin. "After all," as the Prime Minister subsequently wrote, "the Russian armies were suffering fearfully and the campaign was at its crisis" along the Don as well as in the Arctic.[37] Nevertheless, with the further and in this case decisive approval of the President, Churchill went ahead on his long-established plans for what he kept telling Mr. Roosevelt was a second front in the Mediterranean.

The combination of the new British political and military unanimity against crossing the Channel in 1942, with President Roosevelt's instructions to Marshall, King, and Hopkins

---

[37] Churchill, *The Hinge of Fate*, 266–72; *Stalin's Correspondence*, 52–57; cf. Butler, *op. cit.*, Vol. III, 630–31.

demanding some offensive action this same year, inescapably resulted in a halfhearted American military agreement to land in French North Africa by October, 1942. His last attempt in London to delay this decision having failed, General Marshall, with his happy British opposite number, General Sir Alan Brooke, settled at the end of July for an Anglo-American military statement that any landing in North Africa in 1942 "in all probability" made an operation against the Channel impractical in 1943. While neither the President nor the Prime Minister cared yet to admit the consequences to the real second front of their preference for an earlier action in North Africa, the day of reckoning with Stalin could not be evaded indefinitely.[38]

Perhaps for this reason, on July 25 Mr. Churchill resurrected a previously discarded plan for a large-scale amphibious raid upon the French Norman port of Dieppe. As Admiral Mountbatten explained to a naval colleague, "political reasons" had evoked this revival of an operation which General Sir Bernard Montgomery had already opposed reconsidering at all, on the grounds of security leaks. But the politician in the Prime Minister had stressed the need for some seemingly offensive action before the end of the summer.[39]

Carried through on August 19 immediately following Churchill's visit to Moscow, this costly raid had as its avowed aim the discovery of the difficulties inherent in mounting assaults upon the defended ports of France. Whatever it taught the Allies, it certainly discouraged the Russians, while spurring Hitler to increase vastly the fortifications along the French coast, already cited by Churchill to the Russians as

---

[38] Matloff and Snell, *op. cit.*, Vol. I, 278–83; cf. Butler, *op. cit.*, Vol. III, 633–38; Sherwood, *op. cit.*, 602 ff.; Bryant, *op. cit.*, Vol. I, 427–30; Samuel Eliot Morison, *Strategy and Compromise* (Boston, 1958), 37–40.

[39] Colonel C. P. Stacey, *Official History of the Canadian Army in the Second World War* (Ottawa, 1955), Vol. I, 325–41; cf. Terence Robertson, *Dieppe: The Shame and the Glory* (Boston, 1962), 163; Churchill, *The Hinge of Fate*, 509–11; Bryant, *op. cit.*, Vol. I, 487–88; Leasor, *War at the Top*, 216–18.

preventing any such operation in the previous year. Moreover, the thirty-odd largely second-string German divisions stationed in the West could hardly be reinforced at all in the summer of 1942, notwithstanding Hitler's admission after Dieppe that a major Allied landing in France would place Germany "in a generally critical position." Although Allied air attacks were already diverting a large and increasing percentage of Luftwaffe fighter strength west, for the Germans, if not for the British Army, the campaign in Russia necessarily continued to have priority over all other activities.[40]

Churchill's party had arrived in Moscow on August 12, having borrowed W. Averell Harriman from President Roosevelt to assist the Prime Minister in his "somewhat raw job" of explaining to the Russians the absence of a second front in 1942. Losing no time in putting the best face on the matter, Mr. Churchill explained to the glum Soviet Premier that while the shortage of landing craft would limit any cross-Channel assault to only six divisions in 1942, by 1943 the Allies were proposing to put a force of no less than twenty-seven divisions into France. Unfortunately, like almost all statesmen, democratic or totalitarian, Stalin manifested little interest in operations scheduled by the military a whole year ahead. Thus, instead of binding Churchill irrevocably to his new promises, Stalin took issue with the Prime Minister on the supposed British cowardice in refusing to take risks and fight the Germans in 1942.

Insults proving to no avail with Mr. Churchill, who remained calm, the conversation moved to the more mutually satisfactory theme of the British air raids upon Germany. Probably unaware of the ineffectiveness of the Royal Air Force attacks upon German factories in 1942, Stalin waxed enthusiastic over the British air raids directed against the

---

[40] Harrison, *op. cit.*, 136–41; cf. Carell, *op. cit.*, 568; Butler, *op. cit.*, Vol. III, 638–46; Sherwood, *op. cit.*, 626; De La Gorce, *op. cit.*, 429; *Hitler's Table Talk*, 663, Blumentritt, *Rundstedt*, 133–34.

homes of the German proletariat. In this more agreeable atmosphere, Churchill broached the idea of an Allied landing in French Northwest Africa, landings which he promised would take place in October, 1942.

The Prime Minister's dangerous emphasis to the effect that success in North Africa this year would alone make possible a serious attack upon Germany in 1943 seems to have turned the trick in arousing Stalin's momentary interest in the North African operation. Of course, as the official British Historian may have implied, it is difficult to understand how Mr. Churchill's conscience remained clear that on this occasion he did not mislead Stalin regarding crossing the Channel in 1943. To be sure, the Prime Minister may not yet have admitted to himself that Marshall and Brooke were correct in saying that his North African landings in 1942 in all probability rendered a cross-Channel operation impossible in 1943, but this was hardly an excuse for saying precisely the opposite to Stalin.[41]

On the next day, August 13, however, Soviet disappointment was again manifest. After further recriminations concerning what the Russians persisted in treating as a British promise to cross the Channel in 1942, Stalin submitted a formal *aide-mémoire* of protest. This document read, in part, as follows: ". . . I [Stalin] and my colleagues believe that the year 1942 offers the most favorable conditions for a second front in Europe, seeing that nearly all the German forces—and their crack troops, too—are tied down on the Eastern Front, while only negligible forces, and the poorest, too, are left in [western] Europe. It is hard to say whether 1943 will offer as favorable conditions for opening a second front as 1942."

---

[41] Churchill, *The Hinge of Fate*, 473–83, 659; cf. Butler, *op. cit.*, Vol. III, Part II, 542–43, 663; Sherwood, *op. cit.*, 616–18; *The United States Strategic Bombing Survey*, ii, *Foreign Relations of the United States, 1942*, Vol. III, 618–22.

In a reply, supported by Mr. Averell Harriman for the Americans, the Prime Minister correctly denied having promised to cross the Channel in 1942. He then asserted that his North African landing would bring "more aid to Russia than any other plan," as well as prepare the way "for real action in 1943." In conclusion, Mr. Churchill recommended that Stalin's wisest course was to employ the second-front publicity as a cover plan for landing in North Africa, and to proclaim, as Churchill himself intended to do, the African operation a second front when it opened this autumn.[42]

A description of the principal protagonists to these brutal discussions, drawn at the time by so Russophobe an observer as Sir Alan Brooke, is revealing. Noted Brooke: "The two leaders, Churchill and Stalin, are poles apart as human beings. . . . Stalin is a realist if ever there was one; facts only count with him. Plans, hypotheses, future possibilities, mean nothing to him, but he is ready to face facts, even when unpleasant. Winston, on the other hand, never seems anxious to face an unpleasantness until forced to do so. He appealed to sentiments in Stalin which do not, I think, exist."

The Chief of the Imperial General Staff likewise respected his Soviet opposite number, General Shaposhnikov, whom, however, he considered a pathetic figure fast dying of some ailment. Marshal Voroshilov, however, Brooke deemed an incompetent sycophant of Stalin and a liar to boot. The pessimistic Brooke believed neither that the Red Army would hold the Caucasus nor, as Stalin and Voroshilov had declared, that it had twenty-five well-entrenched divisions with which to do so. Significantly, Churchill was more optimistic.[43]

Having gauged each other's mettle, Churchill and Stalin

---

[42] *Stalin's Correspondence*, 60–63; Churchill, *The Hinge of Fate*, 490–92; cf. Standley, *op. cit.*, 213.

[43] Bryant, *op. cit.*, Vol. I, 460–70; cf. J. Kennedy, *op. cit.*, 264, 275; Churchill, *The Hinge of Fate*, 487–88, 495; Sir Ian Jacob, "Churchill as a War Leader," in *Churchill by His Contemporaries: An Observer Appreciation* (London, 1965), 89–91; Fleet Admiral William D. Leahy, *I Was There* (New York, 1950), 122.

parted, Churchill not escaping from an utterly unmerited Stalin taunt concerning the Royal Navy's lack of glory in refusing to convoy war matériel to Soviet Arctic ports at the current exorbitant rate. The basic trouble, of course, was that unless the British were willing to endure high sacrifices in some respect on behalf of Russia, the Soviets, who were losing so many times more than any possible British losses, could not be expected to forgive their Ally for her more protected posture.

Not surprisingly, upon hearing of this contretemps, President Roosevelt hastened to assure Stalin that Americans appreciated that Russia was bearing the brunt of the fighting and were filled with admiration for her efforts. But on the return flight to Teheran, to Field Marshal Sir Archibald Wavell, a Russian-speaking member of the British mission, went perhaps the last word at the time on Churchill's first visit to Moscow. In one of his less distinguished forays into his normally private world of poetry, Wavell wrote up a ballad the refrain of which ended:

> It's not so hot a thing to have to sell;
> No Second Front in 1942 . . .
> I've got away with what I came to sell;
> No Second Front in 1942.[44]

In reality, whether the Allies had gotten away with no second front in 1942 depended upon what happened along the Volga and the Don over the next few months.

---

[44] Bryant, *op. cit.*, Vol. I, 473–74; cf. Churchill, *The Hinge of Fate*, 497–502; Sherwood, *op. cit.*, 621–22.

"I am not afraid of military reverses. Your empire has two powerful defenders in its vastness and its climate. The Emperor of Russia will always be formidable in Moscow, terrible in Kazan, and invincible in Tobolsk."[1] Advice to the Czar, 1812

"I insist categorically on Stalin's recall. The Tsaritsyn [Stalingrad] front is in a bad way despite the abundance of troops. I leave him (Voroshilov) as commander of the Tenth (Tsaritsyn) Army on condition of obedience to the commander of the southern front."[2] TROTSKY, to LENIN,
October 4, 1918

"I know how to die, but I shall never cede one inch of territory. Your sovereigns, who were born upon the throne, can allow themselves to be beaten twenty times, and will always return to their capitals. I cannot do that; I am a self-made soldier."[3]
NAPOLEON, 1813

"It is a mark of genuine passion that it destroys its possessor when its object becomes unattainable."[4] CARL BURCKHARDT

[1] M. Florinsky, *Russia: A History and an Interpretation* (New York, 1959), Vol. II, 675 n.

[2] Trotsky, *My Life*, 443.

[3] Harold Nicolson, *The Congress of Vienna: A Study in Allied Unity, 1812–1822* (New York, 1961), 44.

[4] Carl J. Burckhardt, *Richelieu: His Rise to Power* (New York, 1964), 83.

CHAPTER VIII

The Fall of Halder

August 4–November 19, 1942

ON AUGUST 4, Hitler wrote Mussolini to explain that while he would do what he could for the stalled Axis offensive in Egypt, he required his air transport still more for the "vast unroaded zone" along the lower Don, where, in bad weather, fuel for his Panzer striking armies frequently had to be supplied by air. Although the Chief of Staff of the Italian Army thought that matters were going well for the Germans in Russia, he no longer believed that the Axis could fully defeat their enemies. Instead, the Italian Chief of Staff broached to Count Ciano an idea to become endemic in the future memoranda of Germany's major allies, namely, inducing the Soviets to make a separate peace with the Axis Powers, presumably along the lines of Brest-Litovsk in 1918.[5]

The newly reinforced German drive on Stalingrad was indeed going well during the first week of August. The Fourth Panzer Army, now across the Don, struck rapidly up the river toward Stalingrad along the railway from the southwest, a direction of assault well calculated to take the Red Army by surprise. Against the opposition of the weak Fifty-first Soviet Army, recently rushed up from the Caucasus, this strong German Panzer army advanced from Kotelnikovo on August 2 to within only forty miles of Stalingrad by August 9. There the Fourth Panzer Army was halted by shortages

[5] F. W. Deakin, *The Brutal Friendship* (London, 1962), 21; cf. *The Ciano Diaries*, 510–11; Alfieri, *op. cit.*, 188–91.

of fuel and of tanks, notwithstanding a superiority in strength over the Russians of at least two to one. As Hitler had observed to Mussolini, the Germans were now operating in a region where the lack of adequate communications was more reflective of Asian Russia than of the poor enough standards of European Russia.

A similar dependence upon a single rail line with no paved roads was enervating the advance of the Sixth German Army directly upon Stalingrad from the west. Fortunately for its inexperienced commander, General Paulus, a conflict within the Soviet Front and Army commands opposing his sector enabled his army to defeat the Sixty-second and Sixty-fourth Soviet Armies piecemeal within the great bend of the Don. Although, as usual, the unfortunate commanders of these two Soviet armies would be replaced, their attempts to retreat across the Don before being trapped again by the swift German encirclements seem realistic rather than simply defeatist, as one of their successors has charged.

By 1942, it should be noted, it took several Soviet armies, organized in what was still termed a "Front," to equal a single German Army. As a consequence of the desperate shortage of trained officers for the Red Army resulting from the appalling losses of 1941, the Corps had long since been eliminated from the Russian command structure, thus, in effect, down-grading Soviet Armies to the strength of their own former Corps. Above these so-called Armies were the Fronts, in practice now amounting to the equivalent of the former Russian Armies. When necessary during 1941/42, an organization termed a "Direction" served as a Soviet Army Group, uniting several fronts in what often became an exceedingly provisional and flexible command structure at the highest level.[6]

Meanwhile, south of the Don in the enormous reaches of the Kuban and North Caucasus, as anticipated by German

---

[6] Yeremenko, *op. cit.*, 70–122; Halder, *War Diary*, Vol. VII, 369; Werth, *op. cit.*, 443–48; Philippi and Heim, *op. cit.*, 155–56; Chuikov, *op. cit.*, 41–54; Carell, *op. cit.*, 506–12, 544–47.

Intelligence, Army Group A was moving rapidly ahead against initially negligible resistance. On August 9, General Ewald von Kleist's First Panzer Army had captured Maikop, the nearest of the oil fields listed as its summer objectives. Unfortunately, Maikop's whole output, even after the eventual restoration of its badly damaged facilities, could only amount to 8 per cent of the total production of the U.S.S.R.

By the end of the month, Kleist's Panzer army had reached the Terek River only sixty miles from the next oil field at Grozny. At the same time, what Hitler had left of the Eleventh German Army on the Crimea was at last about to cross the Kerch Strait and strike at the Soviet naval bases of Novorossiisk and Tuapse on the Black Sea. But by this date the consequences of what Stalin would characterize as Hitler's effort "to chase two hares at once" (that is, in the Caucasus and toward the Volga) was about to catch up with the ever more divergent German drives. Like the Fourth German Panzer Army bogged down southward of Stalingrad, the drive of the First Panzer Army was halted by shortages of fuel and tanks.

Almost simultaneously, despite the unreliability of the Moslem Caucasian elements of the Red Army, approximately twenty Soviet divisions, reinforced with a heavy concentration of Air Force bombers, established a firm line in the rugged foothills of the North Caucasus against the now far-flung and attenuated German offensive. The fact of the matter was that German logistics were not up to sustaining any offensive ranging more than three hundred miles beyond the severe communications bottleneck at Rostov-on-Don.[7]

During these seemingly successful German drives of August, 1942, Hitler and his Army High Command finally took realistic measures to reduce the growing partisan movement

[7] Standley, *op. cit.*, 443; cf. Blau, *Russia*, 158–68; Hart, *The Other Side of the Hill*, 220–21; Halder, *War Diary*, Vol. VII, 372; Carell, *op. cit.*, 512–33; Lieutenant General Max Börk, *Comments on Russian Railroads and Highways* (Washington: Office of the Chief of Military History, undated), 32–38.

behind the German lines in the thickly wooded and hostile regions of their Army Group Center. A combination of a ruthless draft of labor with a continued Nazi refusal to carry out promises to abolish the collective farm system was driving much of the younger and more vigorous population of these areas of Great Russia proper still occupied by the Germans into the eager hands of the Soviet-controlled partisans. Juster treatment of the rural population, as well as provisions for the maintenance of a bare minimum of the economic necessities of life, would reassure the peasantry somewhat, while on an informal basis the man-hungry German Army began accepting more and more Soviet volunteers for its various sustaining services.

By August, 1942, these so-called Hilfswilligen amounted to a half million Soviet citizens, a number destined to grow rapidly until 1943. At the same time, more or less independently of Nazi authority, the German Army also initiated the first of many subsequent efforts to organize outright combat units of Soviet citizens under the leadership of the recently captured Russian general, Andrei Vlasov. With the exception of certain Moslem formations in the Crimea and North Caucasus, however, Nazi Herrenvolk policy in Russia would prevent a more effective German Army exploitation of Vlasov's easily overestimated anti-Soviet potential.[8]

On August 12, the Soviet High Command received its usual accurate information regarding German intentions through its espionage net in Switzerland. This informed Moscow of the disputes raging within the O.K.W., including the insistence of Hitler and Goering upon a renewed attack on Stalingrad in spite of the prevailing German military sentiment that any further such offensive toward the Volga would be useless, while one toward the Caucasus was not apt to succeed. In anticipation of this renewal of the German attack

---

[8] *Hitler's War Directives*, 132–35; R. Fischer, *op. cit.*, 33–45, 179; Howell, *op. cit.*, 100–22; Ehrenburg, *op. cit.*, Vol. V, 48 ff.; Carell, *op. cit.*, 409–12; A. Dallin, *German Rule in Russia*, 209 ff.

upon such a vital nodal point of Soviet communications as Stalingrad, the Stavka was already rushing reserves from northern Russia to the Lower Volga. On August 10, it belatedly subordinated the Stalingrad Front command (then along the Don) to that of the Southeast Front under General Yeremenko.[9]

While the Stavka was preparing to succor Stalingrad, General Franz Halder was beginning to reflect a mounting anxiety over the now enormously extended left flank of Army Group A along the Don. Gradually being fleshed out with the inferior armies of Germany's unenthusiastic allies, the Don line had been easily traversed by Stalin's offensive against White General Wrangel in 1920. When on August 16 Halder had, with unusual subtlety, shown Hitler an old Russian map illustrating this former Stalin offensive, the Fuehrer promptly ordered a German Panzer division into reserve behind the Eighth Italian Army on the Don.

Shortly reinforced with infantry drawn off from the attack on Stalingrad, these German units sufficed to enable the already demoralized Eighth Italian Army to stave off an attack by the First Soviet Guards Army on August 22. Like the Red Army in Stalingrad itself, the Soviet forces near and along the Don at this period lacked air support and had not even much ammunition. Significant for the future, however, with the approbation of General Warlimont's Operations Staff in the O.K.W., Hitler concluded that the best defense of the Don line lay in the rapid seizure of Stalingrad with the consequent release of the German assault forces for such defensive missions on the Don only thereafter.[10]

Preceded by a vigorous revival of the attack upon the Fourth Panzer Army on his right flank, the operation order for the assault upon Stalingrad issued by General Paulus on

---

[9] D. Dallin, *op. cit.*, 211; Yeremenko, *op. cit.*, 86–98.

[10] Warlimont, *op. cit.*, 255; Goerlitz, *Paulus*, 60–61; *Collection of War Experience Materials*, 50; Blau, *Russia*, 164–65; Hart, *The Other Side of the Hill*, 225; *Le Operazioni del C.S.I.R. e dell'Armir, July, 1941–October, 1942* (Rome: Ministry of Defense, 1947), 154 ff.

August 19 foresaw stern Soviet resistance, both in the built-up areas of the city and in terms of heavy counterattacks from the north on the left flank of Paulus' Sixth Army. Nevertheless, accompanied by a tremendous Luftwaffe raid upon the pitifully vulnerable civilians and oil tanks of Stalingrad, by August 23 the Sixth Army had crossed the Don and thrust a five-mile-wide corridor through to the Volga north of Stalingrad.[11] At this juncture the flaming and panicky city was defended by little more than N.K.V.D. troops and four infantry brigades hurriedly commandeered by Yeremenko's Front while on their way south to the Caucasus.

More serious Soviet counterattacks against the extended and precarious German salient at Rzhev near Moscow in the area of Army Group Center now accentuated the growing tension within Hitler's headquarters, currently at Vinnitsa in the Ukraine. On August 8, Field Marshal Guenther von Kluge, commanding Army Group Center, had asked for the release of two Panzer divisions already in his sector with which to relieve the Soviet pressure on Rzhev. Insisting upon reserving these divisions for a still entirely unplanned offensive against Moscow at some time in the future, Hitler stubbornly refused their release. Kluge marched out of the Fuehrer's headquarters after telling Hitler that he must then assume the responsibility for what might happen, only to be blamed just the same a fortnight later when matters in his command went still further astray.

On this same August 8, Field Marshal Georg von Kuechler, Leeb's successor as commander of Army Group North, asked the Fuehrer for further reinforcements for the proposed attack upon Leningrad in September, Operation *Nordlicht*. Claiming that there was a Soviet superiority of almost two to one in his sector, Kuechler also demanded another month

---

[11] Chuikov, *op. cit.*, 61–62; Yeremenko, *op. cit.*, 123–65; Heinz Schröter, *Stalingrad* (London, 1958), 27–34; *Collection of War Experience Materials*, 51–55; Carell, *op. cit.*, 547–59.

with which to complete his preparations, already including the largest employment of artillery envisaged since Verdun. Characteristic of the Fuehrer's attitude toward Leningrad was his demand that the aerial and artillery bombardment of the city produce "the greatest fireworks the world had ever seen."

Since the preparations needed for such an elaborate show would have halted Hitler's additional project of cutting the Murmansk railway at Kandalaksha (Operation *Lachsfang*) this same autumn, Hitler and Jodl insisted upon September 10 as the latest date for the inauguration of *Nordlicht*. At Jodl's suggestion, within another two weeks the reluctant Kuechler would be by-passed entirely as commander for *Nordlicht* by Erich von Manstein, who had recently received his Marshal's baton for the successful siege of Sevastopol. Nevertheless, far from welcoming his new task, Manstein told Halder on August 24 that he would prefer to keep all of his Eleventh Army in southern Russia as a mobile reserve for the offensive there.[12]

Although not yet this pessimistic, Halder was already arguing with Hitler against superimposing the Leningrad offensive upon those toward Stalingrad and the Caucasus. Halder pleaded for the abandonment, at the very least, of the exposed Rzhev-Vyazma salient on the central front, in order to free troops for the numerous weak offensives demanded by Hitler elsewhere. Before the eyes of the aghast Manstein, Hitler furiously replied to his Chief of Staff: "You always come here with the same proposal, that of withdrawal." After some further disparaging remarks about the quality of the German combat soldier in Russia, Hitler ended his tirade by declaring that he expected his "commanders to be as tough as the fighting troops." Controlling his own temper with difficulty, Halder frigidly answered: "I am tough enough, my Fuehrer. But out there brave men and young officers are

---

[12] *Kriegstagebuch des Oberkommandos der Wehrmacht, 1942*, Vol. II, Book 1, 68; cf. Warlimont, *op. cit.*, 251; Ziemke, *op. cit.*, 233–34.

falling in thousands simply because their commanders are not allowed to make the only reasonable decisions and have their hands tied behind their backs."

Before such a blunt statement Hitler recoiled, and fixing his Chief of Staff with a long, malevolent stare, muttered hoarsely: "General Halder, how dare you use language like that to me! Do you think you can teach me what the man at the front is thinking? What do you know about what goes on at the front? Where were you in the First World War? And you try to pretend to me that I don't understand what it's like at the front. I won't stand that! It's outrageous!"[13]

Halder had further infuriated Hitler with his reiterated warnings concerning Soviet tank production, which he now estimated at 1,200 monthly, against a German production of barely 350 a month. In point of fact, however, quite apart from the 4,500 tanks shipped to Russia from Britain and America over the previous year, Stalin had asserted to Churchill this August that Soviet tank production was already 2,000 a month, a statement which he would repeat at the end of the war. Halder also informed Hitler of the General Staff conclusion to the effect that the Red Army was assembling a million and a half men at Stalingrad and along the Don, an unmistakable indication of future Soviet intentions for a large-scale offensive in this region. Not surprisingly, at the end of August Hitler charged his highest Army commanders with "intellectual conceit, mental inadaptability, and an utter failure to grasp essentials."[14] There is equally no cause for wonder that Halder would eventually write that "Hitler's decisions had ceased to have anything in common with the principles of strategy and operations as they have been recog-

---

[13] Warlimont, *op. cit.*, 251–52; Heusinger, *op. cit.*, 129–30; cf. Halder, *War Diary*, Vol. VII, 358; Manstein, *Lost Victories*, 261–62.

[14] Halder, *War Diary*, Vol. VII, 386; cf. his *Hitler als Feldherr*, 51–52; Churchill, *The Hinge of Fate*, 501; Stettinius, *op. cit.*, 232–33; Cherniavsky, *loc. cit.*, 555; *The United States Strategic Bombing Survey*, 278. Soviet tank production rapidly increased throughout 1942 as their factories were settled down in their new eastern bases, but whether it was as high as Stalin claimed is another matter.

nized for generations past. They were the product of a violent nature following its momentary impulses, [a nature] which recognized no limits to possibility and which made its wish the father of its acts. . . ."[15]

Unfortunately for Hitler's continued ability to override General Staff warnings, on August 27 the Second Soviet Shock Army opened a strong offensive on the Leningrad and Volkhov fronts, an offensive designed to re-establish a Russian land link with the besieged but no longer starving metropolis on the Neva. Within the next few weeks, as Hitler watched helplessly, first the reinforcements destined for future operations against the Murmansk railway at Kandalaksha were thrown into the front lines to stem the Soviet assault, and finally the reserves gathered for the German seizure of Leningrad itself were consumed in the maelstrom along the Volkhov River.[16] While by October the Germans had managed to throw back the Soviet attack with heavy losses to the latter, what had already taken place on the Finnish front in late 1941 was now occurring in northern and central Russia, namely, the gradually expanding loss of the initiative to the far from defeated Red Army.

Not content with having alienated both the O.K.H. and his Army Group commanders, by September 7 Hitler's increasingly frantic defiance of reality led him into a row with his always devoted admirer in the O.K.W., General Alfred Jodl. Following an almost unprecedented personal visit to Field Marshal Wilhelm List's Army Group A headquarters, Jodl had made the mistake of justifying the slowing down of List's mountain offensive toward the fiercely defended Soviet Black Sea ports of Tuapse and Novorossiisk. While the normally docile Jodl would never repeat this outburst, the immediate result was his temporary disgrace, not to mention the replacement of List in his Army Group A command by the Fuehrer himself. Refusing to dine hereafter with any officers

---

[15] Halder, *Hitler als Feldherr*, 50.

[16] Ziemke, *op. cit.*, 234–35; Manstein, *Lost Victories*, 262–67.

of the O.K.H. or O.K.W., Hitler planned to replace Jodl with General Paulus of the Sixth Army when the latter had completed the conquest of Stalingrad.

At the same time, Halder also heard that he would shortly be superseded himself. During this crisis all work at Hitler's appropriately named "Werewolf" headquarters in the Ukraine seemed paralyzed, and the Fuehrer shut himself up in his sunless blockhouse all day, emerging only at night when he would not have to see his hated generals. In this hysterical atmosphere, when on September 11 Halder flatly refused to write out an order forbidding retreat under any tactical circumstances, Hitler wrote out the order himself. Two days later, emboldened by a more favorable Intelligence report regarding the state of Red Army reserves, Hitler ordered Army Group B to plan the pursuit of the Soviet forces both up and down the Volga following the expected Soviet defeat at Stalingrad.[17]

When on September 24 Halder saw his Fuehrer for the last time, Hitler explained that half of his nervous exhaustion was due to the obtuseness of his Chief of Staff. What the Reich needed now, Hitler went on, was more National Socialist enthusiasm, rather than professional military ability. In any event, the Fuehrer was determined to enforce his will over the Army. As General Adolf Heusinger of the O.K.H. has written: "A world separated Hitler from the General Staff. His disdain for intellectual work, his undue preference for the purely practical, his exaggerated estimation of the importance of will-power rather than of objective truth," all kept the Fuehrer from understanding the essential purposes and functions of a General Staff.[18]

Furthermore, at a point when Hitler had evidently begun to lose faith in himself and in his great campaign to extirpate

---

[17] Blau, *Russia*, 166–67; Warlimont, *op. cit.*, 256–57; Philippi and Heim, *op. cit.*, 153; Halder, *War Diary*, Vol. VII, 372; Carell, *op. cit.*, 535–36; Heusinger, *op. cit.*, 126–37; *Lossberg*, *op. cit.*, 120–25, 151–52.

[18] Heusinger, *op. cit.*, 133–37; cf. Halder, *War Diary*, Vol. VII, 397.

Bolshevism, the presence of such obvious mistrust, not to say covert hostility, as that of Franz Halder, had become intolerable. Indeed, Hitler's military acolyte, General Jodl, had justified not openly opposing the Fuehrer on the revealing grounds that this would shake the dictator's self-confidence, the principal foundation of his personality and activities. In any case, Halder's replacement, Lieutenant General Kurt Zeitzler, was both energetic and an optimist, a combination after the Fuehrer's heart in this period of gloom and stagnation in the High Command. As in the sarcastic explanation at this juncture of the anti-Nazi Chief of the Abwehr, Admiral Canaris: "We don't need a genius as Chief of Staff, for we've got the Fuehrer."

Appointed with the subtle support of that inveterate enemy of the Army, Hermann Goering, Zeitzler immediately demanded radiant confidence and faith in the Fuehrer from every General Staff officer. But as far as any improvement in the operations of the General Staff went, Zeitzler's appointment made matters worse. Instead of achieving the long-sought unity of the O.K.H. and O.K.W., and with it of their separate and competitive theaters of war, Zeitzler soon settled for a total exclusion of the O.K.W. from his own O.K.H. Russian theater, forbidding the O.K.W. even the most essential information regarding the eastern theater. While this served to uphold Hitler's principle of dividing and thus ruling the German Army, it meant that hereafter German divisions were frequently transferred from the peaceful O.K.W. theaters of the West quite unprepared for the brutal combat in the East into which they were suddenly plunged. Moreover, that mortal antipathy of most politicians, long-range strategic planning, was effectively dissipated into the short-range and wasteful improvisations so characteristic of the strident and vulgar personality of the Fuehrer.[19]

[19] Abshagen, *op. cit.*, 208; cf. Warlimont, *op. cit.*, 257–66; Heusinger, *op. cit.*, 138; Guderian, *op. cit.*, 275; Blau, *Russia*, 167; Manstein, *Lost Victories*, 80; *Kriegstagebuch des Oberkommandos der Wehrmacht, 1942*, Vol. II, Book 1, 8–9.

As Churchill was leaving the Soviet Union in August, he had seen many Poles, both military and civilian, being evacuated from the Soviet Union by way of Persia. Half-starved and embittered, these refugees of war had been allowed to leave Russia by Stalin in negotiations commencing the previous December. The Russians had evidently despaired of winning effective Polish military support on their own front, and in this period of defeat good relations with their British Ally were not to be jeopardized by unnecessary quarrels with the Poles. While the Poles were gratefully straggling out through Teheran, American engineers were arriving in Persia to improve vastly its crucial role as an invulnerable overland supply route to the Soviet Union. But if resenting the departure of the Poles, the Russians still procrastinated on accepting Allied Air Forces, let alone British troops, in their zealously guarded Caucasian oil regions. The Soviets apparently remembered all too well the almost simultaneous arrival of the Germans, Turks, and British in the Caucasus in 1918/19, and preferred to take no risks of losing control of their precious oil fields in any such fashion again.[20]

Once back in London, in mid-September, Churchill began again to harry his Chiefs of Staff concerning the possibilities of that old favorite of his, an amphibious operation in northern Norway for the sake of cutting the heavy Allied shipping losses on the Arctic convoys to Murmansk. Claiming that he had promised something of this kind to Stalin, the Prime Minister also admitted that his competitive North African expedition was no substitute for a cross-Channel assault in the next year, a point which he now conceded the United States Army had been making all along. In addition to accepting the resignation from the War Cabinet of that politically dangerous advocate of a second front, Sir Stafford Cripps, on September

[20] Lieutenant General W. Anders, *An Army in Exile* (London, 1949), 122 ff.; Kot, *op. cit.*, 149 ff.; Werth, *op. cit.*, 686 ff.; Motter, *op. cit.*, 179 ff., C. H. Ellis, *The Transcaspian Episode, 1918–1919* (London, 1963), 18 ff.; *Foreign Relations of the United States, 1942*, Vol. III, 101, 133–34, 681; Eden, *op. cit.*, 323 ff.

22 Mr. Churchill wrote President Roosevelt that his "persisting anxiety" remained Soviet Russia. The need to suspend new sailings of the Arctic convoys until the North African operation had been mounted was further accentuating the fears of the British and American governments concerning the Soviet reaction to this latest blow.[21]

Stalin's reply was not long in forthcoming. Preceded in September by leaks to the press through his Ambassador in Britain, Ivan Maisky, as well as through such itinerant American politicos as Wendell Willkie, then being feted in Moscow, on October 3 Stalin wrote an unusual letter to an American correspondent in Moscow, Henry C. Cassidy. In this heavily publicized statement, the Soviet ruler affirmed that Allied aid to the Soviet Union had so far been of little value. While this might embody elements of truth, given the relatively poor quality of the combat matériel if not of the general economic assistance so far provided, such statements were not the best way of laying the ground for a new Soviet request on October 5 for more planes for the still desperately short Stalingrad sector.

On October 9, the President and the Prime Minister answered Stalin, Roosevelt offering again his unwanted American Air Force formations for the Caucasus and Churchill his own version of a second front in North Africa. Ten days later the official Communist newspaper, *Pravda*, published an article on Rudolf Hess suggesting that Great Britain was a secure refuge for escaping Nazi gangsters. By the end of the month, the President had decided that the Russians did not "use speech for the same purposes" as their Allies. More to the point, the Prime Minister had concluded that it would be "a great mistake to run after the Russians in their present mood." Churchill was not deluding himself; the Soviets indeed sought serious sacrifices on the part of their relatively unscathed

---

[21] Leighton and Coakley, *op. cit.*, 583; cf. Bryant, *op. cit.*, Vol. I, 500–5; Churchill, *The Hinge of Fate*, 557–71; Captain S. W. Roskill, *History of the Second World War: The War at Sea, 1939–1945*, Vol. II (London, 1956), 288 ff.

allies and were no longer willing to be fobbed off with promises of a glowing future or with ineffective or irrelevant gestures in the present.[22]

Meanwhile, in Stalingrad itself, the military situation was coalescing day by day. At the beginning of September, in a desperate effort to gain time to strengthen the defenses of the city, three new Soviet armies with insufficient artillery and green troops were thrown piecemeal into a costly offensive from the north of Stalingrad. Although this feeble offensive weakened the German Army and air concentration upon Stalingrad somewhat, by September 12 the Sixth German Army was fighting its way into the streets of the elongated but dangerously narrow city.

This same day, Vasili Chuikov was appointed by the Front commander General Yeremenko and his political deputy, Nikita Khrushchev, to take over the rather demoralized Sixty-second Army from his less acquiescent predecessor, Lieutenant General A. I. Lopatin. Appointed, unlike Lopatin, for his eager readiness to hang on to Stalingrad at any cost, the morale of Chuikov's Army was not likely to have been stiffened by Stalin's purported desire to delay the evacuation of the Russian civilian population across the Volga. In the supposed opinion of the Soviet ruler, the Red Army was more likely to fight for a living town than for an empty one.[23]

In any event, the Sixty-second Army held on to the soon shattered city with the aid of heavy artillery protection from beyond the mile-wide Volga as well as of a constant flow of infantry reinforcements commencing in mid-September. As

---

[22] Churchill, *The Hinge of Fate*, 572–82; cf. Sherwood, *op. cit.*, 636–42; Woodward, *op. cit.*, 198–200; Standley, *op. cit.*, 290–98; *Foreign Relations of the United States, 1942*, Vol. III, 466 ff., 638–47, 724–26, 745; Eden, *op. cit.*, 394–99.

[23] Hanson W. Baldwin, "The Battle That Turned the Nazi Tide," *New York Times* (New York), April 13, 1963, 56; *Collection of War Experience Materials*, 55–58; Carell, *op. cit.*, 560–65. The contrast between Chuikov's harsh version, *op. cit.*, 75–86, and Yeremenko's gentler account, *op. cit.*, 191–98, of Lopatin's relief is striking for Soviet historiography, even to a difference in dates.

early as September 20, General Paulus' attacking Army was succumbing to exhaustion, and by the last week of the month new Soviet counterattacks to the south of the city further relieved German pressure upon Chuikov's sacrificial garrison. For this was the role of the Sixty-second Soviet Army; by its weakness and apparent desperation it was ideally situated to attract and then to tie down more and more of the already inadequate reserves of German Army Groups A and B.

Contrary to the postwar assertions of Marshal Yeremenko, however, both the Axis troops on the spot and their superiors soon enough sensed the significance of what was happening in the Stalingrad slaughterhouse. For example, on September 24, the Rumanians complained to the German High Command that their Third and Fourth Armies, now left guarding the extended Axis flanks along the Don and south of Stalingrad, were hopelessly weak and without mobile forces or antitank weapons with which to hold their immense frontages. In fact, units of the Fourth Rumanian Army had already been badly knocked about during a Soviet counteroffensive south of Stalingrad in late September, and the Red Army had gained valuable information at that time concerning these obvious Achilles' heels of the Reich.[24]

The command staffs of German Army Groups A and B added their voices to the growing alarm among the soldiers at the end of September. Army Group B now requested the evacuation of Stalingrad and a retirement to a short and strong defense line beyond the Don for the winter. This would free German divisions with which to brace up the three weak Axis armies along the Don. Although Hitler himself had previously told Reich Propaganda Minister Goebbels of his intention to go into winter quarters by October, 1942, regardless of what the Soviets did, the Fuehrer had predicated this remark of the previous spring upon the successful conquest of no less than the Caucasus, Leningrad, and Moscow.

---

[24] Yeremenko, *op. cit.*, 225–48; Blau, *Russia*, 168; Werth, *op. cit.*, 455–61; Carell, *op. cit.*, 566–77.

In short, in Hitler's inverted logic, notwithstanding his failure again this year to defeat the Red Army decisively, he nevertheless chose to run the grave risk of continuing ever more overextended and difficult offensives in the face of the approaching winter. As with almost all politicians, the pursuit of prestige meant more to Hitler than adherence even to his own strategic views; after all, prestige is the life blood of politics and strategy only an annoying, but subordinate, mechanism to far greater statesmen than Adolf Hitler.[25]

With the coming of October, even such conformist newcomers in the German High Command as Paulus, and Halder's replacement as Chief of the Army General Staff, Kurt Zeitzler, grew concerned; the evidence of Soviet offensive intentions was becoming overwhelming. Paulus further recognized that the infantry replacements available to him only through the Dnieper and Don railway-bridge bottlenecks were quite insufficient for the complete conquest of Stalingrad. To be sure, in mid-October his depleted and exhausted troops caught the Russians by surprise and with the aid of air superiority managed to reach the Volga at a new point on a front of several kilometers. It was to be the last significant German success in the Sixth Army sector; the initiative was now more and more shifting over to Yeremenko's expanding forces.

On October 2 and 3, General Zeitzler, who so far had kept his Fuehrer happy with a series of makeshift tactical expedients, now proposed the formation of larger reserves for Army Groups A and B against the ever more certain Soviet counterattack. With Jodl's support, Zeitzler opposed further costly fighting for the ruins of Stalingrad. Hitler refused his new Army Chief of Staff brusquely, admitting for the first time that he sought the fall of Stalingrad for reasons of morale alone. Despite what he called the Army's familiar anxieties over "half-measures," Hitler was still determined that Communism be "deprived of its grail" on the Volga.

[25] Goebbels, *op. cit.*, 136; *Reverses on the Southern Wing, 1942–1943*, Historical Division, H.Q. U.S. Army Europe (Heidelberg, undated), 11–12.

The warnings of Army Group B that the principal Red Army assault was to be expected on the lower Don sector of the Third Rumanian Army also met with Hitler's plausible, if irrelevant, objection that any Soviet counterattack would be more apt to have as its objective breaking through the Italian Eighth Army higher up on the Don in the hope of trapping the whole of Army Groups A and B at Rostov. Wisely, however, the Stavka, now evidently under General Zhukov's professional influence, had rejected any such over-ambitious scheme, a scheme only too reflective of the unduly optimistic Soviet plans in their previous winter offensive.[26]

In one of his many efforts to denigrate the acumen of his professional German opposite numbers, Marshal Yeremenko has referred slightingly to another aspect of the German Army's efforts to bring Hitler to reason on Stalingrad in good time. This was the German Army's clever argument that since Paulus' Sixth Army had already stopped Soviet commercial traffic on the Volga as well as having destroyed almost all of Stalingrad's important factories, the Germans had thus achieved their original objectives in this region. Consequently, in this convenient rationale, the Fuehrer could now afford in any event to retire with his pride intact during the dangerous winter months when the Volga was solidly frozen over.

Apart from the fact that the prestige of capturing and holding the city flaunting his great rival's name had in itself become Hitler's real objective, Volga River military traffic had of course never entirely ceased or the three Soviet armies still hanging on west of the river in the thin ribbon of the Stalingrad area could never have survived without supplies. Everything these heroic armies required, down to their endless flow of infantry replacements for the new Verdun on

---

[26] *Kriegstagebuch des Oberkommandos der Wehrmacht, 1942*, Vol. II, Book 1, 67; cf. *Reverses on the Southern Wing*, 12–16; Greiner, *op. cit.*, 412 ff.; Goerlitz, *Paulus*, 191–93, 226–27; Blau, *Russia*, 169–71; Yeremenko, *op. cit.*, 225–74; Hart, *The Other Side of the Hill*, 224–26; Warlimont, *op. cit.*, 266; General Kurt Zeitzler, "Stalingrad," in *The Fatal Decisions*, 138 ff.

the Volga, had to traverse the great river both before and after it gradually froze solid by mid-December. Moreover, the slightest German retreat from the river would have opened it again to Soviet commercial traffic in the spring.

The worst aspect of the matter was that, as General Thomas, the German Army Economics Chief, pointed out at this juncture in a memorandum most unpopular with his Nazi superiors, in all probability nothing less than the actual occupation of the Baku oil fields themselves would have been required to cripple the Soviet economy and war machine. Even the conquest of Astrakhan at the mouth of the Volga on the Caspian Sea, still so hopefully envisaged in this period by Hitler as an operation for the spring of 1943, could not have fully interdicted the transport of Soviet oil supplies north from Baku through other Caspian seaports and by rail thereafter. In other words, as Yeremenko more objectively points out, the German Army never really had the strength to cripple the Soviet Union in 1942 by a strategy of economic war in the southern reaches of that vast empire. The Western Allies, too, would discover that the politically popular economic road to military success was initially long and eventually disappointing.[27]

In the latter part of October, Yeremenko's left wing south of Stalingrad renewed its attacks on the Fourth German Panzer Army and the adjacent Rumanians in order to relieve pressure on Stalingrad, while on the Don the Third Rumanian Army reported that the Russians were building bridges across the river at numerous points. But with Hitler, the Eighth Italian Army higher up on the Don at Boguchar feared for their sector as the more likely scene for the Soviet winter offensive. In any event, rejecting again the plea of the at last thoroughly alarmed General Paulus for the retirement of his Sixth Army as far as Kharkov, Paulus' jumping-off point for

---

[27] Blau, *Russia*, 174; Yeremenko, *op. cit.*, 218–27; Major General V. F. C. Fuller, *The Second World War, 1939–1945* (New York, 1949), 185; Zeitzler, *loc. cit.*, 145.

the whole 1942 campaign, on November 1 Hitler and his O.K.H.-O.K.W. joint headquarters quit their Ukrainian base at Vinnitsa and returned to winter quarters in East Prussia. By this late date, unquestionably it would have been difficult to effect any large-scale German retirement such as Paulus advocated, in the face of the growing Soviet concentrations and the bad state of the roads. Furthermore, Hitler evidently hoped to the end that his total occupation of Stalingrad might bring in the Turks or the Japanese as much-needed allies for his stalemated campaign in the East.[28]

Unfortunately for convincing Hitler at the last moment of the need for at least some countermeasures against the impending Soviet offensive, during the first week of November, German intelligence agencies fluctuated uncertainly between their well-founded fears of the growing Soviet preparations opposite the Third Rumanian Army and over a new anxiety, perhaps engendered by a Soviet cover plan, concerning a possible Red Army offensive in the Moscow region instead. Moreover, many of the new German infantry reserves currently moving to Russia had been hurriedly formed from Goering's vast reserves of high-grade, but untrained manpower in the Luftwaffe. Rather than put these into the veteran, but badly depleted, regular German Army divisions, the jealous Luftwaffe chief had offered this fresh manpower only on the condition that it would remain under his organizational control without any integration whatsoever with the purportedly reactionary Army.

Finally, however, when the Fuehrer's attention was temporarily distracted by the Allied landings in French North Africa, between November 9 and 15, two weak German Panzer divisions and a still weaker Rumanian armored unit were ordered into reserve behind the Third Rumanian Army.

[28] *Collection of War Experience Materials*, 59; Blau, *Russia*, 175; *Reverses on the Southern Wing*, 21–22; Greiner, *op. cit.*, 415–17; Baldwin, "The Battle That Turned the Nazi Tide," 59; Chuikov, *op. cit.*, 134; *The Ciano Diaries*, 536; *Le Operazioni del C.S.I.R. e dell'Armir*, 187 ff.; Clark, *op. cit.*, 242–47.

Unhappily, it had taken Army Group B so long to obtain Hitler's permission for these belated actions that one of the German armored divisions, the principal component of the XLVIIIth Panzer Corps commanded by Major General Ferdinand Heim, had not yet arrived at its new post by the date the Russian offensive began in this sector.[29]

With the overwhelming defeat of Erwin Rommel finally achieved at El Alamein, at the beginning of November Mr. Churchill felt sufficiently emboldened to congratulate Stalin on what he called "the decisive defeat of Hitler's second campaign against Russia." Stalin replied officially on November 8, thanking the Prime Minister for his renewed offer of Allied Air Force fighter squadrons for the still plane-short Soviet Caucasus—after all, Allied planes could not seize Soviet territory, although in the upshot the rapid Soviet recovery at Stalingrad in the near future would still enable Stalin to evade Churchill's offer.

The Prime Minister's compliments, however, must have afforded Stalin great satisfaction when he recalled the open criticism of his rival Marshal Tukhachevsky in 1932 to the effect that his much-vaunted defense of Tsaritsyn (renamed Stalingrad) during the Soviet Civil War had been a vast mistake. Now the world would see who was justified on this occasion and the successful second defense of the vital artery on the Volga would serve to vindicate to some degree the author of the great purge, even in the eyes of his many enemies among the Soviet military.[30] Stalin had also endeavored to conciliate the Red Army with the decree on October 9 abolishing the political deputies to all Soviet commanders.

---

[29] *Reverses on the Southern Wing*, 14–23, 205–8; Zeitzler, *loc. cit.*, 138–47; Blau, *Russia*, 171–73; Greiner, *op. cit.*, 415–17; Goerlitz, *Paulus*, 194, 218, 227 n.1; Warlimont, *op. cit.*, 265–66; Schroeter, *op. cit.*, 55–66; Carell, *op. cit.*, 577–80.

[30] *Stalin's Correspondence*, 73–74; cf. Alexandrov, *op. cit.*, 50; Werth, *op. cit.*, 489–90; *Foreign Relations of the United States, 1942*, Vol. III, 463–64, 672.

The steadfast loyalty of the vast bulk of the Soviet Officer Corps, along with the growing shortage of trained officers, likewise contributed to this always significant gesture.

Stalin's real answer to Churchill's renewal of their correspondence was to be found in his important speech of November 6, celebrating the twenty-fifth anniversary of the October Revolution. In this proud statement to the Soviet people, as usual Stalin attributed the continued German successes in Russia in 1942 to the absence of an Allied second front in the West. Although manifesting optimism regarding the future of the Allied coalition against Hitler. Stalin also referred ironically to the British achievement in Egypt, where he did not omit to point out that the British were fighting "only four—yes, four German, and eleven Italian divisions." In another declaration, on the next day, the Soviet ruler hinted that Russia, too, would have reason to rejoice in the near future.[31]

Perhaps for this reason, and just after hearing of the for him unexpected Allied landings in Northwest Africa, on November 8 Hitler likewise made one of his more revelatory speeches. To his old Party comrades in Munich he defended himself against the charge that his insistence upon staying in the city which "happens to bear the name of Stalin" was as costly to the German Army as Verdun, a charnel house still reeking of futility, rather than glory, to the uneasy German public. But for the future, also, Hitler warned that he would not be another Wilhelm II, a weak ruler who had surrendered the Reich's eastern conquests at the point of their greatest extent, due to his soldiers' sudden desire for a capitulation in the West.

"Ever since I was a boy," concluded the Fuehrer, "it has always been my habit—originally, perhaps, a bad one, but in the final resort a virtue—to have the last word. All our enemies may rest assured that while the Germany of that

[31] Werth, *op. cit.*, 490–91; cf. Feis, *Churchill, Roosevelt, Stalin*, 95.

time [1918] laid down its arms at a quarter to twelve, on principle I have never finished before five minutes past twelve."[32]

Hitler had reason to defy his enemies at home as well as abroad. After the crushing Axis defeat at El Alamein, on November 6 Mussolini had told the Germans that a separate peace with Russia had to be arranged as soon as possible, a point on which the Duce had much sympathy within the German Army High Command. At this juncture, Foreign Minister Ribbentrop suggested initiating some such negotiations through Madame Kollontai, the Soviet Ambassador to Sweden. Hitler turned down his Russophile Foreign Minister in a rage, the thought of giving up Soviet territory proving as unpalatable to him for reasons of diplomatic negotiation as for those of strategic necessity.[33]

To compound these fundamental errors with respect to Russia, at the beginning of November Hitler had also rejected a desperate appeal from Rommel in Egypt to permit a timely retreat of his already defeated forces. This refusal thus accentuated the Germans' embarrassment when they, if not their Italian Ally, were caught by surprise by the Allied landings in Northwest Africa on November 8. Contrary, however, to the expectation of the German command in Italy, improvised measures enabled the O.K.W. to carry out Hitler's decision on November 9 to seize an Axis bridgehead in Tunisia, an old aim of Mussolini's in any event.[34]

Within ten days another old advocate of German strategic dispersion in the Mediterranean, Grand Admiral Erich Raeder, had joined the fray. Forgetting Malta for the moment, the German Navy chief now enthusiastically informed his Fuehrer that "Tunisia always was and still is the decisive

---

[32] Bullock, *op. cit.*, 630; cf. Zeitzler, *loc. cit.*, 145; Jacobsen, *op. cit.*, 354–56; Goerlitz, *Paulus*, 67.

[33] Ribbentrop, *op. cit.*, 169; Heusinger, *op. cit.*, 140–41; Deakin, *op. cit.*, 84; Hesse, *op. cit.*, 154–55; Kleist, *op. cit.*, 235 ff.

[34] Warlimont, *op. cit.*, 268–72; Kesselring, *op. cit.*, 142 ff; *The Ciano Diaries*, 538–47; *Les Lettres Secrètes*, 135–40.

key position in the Mediterranean. . . . It is . . . a simple task to supply our Armored Army since our [communication] lines are short." Raeder's last assertion was at that very moment in the process of being refuted by the prohibitive cost of convoying the new Axis forces by sea to Tunisian ports. Furthermore, the hasty diversion of some four hundred German fighter and transport planes from Russia to help sustain Hitler's belated new commitment across the Mediterranean was to play havoc with the Luftwaffe at Stalingrad in the near future.[35]

Small wonder that in a brief thaw Stalin smiled upon the seemingly spectacular achievements in Africa of his Western allies, not yet recognizing the appalling price in Russian lives to be paid for the further delay in a second front which the new African operation would inescapably evoke. And Hitler's foolhardy refusal, while under the impact of the Allied surprise, to cut his losses in Africa in order to concentrate on the decisive theater in the East foreshadowed the imminence of the still greater follies at last about to drown the German hopes of victory in the Second World War.[36]

---

[35] *F.C.G.N., 1942*, Vol. I, 126; cf. Ruge, *op. cit.*, 330–32; Lee, *op. cit.*, 126–36; *Collection of War Experience Materials*, 317 ff.

[36] *Stalin's Correspondence*, 75; Henry C. Cassidy, *Moscow Dateline* (Boston, 1943), 301–2; Gallagher, *Soviet History*, 28; Warlimont, *op. cit.*, 277; *Foreign Relations of the United States, 1942*, Vol. III, 478–79, 660.

"The campaign of 1812 has taught us . . . that the probability of final success does not in all cases diminish in the same measure as battles, capitals, and provinces are lost . . . but that a nation is often strongest in the heart of its country if the enemy's offensive power has exhausted itself, and with what enormous force the defensive then springs over to the offensive."[1] CLAUSEWITZ

"I am speaking of the counteroffensive after a successful enemy advance which, however, failed to yield decisive results, during which the party on the defensive collects forces, launches a counteradvance and inflicts upon the antagonist a decisive defeat. I think that a well-organized counteroffensive is one of the most interesting forms of offensive."[2]

STALIN, letter to COLONEL RAZIN,
February 23, 1946

"When our neighbors hear what has happened, they will say it was not into a foreign country that the Swedish Army and the Swedish power ventured, but rather into some mighty sea! They have fallen in and disappeared, even as lead is swallowed in water."[3] Address to PETER THE GREAT after the battle of Poltava, 1709

"Her losses have been inconceivably greater than those of all the other nations put together. Russia has now the right to demand of the Allies that they bring greater force of arms to bear."[4] KERENSKY, October, 1917

[1] Clausewitz, *op. cit.*, Vol. I, 230–31.
[2] Dexter, *loc. cit.*, 45.
[3] R. Waliszewski, *Peter the Great* (London, 1896), 326.
[4] John Reed, *Ten Days That Shook the World* (New York, 1934), 330.

CHAPTER IX

Counteroffensive on the Don

November 19, 1942—Spring, 1943

UNDER the cover of a snowstorm, and sustained by a superiority of more than two to one in tanks, troops, and new-model planes, the first manifestation of what Stalin had long before defined as the permanently operating factors of war made its appearance before dawn on November 19. Organized over the preceding weeks by the Stavka representatives, Generals Zhukov, Alexander Vasilevsky, and Nikolai Voronov, this first effectively controlled counteroffensive of the Red Army was unveiled on the Southwest Front of General Nikolai Vatutin, and on the Don Front of Lieutenant General Constantine Rokossovsky. The Soviet attack rapidly penetrated most of the expectant Third Rumanian Army on a wide front. Twenty-four hours later, and a day earlier than this experienced Front commander had desired, on November 20 Yeremenko's Stalingrad Front struck against the equally expectant and demoralized Fourth Rumanian Army southwest of Stalingrad with equal success.

Despite isolated examples of gallant resistance on the part of General Lascar's Corps in the Third Rumanian Army along the Don, on the whole the poorly equipped Rumanian forces panicked and collapsed as promptly as anticipated. By the afternoon of November 22, the northern and southern pincers of the great Soviet counteroffensive had finally closed at Kalach on the Don, completely severing all German overland communications with the west. Both the Paulus Sixth Army and elements of the Fourth German Panzer Army, comprising most of twenty German divisions, in addition to two Rumanian divisions, were abruptly cut off from their already inadequate rail-borne supplies, not to mention their stockpiles in the rear.[5]

Upon hearing of the long-awaited Soviet offensive, General Paulus had immediately called off the feeble assaults of his Sixth Army within the ruins of Stalingrad, and turning most of his men about, tried to prepare to face the flood of Rokossovsky's forces by-passing the left flank of his Army far to his rear. In East Prussia the Chief of Staff of the Army, General Zeitzler, sent an urgent message to Hitler, then in Bavaria, seeking permission to release General Heim's XLVIIIth Panzer Corps to Army Group B in order to provide a mobile Panzer reserve to brace the collapsing Third Rumanian Army. Finally successful in this petty and long overdue endeavor, Zeitzler found the Fuehrer adamant against allowing a hurried retreat of the Sixth German Army from Stalingrad before the jaws of the Red Army trap had closed. As Hitler wrote Mussolini on November 20, he was "one of those men who in adversity simply became more determined." In short, like Stalin in 1941, Adolf Hitler was about to reveal his utter incapacity to fight defensive warfare, a type of war peculiarly difficult for a demagogue with weak nerves.[6]

Not content with rejecting a rational role for the Sixth Army, Hitler now sent a series of messages from his peregrinating O.K.W. headquarters directly to General Heim's

---

[5] Gallagher, *Soviet History*, 42–43; *The Great Patriotic War*, Vol. III, 20 ff.; Yeremenko, *op. cit.*, 346–78; Carell, *op. cit.*, 581–86; Goerlitz, *Paulus*, 202–3, 242–49; Manstein, *Lost Victories*, 293; Cherniavsky, *loc. cit.*, 551; Boris Telpuchowski, *Die sovjetische Geschichte des Grossen Vaterlaendischen Krieges, 1941–1945* (Frankfurt am Main, 1961), 177 ff.; *Reserves on the Southern Wing*, 17, 31, 175–76, 208–12; *Collection of War Experience Materials*, 68–86, 153–78, 215–32, 261; *Foreign Relations of the United States, 1942*, Vol. III, 673–77; Horst Scheibert, *Zwischen Don und Donez; Winter, 1942–43* (Neckargemuend, 1961), 20 ff.; Mario Fenyö, "The Allied Axis Armies and Stalingrad," *Military Affairs* (Washington), Summer, 1965, 63–66.

[6] Warlimont, *op. cit.*, 273–77; cf. Zeitzler, *loc. cit.*, 147–49; Goerlitz, *Paulus*, 195.

XLVIIIth Corps, thus by-passing the intervening chain of Army commands. But the Fuehrer's frequent, outdated, and absurdly unrealistic orders regarding the direction of Heim's attacks were contradicted by the instructions of Army Group B for a quick retreat, thus saving Heim's weak corps from complete destruction at the hands of the vastly superior Soviet forces flooding south across the Don. But a fortnight later the unhappy General Heim would find himself in a Berlin prison, demoted to private, as a most necessary scapegoat for the Fuehrer's too public error on Stalingrad. Hitler also needed somebody else to blame for the trapping of Rumanian General Lascar's Corps, a Corps to which he likewise had refused to give orders in time for its retreat, notwithstanding a desperate personal plea to this effect from the Rumanian dictator, Marshal Antonescu.[7]

More realistically, on November 20 Hitler decided to carry out a long-contemplated O.K.H. desire to set up a new Army Group Don. Such an additional group would relieve General Maximilian von Weichs of the excessive burden of commanding seven armies, four of which were not German, in his existing Group B. Instead of giving this new command to the Rumanian dictator, Marshal Antonescu, as originally envisaged, the great crisis at Stalingrad impelled Hitler to recall Field Marshal Erich von Manstein and his Eleventh Army staff from northern Russia to head the new Army Group Don. Under the brilliant Manstein were placed the Paulus Sixth Army and the Fourth German Panzer Army, as well as what would survive of the Third and Fourth Rumanian Armies. This left under the semi-scapegoat, General Baron von Weichs, only the Second German, Second Hungarian, and Eighth Italian Armies, still located in that order along the upper Don.[8]

---

[7] Goerlitz, *Paulus*, 242–49; Schroeter, *op. cit.*, 65–72; Zeitzler, *loc. cit.*, 155–57; Heusinger, *op. cit.*, 144; *Reverses on the Southern Wing*, 25–30.

[8] Zeitzler, *loc. cit.*, 168; Manstein, *Lost Victories*, 292–94; *Heusinger*, *op. cit.*, 144–45; *Kriegstagebuch des Oberkommandos der Wehrmacht, 1942*, Vol. II, Book 1, 83.

On November 21, Hitler ordered General Paulus to establish a so-called Fortress Stalingrad, with his Sixth Army headquarters henceforth to be located inside the embattled city itself. Perhaps too late, Paulus replied directly the next day reporting his encirclement and requesting his freedom of decision on the question of a retreat in view of his shortage of supplies of all kinds. The Sixth Army commander had hesitated in reaching this conclusion because of the difficulties of any such breakout, particularly with the burden of some 15,000 German war wounded currently in the field hospitals of Stalingrad. Nevertheless, General Weichs, still Paulus' immediate superior pending the arrival of Manstein, endorsed the Sixth Army commander's request for a retreat on the grounds that air supply was not feasible, while a relieving force could not be made ready before the presumed exhaustion of the Sixth Army's supplies.[9]

Paulus has been severely criticized within the German Army, both at the time by his frantic principal subordinate, Lieutenant General Walther von Seydlitz, and subsequently by Field Marshal von Manstein, for not simply ignoring the Fuehrer's orders and breaking out anyway. Indeed, Seydlitz would shortly endeavor to force Paulus' hand by ordering on his own accord his LIth Corps on the left flank of the Sixth Army to retire from its snug dugouts in preparation for the anticipated breakout. During the previous winter, when the isolated German position at Demyansk had been surrounded by the Russians, Seydlitz' successful relief force had been greatly assisted in reopening a land link to Demyansk by a simultaneous breakout operation on the part of the encircled garrison there.

Since to present Hitler with a *fait accompli* in the much-cited tradition of General Yorck in December, 1812, was scarcely in the character of so uncertain a staff officer in high command as Paulus, the only result of Seydlitz' insubordinate

---

[9] Schroeter, *op. cit.*, 81–97; *Reverses on the Southern Wing*, 35–40; Goerlitz, *Paulus*, 231; Carell, *op. cit.*, 589–90; Clark, *op. cit.*, 255–57.

endeavor was the loss of a strongly fortified line as well as of one of his retreating divisions. For that matter, when the suspicious Fuehrer then split the command at Stalingrad between Paulus and Seydlitz, the latter promptly lost all desire to take the lead in an open rebellion against Hitler. The choice between loyalty to a civilian superior and that to one's own military subordinates is always an agonizing one for any general officer, and especially to an officer so painfully conscious of the lack of confidence of his superiors in his own capacity for command as Friedrich Paulus.[10]

When Hitler finally reached his regular headquarters, the so-called "Wolf's Lair" at Rastenburg in East Prussia, at midnight on November 22/23, he found the anxious General Zeitzler waiting up for him. Against the opposition of the Fuehrer's entourage, Zeitzler insisted upon seeing Hitler to ask once again for the immediate release of the Sixth Army. After some play-acting in the grand manner of Frederick the Great, Hitler broached as an alternative an O.K.W. suggestion for bringing up one or two Panzer divisions from the Caucasus to the relief of Stalingrad. When Zeitzler pointed out the inadequacy of any such project, both in the time required to mount it as well as in its intrinsic weakness compared to the Russians, Hitler lost his temper. Banging on the table, the Fuehrer dropped all pretense of reason and cried: "I won't leave the Volga! I won't go back from the Volga."

The next day Paulus sent another despairing appeal to the O.K.H. for permission to fight his way out of the trap, regardless of losses in men and matériel, and Zeitzler again saw Hitler in behalf of the Sixth Army Chief. After a nerve-racking hesitation, Hitler finally made use of Zeitzler's enemies in the O.K.W., Field Marshal Keitel and General Jodl, in an attempt to browbeat the Army Chief into acquiescence. With the full support of the O.K.H. planning and intelligence

---

[10] Carell, *op. cit.*, 397–405, 595–98; Goerlitz, *Paulus*, 69–72, 221–33; Manstein, *Lost Victories*, 303; Schroeter, *op. cit.*, 108–11; Heusinger, *op. cit.*, 149–50; Jacobsen, *op. cit.*, 358–61.

staffs, however, Zeitzler continued to plead for Paulus. Indeed, Zeitzler went further and notified the greatly relieved Army Group B to initiate the preparations for a breakout on the part of the Sixth Army. So eager was the Commander in Chief of Army Group B, General von Weichs, to carry out this authorization that he proposed to go ahead on its execution even without Hitler's specific approval to do so.

Hitler stopped these Army efforts to by-pass his authority by radioing Paulus directly to stay where he was until relieved by Manstein's new Army Group Don. Then, in collusion with Hermann Goering, and Goering's fatally acquiescent Chief of Staff, Major General Hans Jeschonek, Hitler obtained a qualified Luftwaffe promise to fly five hundred metric tons of supplies to Stalingrad every day. In undertaking this particular evasion of logistic reality, Hitler and the Luftwaffe Chiefs had been undoubtedly influenced by the success of the Demyansk airlift in the previous winter, when six temporarily cut-off German divisions in northern Russia were supplied by air for seventy-two days until relieved.

Like Zeitzler and Weichs, Baron von Richthofen, the commander of the Fourth Air Fleet, who was expected to carry out the Luftwaffe promise to supply Stalingrad, had already informed his superiors that it was out of the question. Nevertheless, in his desire to regain his old position with Hitler, Goering chose to disregard this and other such warnings. For a Luftwaffe already vastly overcommitted by the effort to sustain Tunisia by air, the prospects of supplying the approximately 330,000 soldiers and supporting civilians of the Stalingrad pocket under winter conditions with more than 20 to 40 per cent of the amount of Goering's glib assurances would prove quite illusionary.[11]

---

[11] Zeitzler, *loc. cit.*, 161–69; cf. Goerlitz, *Paulus*, 233–41; Schroeter, *op. cit.*, 102–8; *Collection of War Experience Materials*, 263; Halder, *Hitler als Feldherr*, 53–54; Heusinger, *op. cit.*, 145–52; Greiner, *op. cit.*, 424 ff.; Manstein,

When Manstein at last assumed command at his new Army Group Don headquarters on November 27, he found two doleful letters awaiting him. The first, from General Paulus, thanked him for previous assurances of help in getting the Sixth Army out of its "mess" and explained that, despite Hitler's *de facto* assumption of direct operational command over his Army, Paulus had received no recent information or orders beyond that of hanging onto even his most untenable positions everywhere. Paulus had also received very few supplies from the still unorganized airlift.

Manstein's other letter was from the Rumanian dictator, Marshal Antonescu. Antonescu complained that after disregarding the Rumanian warnings of Soviet counteraction, as a result of the Rumanian collapse, the Germans were now treating his troops with brutality and contempt. Since only four of the original twenty-two Rumanian divisions in their Third and Fourth Armies were still fit for action (nine others having fled and nine more having been destroyed), this particular German reaction was not surprising, however much the Reich might be dependent upon the poor infantry of her faint-hearted ally in Russia.

Manstein soon concluded that he could not afford to wait long for additional German relief forces to be assembled from France and the Caucasus or the Sixth Army would be starved out. Moreover, he now advocated a breakout of the Sixth Army when his relief force had approached Stalingrad. In addition, Manstein foresaw the need for the rationalization and drastic shortening of the whole Eastern Front, including the abandonment of the Caucasus, to free manpower so desperately lacking along the Don.

At least the able new Army Group commander was benefiting from the rough handling of the Soviet IVth Cavalry

---

Lost Victories, 315–18; Kilmarx, *op. cit.*, 186–87; Warlimont, *op. cit.*, 282–84; *Reverses on the Southern Wing*, 41–47, 360 ff.; Adolf Galland, *The First and the Last* (New York, 1954), 205–6; Jacobsen, *op. cit.*, 357.

Corps near Kotelnikovo, south of the Don, in the region of his proposed relief offensive. At the last minute, during the week commencing on November 27, the 6th German Panzer Division, in the very process of detraining from France, had rescued the remnants of the five Rumanian divisions still guarding this area. Well might General Yeremenko bemoan the absence of an Allied second front in the West, however absurd his explanations for the Allied inaction may have been.[12]

Manstein's operational order for the relief of Stalingrad was issued on December 1 under the code name *Winter Gale*. It envisaged an attack by General Hoth's Fourth Panzer Army in a direction unexpected by the Russians, up the railway south of the Don from Kotelnikovo toward Stalingrad. Since only five worn-down divisions of the Fifty-first Soviet Army would oppose Hoth's attack, as against the fifteen Soviet divisions north of the Don along the recently improvised Chir River line, there was some real hope for success in the event of an early German start.

Unfortunately for the Germans, another twelve days would be required before Hoth could assemble all three Panzer divisions assigned to his striking force, and even then his total number of tanks would amount to only some two or three hundred, truly a pitiable figure with which to undertake the most important German action in the war at this stage. Both Hitler and Army Group A in the North Caucasus had procrastinated on contributing to Hoth the Caucasian Army Group's hitherto largely wasted Panzer divisions, while the Panzer forces north of the Don were desperately needed to hold the improvised Chir line against increasing Soviet attacks. Furthermore, most of Hoth's infantry consisted of the

---

[12] Goerlitz, *Paulus*, 234–49; Jacobsen, *op. cit.*, 362–63; cf. Manstein, *Lost Victories*, 304–25; Schroeter, *op. cit.*, 112–16; Zeitzler, *loc. cit.*, 168–70; *Foreign Relations of the United States, 1942*, Vol. III, 671; *Collection of War Experience Materials*, 109–10, 181–98; Yeremenko, *op. cit.*, 381, 405–7; *Reverses on the Southern Wing*, 47–51, 220–22; Scheibert, *op. cit.*, 48 ff.

still demoralized Rumanians and his German infantry component principally consisted of untrained Luftwaffe units without any artillery at all. Secretly, of course, Manstein contemplated a Sixth Army breakout when the Fourth Panzer Army had struggled as close to the pocket as possible, whatever Hitler might continue to order to the contrary.[13]

Meanwhile, on November 27, perhaps nervous over German intentions, Stalin had ordered the Stavka representative in the field, General Vassilevsky, to clean up the encircled Sixth German Army before advancing further to the west. As a component of a more ambitious program eventually aimed at cutting off Rostov, General Rokossovsky's Front commenced Operation *Saturn* against the weak northwestern flank of the Sixth Army on December 2. Because of the inability of Yeremenko's Stalingrad Front to assist in this operation due to the difficulty of supplying Yeremenko's forces across the ice-choked Volga, Rokossovsky's assault had failed by December 9. At the same time, by slaughtering his horses and thus sacrificing his mobility still further, Paulus now gained the food resources with which to await Hoth's relief force. The Germans thus still had some cause for cheer when the seven Soviet armies surrounding Paulus could not destroy him with dispatch, although it must be recalled that by German standards the five elite corps currently comprising their Sixth Army were the approximate equivalent of five Soviet armies in manpower and resources.[14]

With the aid of freezing weather and the arrival of all of its air—if not tank—support, on December 12 Operation *Winter Gale* finally took off for the relief of Stalingrad. Full

---

[13] Manstein, *Lost Victories*, 320–29; *Reverses on the Southern Wing*, 49–55, 223–27; Schroeter, *op. cit.*, 116–19; Seth, *Stalingrad*, 211–14; General Frido von Senger und Etterlein, *Neither Fear nor Hope* (London, 1963), 62–64; Goerlitz, *Paulus*, 252 ff.

[14] *The Great Patriotic War*, Vol. III, 43 ff.; *Collection of War Experience Materials*, 130–35; Yeremenko, *op. cit.*, 382–85; Chuikov, *op. cit.*, 213–36; Manstein, *Lost Victories*, 324–26; Goerlitz, *Paulus*, 251.

of confidence, Hitler informed his intimates that the first phase of the Soviet counteroffensive was over without having achieved any decisive results, except for the capture of some 94,000 men, mostly Rumanian. The Fuehrer reiterated that "under no circumstances" would he surrender Stalingrad, because in such an event "we should never get it back again." In fact Hitler went on to say with Zeitzler's momentary acquiescence: "If we give it [Stalingrad] up, we . . . give up the whole object of this campaign."[15]

Soviet reactions to the belated German attempt to relieve Stalingrad were not long in appearing. Notwithstanding repeated earlier warnings from Yeremenko—warnings previously disregarded by the Stavka representative on the spot, General Vasilevsky—with the actual opening of the German counterattack on December 12, Stalin at last ordered Soviet reinforcements to Yeremenko's front. As a consequence, while the understrength Fifty-first Soviet Army opposing Hoth's Fourth Panzer Army was forced to retire steadily for a week to a river line only thirty miles from the Stalingrad pocket, by December 19, Lieutenant General Rodian Malinovsky's Second Guards Army had begun to reinforce the exhausted Fifty-first Soviet Army. At the same time, the second stage of the long-planned Stavka counteroffensive was launched on December 16/17 against the Eighth Italian Army, still in position along the central Don at Boguchar. For this the Stavka employed no less than four Soviet armies, two of them belonging to the new elite Guards formations.[16]

Before the imminent collapse of the Italians, Manstein had a brief moment in which his chances of establishing a link

---

[15] Warlimont, *op. cit.*, 284–85; cf. Zeitzler, *op. cit.*, 170–71; Griener, *op. cit.*, 429; *Hitler Directs His War*, edited by Felix Gilbert (New York, 1951), 12; Jacobsen, *op. cit.*, 364.

[16] Yeremenko, *op. cit.*, 405–22; Manstein, *Lost Victories*, 329–35; Kilmarx, *op. cit.*, 238–40; *Reverses on the Southern Wing*, 228–35; Clark, *op. cit.*, 268 ff.; Scheibert, *op. cit.*, 33 ff.; *L'8 Armata Italiana nella Seconda Battaglia Difensiva del Don, December 11, 1942—January 31, 1943* (Rome, 1946), 15 ff.; Hillgruber, *op. cit.*, 151 ff.; Fenyö, *loc. cit.*, 66–69.

with the Sixth Army were at their peak. On December 18, he had made another fruitless effort to prepare Paulus for a *de facto* breakout (Operation *Thunderclap*), but the Sixth Army Chief, dominated by his optimistic Chief of Staff as well as by his better-justified fears of losing his whole Army immediately on the open steppe, refused Manstein's suggestions. The next day, Manstein's efforts to force a decision met with Hitler's final rejection, a rejection which sealed the fate of the Sixth Army. Alleging that Paulus' few operational tanks lacked enough fuel for a successful breakout to the now halted Fourth Panzer Army, in effect Hitler condemned the too pliable Paulus and his enfeebled Army to what amounted at best to a diversionary role. At least by its total sacrifice, the Sixth Army might gain time for Army Group A, still kept by Hitler in the Caucasus, to retreat across the Don and restore the desperate situation along the constantly threatened Chir line.[17]

On December 23, Hoth learned that his offensive toward Stalingrad was to be abandoned and his best Panzer division was to be sent north to help redress the Italian collapse on the Don. Too late Hitler released to Hoth another motorized division from Army Group A in the Caucasus; now the Fuehrer was to be faced with the urgent decision to save the whole of Army Group A before the new Red Army assault on the Italians had reached Rostov. Perhaps frightened by an unusually frank interview on December 28 with Panzer General Hans Hube, one of the Corps commanders from the Stalingrad pocket, with the keenest reluctance the next day Hitler authorized the retreat of the entire Army Group A from the Caucasus.

Hube had flabbergasted the Fuehrer by advocating shoot-

[17] Manstein, *Lost Victories*, 332–44; Goerlitz, *Paulus*, 255–56; Schroeter, *op. cit.*, 119–23; *Reverses on the Southern Wing*, 55–61, 237–46; Senger und Etterlin, *op. cit.*, 60–79; Philippi and Heim, *op. cit.*, 195–99; *The Great Patriotic War*, Vol. III, 50 ff.; Zeitzler, *loc. cit.*, 172–73; Heusinger, *op. cit.*, 152–55.

ing Luftwaffe generals for the failure of the airlift as a change from pursuing the usual Army scapegoats. Nevertheless, higher priorities for the faltering airlift to Stalingrad would prove unavailing in a period when a third of all the transport planes flying to Stalingrad were being shot down by increasing Soviet countermeasures. Furthermore, the difficulties caused by flying in abominable winter weather from improvised and ever more distant airfields as the Soviets advanced had not been included by Goering and his Chief of Staff in their original estimate of performance to Hitler.[18]

For the failures of Hoth, the airlift, and the necessity for evacuating the Caucasus, the Fuehrer consoled himself with plans for moving a powerful S.S. corps from France to the relief of Stalingrad later in the winter. What was to happen to the Sixth Army during the interim was not discussed. For that matter Hitler could not even make up his mind whether to pull out Army Group A by way of the ice-choked Kerch Strait to the Crimea or through the gravely threatened communications bottleneck of Rostov.

After much indecision on Hitler's part, the Army Group was split, with its Seventeenth Army component compelled to hold no less than 400,000 men in a luxuriously overmanned bridgehead in the Kuban across the Kerch Strait from the Crimea for the sake of a visionary subsequent renewal of the Caucasian offensive. The retreat of the bulk of General Kleist's First Panzer Army through Rostov worked out well, extensive surreptitious preparations having been made for the operation long before it was finally authorized by Hitler at the end of December. Less fortunately for the Germans, as a direct consequence of Hitler's wishful procrastination, Kleist's Panzers would reach the Don only by February 1,

---

[18] Zeitzler, *loc. cit.*, 173–78; Schroeter, *op. cit.*, 92–94, 123–58; Manstein, *Lost Victories*, 343–79; Heusinger, *op. cit.*, 156–57; Hart, *The Other Side of the Hill*, 230–31; Yeremenko, *op. cit.*, 423–48; Carell, *op. cit.*, 606–14; *Reverses on the Southern Wing*, 61–67, 111–18, 305–21; Lee, *op. cit.*, 126–27; *Collection of War Experience Materials*, 262 ff.; Jacobsen, *op. cit.*, 365–72.

or six full weeks too late to aid Hoth's abortive relief of Stalingrad. But at any rate Kleist's urgently needed Panzer Army had made good its escape before the fall of Stalingrad had released seven more Soviet armies for action against the Ukraine.[19]

The solid freezing-over of the Volga by the end of December finally enabled General Rokossovsky, whose Don Front was now belatedly put in charge of all the Soviet forces surrounding Stalingrad, to bring his heavy artillery and ammunition across the great river. On January 8, Rokossovsky offered the Sixth Army terms of honorable capitulation, with promises—for what they might be worth—of adequate food and medical attention for all German prisoners. Although he probably no longer entertained any illusions concerning the fate of the Sixth Army, Hitler rejected Paulus' new plea for freedom of action. In agreement that this final sacrifice by the Sixth Army was necessary to enable Army Group A to retreat in time, for once, Field Marshal von Manstein approved of the Fuehrer's decision. In any event, only a few thousand men of the Sixth Army would survive the rigors of Soviet prison camps, after Paulus' forces were finally overrun at the end of January.[20]

Rokossovsky's final offensive against Stalingrad, codenamed *Ring*, began promptly on January 10 with a marked superiority in matériel, if not in manpower, over Paulus. Two days later, on January 12, the third step of the great Stavka counteroffensive on the Don was launched, on this occasion principally against the Second Hungarian Army, which still held its position further up the Don from the already defeated Eighth Italian Army. General von Weichs, commander of Army Group B, abruptly found himself with only seven

---

[19] Manstein, *Lost Victories*, 349–98; Schroeter, *op. cit.*, 158–60; *Reverses on the Southern Wing*, 68, 118–62.

[20] Yeremenko, *op. cit.*, 439–49; Zeitzler, *loc. cit.*, 179–83; Goerlitz, *Paulus*, 260–64; Schroeter, *op. cit.*, 174–88; Manstein, *Lost Victories*, 353–54.

weak German divisions to hold a newly improvised front of 180 miles that was to defend the vital rail and industrial center of Kharkov. The Second Hungarian Army was engaged in a rapid retreat, while the surviving remnants of the Eighth Italian Army were about to be withdrawn from the Eastern Front entirely. Hitler's undue reliance upon complete army formations from his weak allies was reaping its reward.[21]

Attacking from the west, by January 17 Rokossovsky's Don Front had captured the Pitomnik airdrome behind encircled Stalingrad, leaving only the small and bomb-cratered field at Gumrak with which to supply the whole Sixth Army. Recriminations now broke out between Paulus and the Luftwaffe over the latter's obvious failure, and Hitler hurriedly appointed Field Marshal Erhard Milch to take command of the practically paralyzed airlift. At the same time, the conspirators against Hitler within the German Army vainly appealed to Paulus to call publicly for the overthrow of Hitler's regime. Manstein was now prepared to assume command of all the Eastern Front for the sake of conducting a more effective strategy of mobile defense, a strategy forbidden by Hitler's rigid linear resistance conceptions which stemmed both from considerations of prestige and from the obsolete doctrines of the First World War.[22]

As usual, however, the perfect conformist Paulus confined his response to new pleas on January 20 and 24, both for freedom of action for his remaining effective troops to break out, and also to surrender his 16,000 unprovided-for wounded, who could no longer be flown out. Although these requests were again supported by Zeitzler and Manstein, on January 24 Hitler once more ordered the Sixth Army to "fight to the last

[21] *Reverses on the Southern Wing*, 70–75, 293; Yeremenko, *op. cit.*, 480; *Collection of War Experience Materials*, 132–42; Schroeter, *op. cit.*, 160–62; Telpuchowski, *op. cit.*, 209 ff.

[22] *Reverses on the Southern Wing*, 321–23; Schroeter, *op. cit.*, 168–90; Manstein, *Lost Victories*, 357 ff.; *Collection of War Experience Materials*, 142–46; Wheeler-Bennett, *The Nemesis of Power*, 533–34.

man" for the sake of saving "the Western World." The next day Hitler ordered another increase in tank production and busied himself with plans for the construction of a stadium at Nuremberg suitable for celebrating the conquest of Russia.[23]

His Army split up into fragments on January 28, Paulus reported that his men, without any food or ammunition to speak of, could not hold out more than a few days. At the advice of his strong-willed Chief of Staff, Major General Arthur Schmidt, on January 31 Paulus surrendered the pocket in which he was personally located. A rain of decorations and promotions from the Fuehrer, including that of Paulus to the rank of Field Marshal, failed to forestall the surrender of the last Sixth Army pocket by February 2.

Refusing Zeitzler's proffered resignation, Hitler was now enraged over the capitulation of Paulus. Bitterly the Fuehrer anticipated that his new Field Marshal would soon be engaging in propaganda for the Russians, not a bad guess. Repeatedly he asked his intimates why Paulus had not killed himself instead of surrendering. After announcing that no more Field Marshal's batons would be granted during the war, Hitler ended his tirade by declaring that his faithful Sixth Army commander had "besmirched" his honor by going into captivity alive. Rarely had the Fuehrer's death wish been crueler or more apparent.[24]

Three days later, on February 5, Hitler admitted to Manstein, whose resignation he may have wished to head off, that he alone assumed the responsibility for the Stalingrad disaster. Although Hitler said that he might have put some of the blame upon Goering's misestimate of the Luftwaffe's potential, he had no intention of saddling his chosen successor with

---

[23] Warlimont, *op. cit.*, 286; Zeitzler, *loc. cit.*, 184–85; cf. Philippi and Heim, *op. cit.*, 199–200; Carell, *op. cit.*, 619–21; Manstein, *Lost Victories*, 358–59; Goerlitz, *Paulus*, 264–72; Klein, *op. cit.*, 203–6.

[24] *Hitler Directs His War*, 19–22; cf. Zeitzler, *loc. cit.*, 185–89; Yeremenko, *op. cit.*, 450–53; Seth, *Stalingrad*, 246–47; Heusinger, *op. cit.*, 158–59; Goerlitz, *Paulus*, 287.

the responsibility for the defeat. Nevertheless, as Manstein has observed, Hitler refused to draw the proper conclusions for future operations from his failure, and Manstein faced his usual struggle to induce him to accept a fresh retirement of Army Group Don upon the Donets Basin. By this period the entire German operational tank strength in the eastern theater had been reduced to less than five hundred tanks.

Perhaps momentarily chastened by his fiasco, Hitler at last allowed his brilliant subordinate to go over to an active defensive with the fine S.S. Panzer Corps, which had finally arrived from France. By the end of February with the aid of retreat, thaws and reinforcements, Manstein had stabilized the front in southern Russia and was making arrangements for his successful counteroffensive toward Kharkov in March. But unhappily for Nazi Germany the Fuehrer's unwonted mood of self-abnegation would not last long thereafter.[25]

Soviet operational inexperience, a further decline in the quality of its infantry, and its still insufficient artillery and transportation had also kept the Red Army from fully exploiting the destruction of the Sixth German Army and the other Axis armies on the southern front over the course of this winter. But the so recently desperate Red Army could be proud of the capture of the first full German field army since 1806, along with twenty-four generals and approximately 108,000 other officers and men still alive in the Stalingrad pocket at the beginning of February, 1943. Close to that number of German soldiers had already died in the pocket by this date, mostly toward the end, and approximately 42,000 German wounded had been flown out before the last airfield was closed down. With the large losses of the Italian, Rumanian, and Hungarian armies outside of Stalingrad added,

[25] Manstein, *Lost Victories*, 365 ff.; *Reverses on the Southern Wing*, 76–88; Captain B. H. Liddell Hart, *Strategy: The Indirect Approach* (New York, 1954), 267, 295; Warlimont, *op. cit.*, 286; Guderian, *op. cit.*, 288; *Kriegstagebuch des Oberkommandos der Wehrmacht, 1943*, Vol. III, Book 1, 66.

the Axis had sustained in attrition the loss of at least 500,000 men between November 19 and February 2, in addition to the equipment of some forty-five divisions.

Truly the Reich was utterly dependent for its continued security upon the Allies' comparative inaction in the West in order to replace in some measure its losses in the East. And doubtless Zhukov, Vassilevsky, and the other Stavka generals deserved the Marshal's batons which they, but not yet the equally deserving commanders in the field, received from Stalin on January 25 for their successful coordination of the complex Stalingrad counteroffensive.[26]

Following the first German reverses on the Don, in early December, in a conversation with Hermann Goering, Mussolini renewed his suggestion of the previous month in behalf of a compromise peace with Russia. On December 16, Mussolini instructed Count Ciano to warn Hitler in a forthcoming interview that the Axis must be prepared to withdraw as many troops as possible from Russia in 1943 to resist the expected Anglo-American assault upon Italy. The Italian dictator also had hopes that the Japanese might intervene to mediate the Soviet-German war.

Hitler, who no longer expected success by the Italians anywhere, received Ciano at his gloomy headquarters at Rastenburg with reproaches for the flight of the Eighth Italian Army, a flight which unhappily for Ciano had commenced two days earlier along the Don. Warming to his current theme of the Reich as the savior of Europe from Bolshevism, Hitler assured the Italian Foreign Minister that the situation in the East would soon again be under control. At the same time, he evidently informed the Japanese through the reluc-

---

[26] Schroeter, *op. cit.*, 208; Goerlitz, *Paulus*, 272 n. 1; Yeremenko, *op. cit.*, 453; Werth, *op. cit.*, 542; Garthoff, *Doctrine*, 46–47, and his "The Marshals and the Party" in *Total War and Cold War*, 246–47; *The United States Strategic Bombing Survey*, 167–68; Manstein, *Lost Victories*, 437–40; Carell *op. cit.*, 622–23; *Reverses on the Southern Wing*, 81–82; Goerlitz, *The German General Staff*, 43; Cassidy, *op. cit.*, 348.

tant Ribbentrop that no proposals for their mediation would be entertained by Germany. In the near future the Fuehrer would reflect as much disgust with the lack of effective assistance against Russia by his Japanese Ally as by his Italian, and would warn Ribbentrop that giving up any conquered territory to the Soviets would be a repudiation of the principles "to which he had consecrated his whole life." Hitler also expressed keen admiration for Stalin's courage in keeping the Soviet Union going throughout the terrible crises of 1941/42.[27]

Stalingrad had its impact, too, upon Germany's only competent ally in the campaign against Russia, Finland, whose Government from early February began to seek for ways out of the war. An immediate benefit for the Soviets would thus be the freeing of this long front from Finnish pressure; from the spring of 1943 the Red Army withdrew forces from the Finnish theater to such an extent that the 400,000 Finns and 170,000 Germans held on this difficult front soon amounted to more than double the number of the Soviet troops remaining opposite them. As on the vastly overstaffed Crimean-Kuban sector in the far south, Hitler's political favoritism foı his flanks would result in the collapse of his vital center. Hitler might continue to express his puzzlement over the seemingly endless supply of Red Army reserves, as well as blaming his allies and his own generals for his defeats, but the moderate Soviet superiority in manpower and equipment at Stalingrad existed only as a result of his own wishful dispersion of German reserves for motives of politics and prestige.

In the north, likewise, the Red Army, concentrating upon essentials, opened a land route on January 18, 1943, to blockaded—but no longer starving—Leningrad. Well might Mussolini reiterate to Hitler in March that since the defeat of the

[27] Maxime Mourin, *Les Tentatives de Paix dans la Seconde Guerre Mondiàle, 1939–1945* (Paris, 1949), 140–44; cf. *Hitler Directs His War*, 12–23; Ribbentrop, *op. cit.*, 169–70; Deakin, *op. cit.*, 102–5; *The Ciano Diaries*, 555–57; Schmidt, *op. cit.*, 260–61; *N.C.A.*, Vol. V, 658–59; Toshikazu Kase, *op. cit.*, 67–68; Cavallero, *op. cit.*, 417.

Soviet Union was no longer possible, the Russian chapter had to be brought to a close by one means or another. The Duce might as well have been appealing to the wind as to the amateur strategist and political fanatic at the head of the Third Reich.[28]

Other politically motivated advocates of strategic dispersion were discovering during the winter of Stalingrad that the pursuit of short-range prestige victories was all too often incompatible with the realization of long-range and decisive strategies for final victory. Already on November 9, a safe few hours after the Western Allies were committed to French North Africa, Winston Churchill warned his cautious Chiefs of Staff that the Russians could not be expected to rest content with small-scale Allied descents upon sundry insular "Sardines" in the Mediterranean throughout 1943 "while Hitler has a third crack at them." A week later the Prime Minister was lamenting that the British planners had "pulled in our horns" to such an extraordinary extent for the next year that he could not "imagine what the Russians will say or do when they realize it." The British Ambassador in Moscow, Clark Kerr, would shortly point out to Mr. Churchill that, in fact, the Soviets might be driven again to a separate peace with Hitler in the event of no serious assistance on the part of their Allies.

Of course, Churchill has cited in his postwar memoirs his brief flurry of anxiety over the possible Soviet reaction to no second front for a third year as evidence to the effect that he was not "invariably hostile" to any such plan and therefore that he had not deliberately deceived or misled Stalin on the burning issue of crossing the Channel in 1943. In reality, by mid-December the British Chiefs of Staff were gratified to discover that the Prime Minister was coming around to their

---

[28] Ziemke, *op. cit.*, 242–49; *Les Lettres Secrètes*, 161–85; Goebbels, *op. cit.*, 263, 280, 313–14, 368, 395, 415, 434–35, 468, 493; Goure, *op. cit.*, 298–99; Mannerheim, *op. cit.*, 460 ff.; Cherniavsky, *loc. cit.*, 551.

opposition to superimposing a new campaign in France upon the one now irrevocably embarked upon in the Mediterranean.

To be sure, Stalin was not making the reassumption of this more customary stance any easier for the Prime Minister. He had already asked both Churchill and Roosevelt again about what he called their promises to land in Western Europe no later than the spring of 1943, and Churchill, at least, admitted to his distrustful Chiefs that he had promised Stalin something of the kind during his visit to Moscow in the previous August.[29]

Although General Marshall remained opposed in principle to wasteful "dabbling" in the Mediterranean, his United States Army planners were no longer united on the cross-Channel alternative in 1943, nor was Admiral Ernest J. King of the United States Navy really behind him. As Churchill had long perceived, King could always be paid off with larger resources for his own Pacific theater. Consequently, with the Prime Minister safely in hand, and with President Roosevelt veering toward the Mediterranean as a consequence of the alleviation of his anxiety regarding Russia, the ground was well laid for the triumph of Sir Alan Brooke's strategy of limited war at the forthcoming Anglo-American conference at Casablanca. Quite preoccupied with the conduct of the Stalingrad counteroffensive, and manifesting growing signs of self-confidence himself, Stalin did not yet recognize the dangers to his own cause in refusing to attend another still exclusively Anglo-American conference.[30]

Alleging that the shortage of shipping and the strength of the German Army in France were the reasons for postponing

---

[29] Churchill, *The Hinge of Fate*, 649–67; cf. Bryant, *op. cit.*, Vol. I, 528–36; *Stalin's Correspondence*, 78–84; J. Kennedy, *op. cit.*, 276–77; Sherwood, *op. cit*, 657–62; *Foreign Relations of the United States, 1942*, Vol. III, 675–76.

[30] Matloff and Snell, *op. cit.*, Vol. I, 364–79; cf. Leighton and Coakley, *op. cit.*, 585–87, 665–66; Churchill, *The Hinge of Fate*, 540, 668–76; General Albert C. Wedemeyer, *Wedemeyer Reports*! (New York, 1958), 174 ff.; *Foreign Relations of the United States, 1942*, Vol. III, 666; Sherwood, *op. cit.*, 662–74.

a cross-Channel operation until 1944, at the Casablanca Conference in late January the Chief of the Imperial General Staff, Field Marshal Sir Alan Brooke, pushed through his preference for a campaign against Italy rather than the Reich. More substantial, if less often stated, reasons for this decision lay in the existing Allied commitment to the Mediterranean since *Torch*, the unreadiness of the United States Army either for combat with the Germans or for staff conferences with the British, the unwillingness of the British armed services to make heavy sacrifices on behalf of Soviet Russia, and, perhaps foremost, the reassuring recovery of the Red Army since Stalingrad. Harry Hopkins might tell the Prime Minister that he felt the results of Casablanca represented "a pretty feeble effort" for Great Britain and the United States in 1943, but notwithstanding their numerous assurances to Stalin, the Combined Chiefs of Staff were insufficiently dedicated to the concept of all-out land war against the German Army to override their British components on the issue of a second front in 1943. Besides the growing probability of knocking Italy out of the war in the near future appealed greatly to statesmen always more aware of prestige factors than of real military achievements.[31]

If, as a direct consequence of the Casablanca decisions, the bulk of the American Army in combat would be fighting the Japanese throughout the year 1943, on the level of policy, likewise, the Western Allies had sharply limited their effectiveness in war against Hitler's Reich. In part motivated by guilt regarding the absence of a second front with its consequent threat of a Nazi-Soviet truce, as well as to some extent evoked by the United States Army's philosophy of absolute war leading thereby to an absolute victory, President

---

[31] Sherwood, *op. cit.*, 691; cf. Bryant, *op. cit.*, Vol. I, 544–61; J. Kennedy, *op. cit.*, 280–85; Maurice Matloff, *United States Army in World War II*, Vol. II: *Strategic Planning for Coalition Warfare, 1943–1944* (Washington, 1959), chap. i.

Roosevelt's enunciation of a policy of unconditional surrender at Casablanca was sprung upon Mr. Churchill without apparent warning. Although the Prime Minister did try to exclude Italy from its provisions—after all he wanted her to surrender soon—he accepted Roosevelt's absolutist policy with respect to the major Axis powers. Having induced the Americans to swallow a British strategy of limited war, the least the Prime Minister could do was to go along with the incompatible American policy of absolutist terms of peace.

The unfortunate effect of the doctrine of unconditional surrender upon the Germans and, in particular, upon the growing resistance of the German Army to Hitler has often been noted. As Hitler pointed out to Erwin Rommel in May, 1943, in conceding that there was little chance left of winning the war, the Fuehrer could still stress that henceforth the Axis was bound to a struggle to the end with the West whether the German generals liked it or not. Certainly, regardless of the Carthaginian peace he actually had in mind for the Reich, Stalin was never so foolish as to commit himself publicly on any negotiations with the Third Reich. Quite the contrary, he could always employ the threat of doing so as a means of extorting more concessions, including a second front, from the Western Allies. But then, notwithstanding Nazi outrages in Russia, the Soviet dictator did not have the same problem with public opinion faced by the elected representatives of a democracy.[32]

To some extent as a consequence of a tendency to continue deceiving themselves concerning the postponement of a second front until 1944, the prevarications of the President and

---

[32] Sherwood, *op. cit.*, 695–97; Churchill, *The Hinge of Fate*, 684–88; Feis, *Churchill, Roosevelt, Stalin*, 108–13; Matloff, *op. cit.*, 16–41; Leighton and Coakley, *op. cit.*, 662; Hanson W. Baldwin, *Great Mistakes of the War* (New York, 1950), 14 ff.; *The Rommel Papers*, 427–28; Goebbels, *op. cit.*, 463–68; Schmidt, *op. cit.*, 261–62, Dulles, *op. cit.*, 171 ff.; Kennan, *Russia and the West Under Lenin and Stalin*, 358–69; Standley, *op. cit.*, 381.

the Prime Minister over the next few months on this basic issue may be condoned. Nevertheless, to declare, as did Roosevelt and Churchill in reporting to Stalin on the Casablanca Conference on January 26, 1943, that the "main [Allied] desire" had been "to divert strong German land and air forces from the Russian front" was pretty raw.[33] That blunt old Tory, the United States Chief of Naval Operations, Admiral King, had more accurately defined the Allied policy at Casablanca vis-à-vis Russia, as one not of "placating Stalin," but of "implementing the Russians to our own interest."[34]

Stalin replied promptly on January 30 to inquire for more details regarding the opening of a second front in Europe in 1943, since he had been permitted to assume that this was still the Western intention. However, by the middle of February, with the slowing down of his winter offensive, the Soviet ruler was becoming disillusioned concerning one of the avowed purposes of *Torch*, namely the bringing of aid to Russia. As in the previous winter, but still more so this year, the Germans were again shoring up their eastern front by bringing up reserves from Western Europe. In his correspondence with Churchill, Stalin estimated these transferred German reserves as amounting to some twenty-seven divisions, including five Panzer divisions. And in an Order of the Day at the end of February, 1943, the Soviet ruler again publicly complained that in the "absence of a second front, the Red Army is fighting the war alone."[35]

On March 11, Churchill sent another long explanation to Stalin to the effect that thirty German divisions remained in western Europe against the sixteen British divisions in the United Kingdom available for an offensive in France. Most of the British Army, pointed out Mr. Churchill, was tied up

---

[33] Churchill, *The Hinge of Fate*, 742–43; *Stalin's Correspondence*, 86–88.

[34] Leighton and Coakley, *op. cit.*, 587 n. 34.

[35] Standley, *op. cit.*, 333–44; cf. *Stalin's Correspondence*, 89–96; Sherwood, *op. cit.*, 701–5; Churchill, *The Hinge of Fate*, 745–46.

in the Mediterranean. Stalin replied to this communication a few days later by raising his figures of German divisions transferred from western Europe to the East to thirty-six, including six armored. Stalin concluded with a warning "in the strongest possible manner how dangerous from the viewpoint of our common cause" it would be to permit any "further delay in the opening of the second front in France. This is the reason why the uncertainty of your statements concerning the contemplated Anglo-American offensive across the Channel arouses grave anxiety in me, about which I cannot be silent."[36]

Not until June, well after the German discovery of the corpses of the missing Polish Army officers at Katyn had blown the always fragile Polish-Soviet relationship sky-high, did Stalin learn that the second front was definitely off until 1944. Protesting about such basic Anglo-American decisions taken in his absence, Stalin's reproaches evoked a furious message from Churchill to the alarmed British Ambassador in Moscow, Sir Archibald Clark Kerr. As in his earlier defensive explanations to Clark Kerr's predecessor in Moscow, Sir Stafford Cripps, the Prime Minister justified British inaction across the Channel in 1943 in terms of the "complete indifference" manifested by the Soviets during Great Britain's hours of extremity in 1939/40. Like Stalin at that time with respect to his own Red Army, Churchill refused to condone what he now termed "a useless massacre of British troops" in order to overcome the suspicions of his distrustful Ally.

The British Government may have been paying the Soviets back for their betrayal of the West in 1939/40, but only Hitler could profit from either of these striking examples of failure in Allied coalition warfare. In reciprocal anger Stalin now refused to see President Roosevelt and would soon recall his ambassadors to Washington and London, Ivan Maisky and

---

[36] *Stalin's Correspondence*, 99–106; Churchill, *The Hinge of Fate*, 747–51. For an objective account of the decline of the German Army strength in the West, see Harrison, *op. cit.*, 142.

Maxim Litvinov respectively. On July 13, 1943, the Soviet dictator went further and set up a so-called Free Germany Committee of captured German officers, as open a repudiation of Roosevelt's unconditional surrender policy as possible. Whether, in his rage and chagrin after so many promises at facing a third German summer assault alone at Kursk in July, Stalin actually opened secret negotiations with the Reich is uncertain. His potential, however, for doing so, or for halting the Red Army at her 1939–41 frontier with Germany, always remained, and may eventually have evoked rather more Allied assistance than had the earlier and far better justified danger of the Red Army's collapse in 1941/42.[37]

---

[37] Woodward, *op. cit.*, 241–43; cf. *Stalin's Correspondence*, 131–41; Sherwood,, *op. cit.*, 734–38; Standley, *op. cit.*, 403–11, 465–68, 498; Kleist, *op. cit.*, 235–84; Werth, *op. cit.*, 635–78, 727–37; Schmidt, *op. cit.*, 269–70.

"A German-Russian alliance means simply the confluence of two streams which run toward the same sea, the sea of world revolution. National Socialism will submit to Gleichschaltung with the Bolshevik world revolution, or will subject that revolution to Gleichschaltung with itself: it amounts either way to much the same thing."[1] RAUSCHNING, 1939

"If the war is to be lost, the nation will also perish. This fate is inevitable. There is no need to consider the basis even of a most primitive existence any longer. On the contrary it is better to destroy even that, and to destroy it ourselves. The nation has proved itself weak, and the future belongs solely to the stronger Eastern nation."[2] HITLER, March, 1945

"Nero, too, was a product of his epoch. Yet after he perished his statues were smashed and his name was scraped off everything. The vengeance of history is more terrible than the vengeance of the most powerful General Secretary."[3]

TROTSKY, 1940

"The redeeming feature of war is that it puts a nation to test. As exposure to the atmosphere reduces all mummies to instant dissolution, so war passes supreme judgment upon social systems that have outlived their vitality."[4] MARX

[1] Rauschning, *The Revolution of Nihilism*, 260.
[2] H. R. Trevor-Roper, *The Last Days of Hitler* (New York, 1947), 82.
[3] Trotsky, *Stalin* (New York, 1941), 383.
[4] Karl Marx, *The Eastern Question* (London, 1897), 318.

CHAPTER X

Gleichschaltung

WITH THE SOVIET recapture of Stalingrad and loss of the whole of Paulus' Sixth Army, the spell which Hitler had exercised over the German Army since 1937 began to break up. No longer did even Propaganda Minister Goebbels dare refer to his Fuehrer as a Feldherr, that is, as a military leader of acknowledged reputation. Within the Army General Staff, General Ludwig Beck's warnings during 1937/38 were recalled and criticism and conspiracy against the now discredited swindler at their head grew apace. Reverting to his earlier days as a lone wolf (his original Party name), Hitler cried to Goebbels that he was now "totally fed up with the generals." He couldn't "imagine anything finer than having nothing to do with them." All generals were "faithless . . . reactionaries," who were "opposed to National Socialism." Truly Hitler required a private scapegoat for his public failure and mortification.[5]

Yet by the spring of 1943 German casualties in Russia were still small as compared to those of the Soviet Union—well under a million in dead and missing as against probably eight or nine times that number for the Red Army. Nevertheless, the Russians had recovered and come back, although at this

---

[5] Goebbels, *op. cit.*, 368–69; cf. Lossberg, *op. cit.*, 120–26; Wheeler-Bennett, *The Nemesis of Power*, 535 ff.; Fabian von Schlabrendorff, *They Almost Killed Hitler*, edited by G. S. Gaevernitz (New York, 1947), 51–61; Poole, *loc. cit.*, 153; *The Ciano Diaries*, 570–71; Halder, *Hitler als Feldherr*, 55.

stage with a still very slight margin in manpower and matériel. So far the Reich had lost only one vital thing in the East, but that loss was mortal. As in the First World War the potentially much stronger coalition of the Reich's enemies had gained the time essential to exploit their inherently greater resources. Hitler's gamble in Blitzkrieg on the basis of a limited war economy had failed as decisively as had Imperial Germany's strategy between 1914 and 1917.[6]

Especially on the Eastern Front is the analogy between the First and Second World Wars revealing. Only because the Western Front was the principal and decisive theater in the First World War, had the poorly led and equipped Czarist armies managed to sustain three years of retreat before collapsing. Moreover, the Czarist forces of 1914–1916 had benefited from a superiority in strength over the Central Powers of about two to one in military manpower. On the other hand, during the decisive period of 1941–1943 the Red Army had fought the Axis with a manpower strength on the Eastern Front ranging from two to eight million, as opposed to an average of somewhat over four million men maintained steadily throughout this period in the East by Germany and her Allies.[7]

In short, both because of its appalling losses in 1941/42 and because of the overwhelming concentration of strength of the Axis in the East at this time, Soviet Russia was never able seriously to exploit its supposed superiority in manpower over its enemies. Nonetheless, to the astonishment of practically every-

---

[6] Goebbels, *op. cit.*, 460; Alexander Dallin, *op. cit.*, 427; Goldsmith, *op. cit.*, 77; Bertram D. Wolfe, "Titans Locked in Combat," *Russian Review* (Hanover), January, 1965, 22 n. 13.

[7] General Erich von Falkenhayn, *General Headquarters, 1914–1916, and the Critical Decisions* (London, 1919), 294; Field Marshal Erich von Manstein, "The Development of the Red Army, 1942–1945," in *The Red Army*, 140–46; Halder, *War Diary*, Vol. VII, 248; Bernard Pares, *The Fall of the Russian Monarchy* (London, 1939), 210 ff., 353 ff.; Cherniavsky, *loc. cit.*, 551–52; General Nicolas Golovine, *The Russian Army in the World War* (New Haven, 1931), 77–93.

one, the Red Army survived and triumphed in what from June, 1941, unmistakably became the principal theater of the Second World War. Czarist Russia had unsuccessfully displayed two Western characteristics in war, i.e., a sincere and self-sacrificing alliance with her Allies and an utterly inadequate initial war-production base. Bolshevik Russia reversed this Czarist pattern and won the war by means of insincere alliances and a far more adequate war-production base from 1939 to 1945. Had Trotsky survived Stalin's executioner, he could hardly have reproached his rival as unrealistic in, at least, these respects.

If the Communist Party under Stalin's leadership also sustained Russian morale and discipline as Nicholas II never could, for that matter the fundamental cause of the Bolshevik achievement of power in 1917 had resulted from the communist leader's more realistic understanding of the meaning of war and violence than was manifested by its more conventional political rivals in Russia. Born as the violent child of Czarist Russia's defeat at the hands of Imperial Germany, the Soviets successfully faced and resolved problems far greater than any met by their Czarist predecessors. After all, conquering insurmountable problems at whatever price in blood and sacrifice was precisely what Stalinist Communism was constructed for. Thus, it was only to be expected that a left-wing Nazi such as Dr. Goebbels would declare in May, 1943, that "the Soviet Union is alive only because it is peopled with Russians and because Bolshevism dominates it as its dictator." Goebbels now realized full well that Nazi folly in driving Great Russia—and, indeed, Slavic patriotism as a whole—under Stalin's terrible wing was destroying the Reich's "only opportunity for bringing the war in the East to a satisfactory end."[8]

If Hitler reaped the benefits of Stalin's defeatist paranoia between 1937 and 1941, the Soviet dictator profited from the

---

[8] Goebbels, *op. cit.*, 328, 395.

consequences of Hitler's stupidity, overconfidence, rigidity and barbarism thereafter. Between 1937 and 1939 Stalin crippled the leadership of the Red Army, while tarnishing the Soviet Union's reputation as a potential Ally of the West. Not content with that, in 1939/40 Stalin proceeded to guard the rear of his mortal enemy, Hitler, when the latter was engaged in disposing of Russia's last potential Continental Allies in western Europe. At the same time, the Soviet dictator was busily engaged in seizing almost worthless territory from Finland and Rumania with the inevitable consequence of earning their deadly enmity as a consequence. Finally, seduced by his own conquests, Stalin advanced the Red Army and Air Force piecemeal too far forward into the recently occupied and still unfortified Baltic States and eastern Poland.

Stalin's halfhearted reversal of policy at the last minute, following his many warnings in the spring of 1941, at least helped to embroil the Germans in the Balkans on the eve of *Barbarossa* as well as to relieve the Soviet rear of an active Japanese threat. On the other hand, the Soviet ruler's Jacobin insistence upon an offensive strategy without major retreats in the summer of 1941 so depleted the Red Army that not until the summer of 1943 could it really mount a successful and sustained offensive against German formations not already cut off from the rear. Of course, by mid-1943 Soviet military inexperience had been in large measure overcome, and a flood of American trucks, food, fuel, and communications matériel had granted to the Red Army the mobility necessary for the reconquest of the Ukraine. Furthermore, as occurred with Hitler during his period of success, when Stalin finally was able to advance, his possible disagreements with the Stavka no longer seem to have been so disastrous in results. Victory is a marvelous catalyst for harmony in the High Command.

For blundering into his unwanted war with the West in 1939, Hitler, too, may properly be condemned, although, as in 1914, the ambiguities of British policy were difficult for the Germans to make out until it was too late. Thereafter over the course of the next twenty months Hitler's grand strategy may best be outlined as taking the form of a gigantic circle. First the Fuehrer's interest was focused directly upon the East in Poland during the early autumn of 1939. Then, with his attention moving northward to Finland that winter, Hitler wisely refrained from intervention in this particular Soviet fiasco—he may, indeed, have anticipated an open Soviet-Western clash during this notably opaque period of the war.

In the spring of 1940, Hitler opened his offensives successively to the north in Norway and then west against the Low Countries, France, and Great Britain. By the autumn of 1940, his concern was already directed southwestward toward Spain, and with the first winter of Il Duce's discontent, Hitler was forced to come to the aid of his weakening Ally. German succor first went directly to the south to Libya-Sicily in January and February, 1941, and by the spring of 1941 to the southeast in the Balkans. Only with the summer of 1941 could Hitler return to his original and fundamental purpose for the Slavic East embodied in the *Barbarossa* campaign. Given the political, strategic, logistic, climatic and economic conditions actually prevailing, his campaign could not possibly have been launched much before June, 1941, nor could it have been undertaken appreciably later with any hope of success.

If Hitler's timing in attacking Russia cannot be held at fault, neither can his underestimation of Soviet war potential be considered surprising in view of the almost universal optimism among his professional advisors concerning Russia's poor chances. Hitler's overconfidence and Stalin's guile, however, led the Fuehrer into his serious miscalculation with the Japanese, a miscalculation which may have cost him the war. Of course, it is perfectly possible that no German policy could have brought Japan in as an active ally; the complete success of *Barbarossa* might have been necessary before Tokyo could overcome its memories of the mortifying encounters with the

Red Army in 1938/39 and launch an all-out attack upon the gravely weakened Red Army in the Far East in either 1941 or 1942.

With the planning for *Barbarossa*, the case against Hitler as a Feldherr grows stronger. In retrospect, at any rate, only Rundstedt's early proposal for an initial German thrust toward Leningrad, followed swiftly by a converging movement upon Moscow, offered much grounds for the adequate logistic support of the German advance. Subsequently, as Halder desired, the Ukraine could have been occupied from the north, thereby exploiting the vital Moscow railway nodal point against the Russians. Thus, the essentially logistic failure of the winter of 1941/42 might have been forestalled regardless of climatic conditions. Even as it was, with Stalin's eager assistance, Hitler's inconsistent and indecisive strategies of 1941 destroyed almost the whole of the original Red Army of June, 1941; a little more professionalism and tank production on the part of the Germans might well have achieved a final decision against the Red Army before winter and the Siberians had arrived.

For the rapidly waning chances of 1942, both a logical resumption of the unattractive offensive upon Moscow and a still more unappetizing return to the short strong line of 1939–41 (as Leeb advocated) were rejected by Hitler in favor of a form of limited economic war against the Soviet Union, as if time no longer mattered for the Reich. Perhaps, in reality, it no longer did following the American entry, and the entire Stalingrad-Caucasus campaign may very well be dismissed as no more than the spectacular final fling of an unsuccessful gambler. Certainly Halder's dismissal and Jodl's temporary disgrace implied as much, as had the Reich's logistic experience in the First World War, when her armies also reached the more easily attainable Caucasus in 1918, but that time also stopped short of the far more essential military goals in the north.

By 1943 the price paid for Hitler's rigid defensive was becoming so obvious that Ribbentrop, Mussolini, and the Japanese openly attempted to mediate the war with Russia as the only possible way out of Hitler's discredited crusade against Bolshevism. After having lost his Italian ally, by September, 1943, Hitler himself would finally agree to the idea of negotiations with the Soviets, but he immediately qualified his acceptance in confessing to his Foreign Minister: "You know, Ribbentrop, if I settled with Russia today, I would only come to grips with her again tomorrow—I just can't help it." Some months later, Hitler reaffirmed this attitude, asserting that Stalin was not in earnest in wanting negotiations with the Reich, because he merely hoped by such discussions to incite the Western Allies to open a second front. As so often in his political insights, the Fuehrer may not have been very far off in this respect.[9]

By 1944, the desperate German Army conspirators against the mounting follies of their Fuehrer, unable to establish contact with the Russians themselves, wished to transfer the best German divisions from the West to shore up the collapsing Army Group Center in the East. There in July, 1944, by the proper strategic employment of massed tank armies and air superiority, the Soviets trapped large numbers of German troops forbidden to retreat by Hitler's orders. As has been pointed out, Hitler's wilful pursuit of policy without strategy had blinded him to the futility of both his policies and improvised strategies. In Stalin's illuminating phrase, "Hitler was a very able man, but not basically intelligent." And in Halder's basic conclusion, Hitler's failure as a Feldherr lay in his incapacity for effective thought in grand tactics, that is, in his inability to combine his passion for technology with the requirements of an over-all strategy.[10]

---

[9] Ribbentrop, *op. cit.*, 170–72; cf. Schmidt, *op. cit.*, 247–70; Hesse, *op. cit.*, 181–86, 212–16; Halder, *Hitler als Feldherr,* 55–57; *N.C.A.*, Vol. VII, 926–27.

[10] Sherwood, *op. cit.*, 782; cf. *Hitler Directs His War*, xxiv; Eden, *op. cit.*, 479; Ansel, *op. cit.*, 328 n. 3; Goerlitz, *The German General Staff*, 464; Dietrich, *op. cit.*, 78, 108–9; Dulles, *op. cit.*, 169–70; *Collapse of*

If, in common with the Nazi movement as a whole, Hitler failed in his conflict with Stalin to a considerable extent because of his fundamental stupidity, his compensatory assertion of the triumph of will power over the objective calculations of strategy led him in time to his bloody conflict with his own Army General Staff. With the final collapse of the Third Reich in the spring of 1945, Hitler no longer minced words with his Chief of Staff, then General Heinz Guderian. He cried: "It is intolerable to me that a group of intellectuals should presume to press their views on their superiors. But such is the General Staff system and that system I intend to smash." On occasion Stalin doubtless had cause to feel the same way, but as the high priest of a deterministic religion Stalin could scarcely repudiate rational military doctrine as crudely as had the Fuehrer of a dogma of avowed emotionalism. Indeed, with Molotov during the 1930's, Stalin appears to have attended the lectures of General Shaposhnikov at the Frunze Military Academy and to have deliberately exposed himself to the ideas of Clausewitz and of subsequent German Army thought.[11]

In spite of the self-defeating barbarism of Nazi policies toward the Russians still advocated by Heinrich Himmler as late as October, 1943, and notwithstanding the Fuehrer's earlier distaste for the idea "that the hour of Russia or the United States had come," Hitler's paranoid identification with the hated Soviet Union becomes unmistakable in the spring of 1945. Refusing Guderian the resources unnecessarily tied up in Norway, Hungary, or Latvia with which to defend Berlin from the Russians, the parvenu Austrian Fuehrer was at last able to complete his final revenge upon Prussia and her

---

Army Group Center, June 22–September 1, 1944, MS (Neustadt: Office of the Chief of Military History, December, 1947), 9 ff., 51 ff.; *Hitler's Table Talk*, 308.

[11] Guderian, *op. cit.*, 397; cf. Manstein, *Lost Victories*, 274–87; Lossberg, *op. cit.*, 123–25; Konrad Heiden, *Der Fuehrer* (Boston, 1944), chap. vii; Garthoff, *Doctrine*, 53–56; Goerlitz, *The German General Staff*, 475–92; *Hitler's Table Talk*, xiv.

aristocratic General Staff by means of the aid of the Red Army. No wonder Hitler's respect for Stalin, and what he termed the Soviet ruler's grandiose deed in creating the Red Army, grew steadily with the Soviet recovery. After all, Stalin was achieving that Gleichschaltung of the Third Reich and Bolshevik Russia which had been predicted by Hermann Rauschning in 1939, a Gleichschaltung which Hitler had failed to achieve himself in his great crusade against the Soviet Union. Hitler's Communist successors in East Berlin would thus be granted ample opportunity to attempt to realize the sordid details of this process on the spot over the next two decades.[12]

The course of official Anglo-Soviet relations before and during the Second World War was far less ambivalent than that of the Germans and the Russians—they ranged from outright hostility to the merely distrustful. Of course, the Conservative governments antedating Churchill both loathed and underestimated the Soviet Union, and the more open-minded Churchill himself had never been forgiven by Stalin for his leading role in the Western intervention in Russia at the end of the First World War. In their grievous and, indeed, well-founded fear of Nazi Germany, the Soviets at first tended to underestimate the military potential of their British Ally, while later on they much overestimated Britain's capacity for offensive action. In short, from 1939 to 1945 the Soviets simply could not credit the far more luxurious standards of Western societies at war as either necessary or sincere. Moreover, a Communist government, born by betraying the Western Powers in 1917, could not really manifest loyalty to a Western alliance from 1939 on, however tragic the consequences of such a betrayal again might be for the Soviet Union in 1941/42.[13]

---

[12] *Hitler's Table Talk*, 327; cf. *N.C.A.*, Vol. IV, 558 ff., 573 ff., Vol. VII, 844; Goerlitz, *The German General Staff*, 486 ff.

[13] Churchill, *The Hinge of Fate*, 493; Djilas, *op. cit.*, 70, 106; Hilger and Meyer, *op. cit.*, 288–340; Winston Churchill, *The Aftermath* (New York, 1929), 261 ff.; Carr, *The Bolshevik Revolution*, 111.

If from the autumn of 1939 Churchill was forced to recognize that Soviet policy was inherently dedicated to a paranoid or absurdly short-range conception of self-interest, the insincerity, vulgarity, and ruthlessness customary to revolutionary regimes further put off a reknitting of effective coalition relations even after Hitler's attack had rendered the Soviet Union an unwilling Ally of Great Britain. Thereafter, Mr. Churchill's inability to exploit fully his still somewhat uncertain control of the Conservative Party, let alone of his dubious Chiefs of Staff on behalf of a second front, would naturally lead to Soviet and American charges of his insincerity on this fundamental issue. Furthermore, as the British Ambassador to the Soviet Union pointed out to the Prime Minister in 1943, the many misleading Western assurances on this score would engender in the Russians a still stronger distrust of the West.

That this was a bona fide Soviet case at the time may be seen from the German records captured by the United States Army, records which reveal that 94 per cent of German Army casualties between June, 1941, and December, 1943, were incurred on the Eastern Front alone. To be sure, the subsequent Soviet charges to the effect that the second front had been deliberately delayed for the sake of weakening the U.S.S.R. partakes of the usual Communist *ex post facto* rationalizations for purposes of anti-Western propaganda, but the Russian sense of betrayal in 1943 was quite as justified as that of the West in 1939.[14] Although British grand strategy was certainly not calculated to injure the Soviet Union in 1942/43, neither was it, as alleged at the time, essentially designed to aid her. Like the Japanese policy vis-à-vis Germany, it was simply conceived and maintained without more than a *pro forma* concern for the basic interests of the Soviet Union.

---

[14] Woodward, *op. cit.*, 243; Gallagher, *Soviet History*, 47 ff.; Chuikov, *op. cit.*, 356 ff.; Stimson, *op. cit.*, 429 ff.; Harrison, *op. cit.*, 142, n. 49; Churchill, *The Gathering Storm*, 448–49, *The Hinge of Fate*, 649–51, 818; *Foreign Relations of the United States, 1941*, Vol. I, 30, 765.

Unlike the Japanese, the British were to be saved by the fortunate survival of their more powerful Ally.

When the British finally compelled by their Allies to invade France in 1944, it was an invasion essentially undertaken in the self-interest of the West, the terrible risk of the collapse of the Soviet Union having long since passed. At this date the Red Army no longer needed more than Western supplies with which to occupy eastern Europe, although the establishment of a second front doubtless facilitated the speed of the Soviet conquest of Poland and the Balkans in 1944/45. But a Western second front might at least still keep the Red Army out of the vital Ruhr and Rhineland, as no Western offensive from the Mediterranean could have ever hoped to achieve.

With the Americans still innocent concerning ultimate Soviet intentions, guilty over the long postponement of the second front, and desirous in any event of Soviet participation in both the Pacific war and the United Nations, after 1944 Stalin had only to cope with the resistance of his British Ally to his policy in Europe. A patient statesman who, unlike Hitler, knew how and when to stop, in the last year of the war Stalin pushed the isolated and weakening British just about as far as he could. When at Warsaw in August, 1944, or at Athens in December of that year he perceived that he had pushed too hard, Stalin withdrew without apologies; such were not for the ruler who was finally realizing the wildest aspirations of the most Slavophile Czar.[15]

Since Stalin's determination, Bolshevik Party discipline, and Great Russian patriotism proved capable of resisting and then

---

[15] Morison, *op. cit.*, 11–12, 52, 59; Djilas, *op. cit.*, 106; Kennan, *Russia and the West*, 358; Leites, *op. cit.*, 517; Churchill, *Closing the Ring* (New York, 1951), 311; Alexander Barmine, *One Who Survived* (New York, 1945), 257–59; *The Public Papers and Addresses of Franklin D. Roosevelt, 1944–45*, edited by Samuel Rosenman (New York, 1950), 99; K. R. Greenfield, *American Strategy in World War II: A Reconsideration* (Baltimore, 1963), 6–22.

driving back Hitler's great crusade, by 1945 Hitler had fully completed the destruction of German hegemony over the Slavic East initiated by his frantic predecessors in Berlin and Vienna during the previous century. The Slavic peoples could at last drive the Germans back to their lines of the early Middle Ages and thus in at least one respect Hitler had successfully fulfilled his rage against the modern world. And in the temporary vacuum of power, created throughout central Europe by Hitler's incompetence and final quasi-madness,[16] Stalin might hope to reconcile the previously dissonant ideological roots of his power, Marxist messianism and Slavophile imperialism. At last over the prostrate body of the Third Reich, Leon Trotsky and the Third Rome might again be one.

---

[16] André François-Poncet, *The Fateful Years, 1931–1938* (New York, 1949), 291.

Bibliography

ABSHAGEN, KARL. *Canaris* (translated). London: Hutchinson, 1956.

ALEXANDROV, VICTOR. *The Tukhachevsky Affair*. London: Macdonald, 1963.

ALFIERI, DINO. *Dictators Face to Face*. New York: New York Univ. Press, 1955.

ANDERS, LIEUTENANT GENERAL WLADYSLAV. *An Army in Exile*. London: Macmillan, 1949.

——. *Hitler's Defeat in Russia*. Chicago: Regnery, 1953.

ANSEL, REAR ADMIRAL WALTER. *Hitler Confronts England*. Durham: Duke Univ. Press, 1960.

ARMSTRONG, JOHN. "Recent Soviet Publications on World War II," *Slavic Review* (Seattle), September, 1962.

——. *Ukrainian Nationalism*. New York: Columbia Univ. Press, 1963.

ASSMANN, VICE ADMIRAL KURT. *Deutsche Schicksal Jahre*. Wiesbaden: Brockhaus, 1950.

——. "The Battle for Moscow: Turning Point of the War," *Foreign Affairs* (New York), January, 1950.

ATKINSON, L. B. "Conflict of Command in the Red Army, 1918–1942," *Military Review* (Fort Leavenworth), July, 1952.

BALDWIN, HANSON W. *Great Mistakes of the War*. New York: Harper and Row, 1950.

——. "Hitler's Power in 1939," *New York Times* (New York), May 9, 1948.

——. "The Battle That Turned the Nazi Tide," *New York Times* (New York), April 13, 1963.

BALLANTINE, JOSEPH W. "Mukden to Pearl Harbor: The Foreign Policies of Japan," *Foreign Affairs* (New York), July, 1949.

BARMINE, ALEXANDER. *One Who Survived.* New York: Putnam's, 1945.

BELOFF, MAX. *The Foreign Policy of the Soviet Union, 1924–1941.* Vols. I and II. London: Oxford Univ. Press, 1955.

BEREZHKOV, VICTOR. "On the Eve of Hitler's Invasion," *Atlas* (New York), January, 1966.

B.D., cited as. *Documents on British Foreign Policy, 1919–1939.* Third Series, Vols. III–VII. Edited by E. L. Woodward and B. Butler with A. Orde. London: H.M.S.O., 1952–54.

BLAU, GEORGE E. *The German Campaign in Russia: Planning and Operations, 1940–1942.* Washington: Dept. of the Army, March, 1955.

——. *The German Campaign in the Balkans: Spring, 1941.* Washington: Dept. of the Army, November, 1953.

BLUMENTRITT, GUENTHER. "Moscow," in *The Fatal Decisions.*

——. *Von Rundstedt: The Soldier and the Man.* London: Odhams, 1952.

BÖRK, LIEUTENANT GENERAL MAX. *Comments on Russian Railroads and Highways.* MS T-7. Washington: Office of the Chief of Military History, undated.

BRYANT, SIR ARTHUR. *The Turn of the Tide, 1939–1943.* London: Collins, 1957.

BULLOCK, ALAN. *Hitler: A Study in Tyranny.* London. Odhams, 1958.

BUTLER, J. R. M. *History of the Second World War: Grand Strategy.* Vols. II and III. London: H.M.S.O., 1957–64.

BUTOW, ROBERT J. *Tojo and the Coming of the War.* Princeton: Princeton Univ. Press, 1961.

CARELL, PAUL. *Hitler's War on Russia: The Story of the German Defeat in the East.* London: Harrap, 1964.

CARR, E. H. *A History of Soviet Russia.* Vol. III: *The Bolshevik Revolution, 1917–1923.* New York: Macmillan, 1953.

——. *German-Soviet Relations Between The Two Wars, 1919–1939.* Baltimore: Johns Hopkins Univ. Press, 1951.

CARROLL, WALLACE. "It Takes a Russian to Beat a Russian," *Life* (New York), December 19, 1949.
CARSTEN, F. L. "The Reichswehr and the Red Army, 1920–1933," *Survey* (London), October, 1962.
CASSIDY, HENRY C. *Moscow Dateline*. Boston: Houghton Mifflin, 1943.
CAULAINCOURT, GENERAL ARMAND DE. *With Napoleon in Russia*. New York: Grosset and Dunlap, 1935.
CAVALLERO, MARSHAL UGO. *Commando Supremo: Diaro 1940–1943 del Capo di S.M.G*. Bologna: Cappelli, 1948.
CHERNIAVSKY, MICHAEL. "Corporal Hitler, General Winter, and the Russian Peasant," *Yale Review* (New Haven), Summer, 1962.
CHUIKOV, MARSHAL VASILI. *The Beginning of the Road*. London: MacGibbon and Kee, 1963.
CHURCHILL, WINSTON. *Into Battle*. London: Cassell, 1941.
———. *Secret Session Speeches*. New York: Simon and Schuster, 1946.
———. *The Second World War*. Vol. I: *The Gathering Storm*. Vol. II: *Their Finest Hour*. Vol. III: *The Grand Alliance*. Vol. IV: *The Hinge of Fate*. Boston: Houghton Mifflin, 1948–50.
———. *The Aftermath*. New York: Scribner's, 1929.
———. *The Unknown War: The Eastern Front*. New York: Scribner's, 1931.
CIANO, COUNT GALEAZZO. *The Ciano Diaries, 1939–1943*. Edited by Hugh Gibson. New York: Doubleday, 1946.
———. *Diplomatic Papers*. Edited by Malcolm Muggeridge. London, 1948.
CLARK, ALAN. *Barbarossa: The Russo-German Conflict, 1941–1945*. New York: Morrow, 1965.
CLAUSEWITZ, KARL VON. *On War*. Vols. I–III. London: Cassell, 1918.
Collapse of Army Group Center, June 22–September 1, 1944. National Archives MS. Neustadt: Office of the Chief of Military History, December, 1947.
[*Soviet*] *Collection of Materials for the Study of War Experiences*. No. 6. National Archives MS. Washington: Office of the Chief of Military History, Dept. of the Army, undated.

Contemporary History in the Soviet Mirror. Edited by J. Keep and L. Brisby. New York: Praeger, 1964.

COULANDRE, ROBERT. *De Stalin à Hitler: Souvenirs de Deux Ambassades*. Paris: Hachette, 1950.

CRAIG, GORDON. *The Politics of the Prussian Army, 1640–1945*. Oxford: Oxford Univ. Press, 1955.

DALLIN, ALEXANDER. *German Rule in Russia, 1941–1945*. London: St. Martin's, 1957.

——. "The North Caucasus," in *Soviet Partisans in World War II*.

DALLIN, DAVID. *Soviet Espionage*. New Haven: Yale Univ. Press, 1956.

DAVIES, JOSEPH E. *Mission to Moscow*. New York: Simon and Schuster, 1941.

DEAKIN, F. W. *The Brutal Friendship: Mussolini, Hitler and the Fall of Italian Fascism*. London: Weidenfeld and Nicolson, 1962.

DEBORIN, G. A. *Second World War*. Moscow: Ministry of Defense, 1958.

DE GAULLE, GENERAL CHARLES. *War Memoirs*. Vol. II: *Unity, 1942–1944*. New York: Simon and Schuster, 1959.

DE LA GORCE, PAUL MARIE. *The French Army: A Military Political History*. New York: Braziller, 1963.

DERRY, T. K. *History of the Second World War: The Campaign in Norway*. London: H.M.S.O., 1959.

DEUTSCHER, ISAAC. *Stalin: A Political Biography*. New York: Oxford Univ. Press, 1949.

——. *The Prophet Armed: Trotsky, 1879–1921*. New York: Oxford Univ. Press, 1954.

——. *The Prophet Outcast: Trotsky, 1929–1940*. London: Oxford Univ. Press, 1963.

DE WITT, C. POOLE. "Light on Nazi Foreign Policy," *Foreign Affairs* (New York), October, 1946.

DEXTER, BYRON. "Clausewitz and Soviet Strategy," *Foreign Affairs* (New York), October, 1951.

DIETRICH, OTTO. *Hitler*. Chicago: Regnery, 1955.

DIRKSEN, HERBERT VON. *Moscow, Tokyo, London*. London: Hutchinson, 1951.

DITTMAR, LIEUTENANT GENERAL KURT. "The Red Army in the Finnish War," in *The Red Army.*

DJILAS, MILOVAN. *Conversations with Stalin.* London: Rupert Hart-Davis, 1962.

Documents and Materials Relating to the Eve of the Second World War, 1937–1939. Vols. I and II. Moscow: Foreign Language Publishing House, 1948.

DORPALEN, ANDREAS. "Hitler, the Nazi Party, and the Wehrmacht in World War II," in *Total War and Cold War: Problems in Civilian Control of the Military.* Columbus: Ohio Univ. Press, 1961.

———. "Hitler Twelve Years After," *Review of Politics* (Notre Dame), October, 1957.

DULLES, ALLEN W. *Germany's Underground.* New York: Macmillan, 1947.

EARLE, EDWARD M. "Lenin, Trotsky, Stalin: Soviet Concepts of War," in *Makers of Modern Strategy.* Also edited by Earle. Princeton: Princeton Univ. Press, 1948.

EDEN, ANTHONY. *The Memoirs of Anthony Eden: The Reckoning.* Boston: Houghton Mifflin, 1965.

EDWARDS, MARVIN. *Stresemann and the Greater Germany.* New York: Bookman, 1963.

Effects of Climate on Combat in European Russia. Washington: Dept. of the Army, February, 1952.

EHRENBURG, ILYA, *Men, Years–Life.* Vol. IV: *Eve of War, 1933–1941.* Vol. V: *The War, 1941–1945.* London: MacGibbon and Kee, 1963–64.

EISENHOWER, GENERAL DWIGHT D. *Crusade in Europe.* New York: Doubleday, 1948.

ELLIS, C. H. *The Transcaspian Episode, 1918–1919.* London: Hutchinson, 1963.

ELLIS, MAJOR L. F. *History of the Second World War: The War in France and Flanders, 1939–1940.* London: H.M.S.O., 1953.

ERFURTH, WALDEMAR. *Die Geschichte des Deutschen Generalstabes, 1918–1945.* Göttingen: Musterschmidt, 1957.

ERICKSON, JOHN. *The Soviet High Command: A Military and Political History, 1918–1941.* New York: St. Martin's, 1962.

ESTORICK, ERIC. *Stafford Cripps.* London: Heinemann, 1949.

FABRY, PHILIPP. *Der Hitler-Stalin Pakt, 1939–1941.* Darmstadt: Fundus, 1962.

F.C.G.N., cited as. *Fuehrer Conferences on Matters Dealing with the German Navy, 1939–1945.* Washington: U.S. Navy, U.S.G.P.O., 1947.

FEILING, KEITH. *The Life of Neville Chamberlain.* London: Macmillan, 1946.

FEIS, HERBERT. *Churchill, Roosevelt, Stalin: The War They Waged and the Peace They Sought.* Princeton: Princeton Univ. Press, 1957.

——. *The Road to Pearl Harbor.* Princeton: Princeton Univ. Press, 1950.

FENYÖ, MARIO. "The Allied Axis Armies and Stalingrad," *Military Affairs* (Washington), Summer, 1965.

FISCHER, GEORGE. *Soviet Opposition to Stalin.* Cambridge: Harvard Univ. Press, 1952.

FISCHER, RUTH. *Stalin and German Communism.* Cambridge: Harvard Univ. Press, 1948.

FOOTE, ALEXANDER. *Handbook for Spies.* New York: Doubleday, 1949.

Foreign Relations of the United States, 1919–1942. Washington: Dept. of State, U.S.G.P.O., 1939–61.

FRANÇOIS-PONCET, ANDRÉ. *The Fateful Years, 1931–1938.* New York: Harcourt, Brace, 1949.

FREUND, GERALD. *Unholy Alliance: Russo-German Relations from the Treaty of Brest-Litovsk to the Treaty of Berlin.* New York: Harcourt, Brace, 1957.

FULLER, MAJOR GENERAL V. F. C. *The Second World War, 1939–1945.* New York: Duell, Sloan, and Pearce, 1949.

GAFENCU, GRIGOIRE. *Derniers Jours de l'Europe.* Paris: Egloff, 1946.

——. *Prelude to the Russian Campaign.* London: Muller, 1945.

GALLAGHER, MATTHEW P. *The Soviet History of World War II: Myths, Memories and Realities.* New York: Praeger, 1963.

———. "Trends in Soviet Historiography of the Second World War," in *Contemporary History in the Soviet Mirror.* New York: Praeger, 1964.

GALLAND, ADOLF. *The First and the Last.* New York: Holt, Rinehart and Winston, 1954.

GAMELIN, GENERAL MAURICE. *Servir.* Vols. I–III. Paris: Plon, 1947.

GARTHOFF, RAYMOND. *Soviet Military Doctrine.* Glencoe: The Free Press, 1953.

———. "The Marshals and the Party," in *Total War and Cold War.*

G.D., cited as. *Documents on German Foreign Policy, 1918–1945.* Edited by P. Sweet, M. Lambert, and M. Baumont. Series C, Vols. I–IV; Series D, Vols. VI–XIII. Washington: Dept. of State, U.S.G.P.O., 1956–64.

Germany and Her Allies in World War II: A Record of Axis Collaboration Problems. Historical Division, H.Q. U.S. Army Europe, undated.

GILBERT, G. M. *Nuremberg Diary.* New York: Signet, 1961.

GISEVIUS, H. B. *To the Bitter End.* London: Cape, 1948.

GOEBBELS, PAUL JOSEPH. *The Goebbels Diaries, 1942–1943.* Edited by Louis Lochner. New York: Doubleday, 1948.

GOERLITZ, WALTER. *History of the German General Staff, 1657–1945.* New York: Praeger, 1953.

———. *Paulus and Stalingrad.* London: Methuen, 1960.

GOLDSMITH, RAYMOND. "The Power of Victory," *Military Affairs* (Washington), Spring, 1946.

GOLOVINE, GENERAL NICOLAS. *The Russian Army in the World War.* New Haven: Yale Univ. Press, 1931.

GORBATOV, GENERAL A. V. *Years Off My Life.* New York: Norton, 1965.

GORDON, HAROLD. *The Reichswehr and the German Republic, 1919–1926.* Princeton: Princeton Univ. Press, 1957.

GOURE, LEON. *The Siege of Leningrad.* Stanford: Stanford Univ. Press, 1962.

GOURE, LEON, and DINERSTEIN, HERBERT. *Moscow in Crisis.* Glencoe: The Free Press, 1955.

GREINER, HELMUTH. *Die Oberste Wehrmachtfuehrung, 1939–1945.* Wiesbaden: Limes, 1951.

GUDERIAN, GENERAL HEINZ. *Interrelationship of Eastern and Western Fronts*. U.S. Army MS T-42. Washington: National Archives, undated.

——. *Panzer Leader*. London: Joseph, 1952.

GUILLAUME, GENERAL AUGUST. *Soviet Arms and Soviet Power*. Washington: Infantry Journal Press, 1949.

GWYER, J. M. *History of the Second World War: Grand Strategy*. Vol. III, Part I. London: H.M.S.O., 1964.

HALDER, GENERAL FRANZ. *Hitler als Feldherr*. Munich: Dom, 1949.

——. *War Diary*. MS at Foreign Policy Assoc. New York, undated.

HALLGARTEN, W. F. "General Hans von Seeckt and Russia," *Journal of Modern History* (Chicago), March, 1949.

HANFSTAENGL, ERNST. *Unheard Witness*. New York: Lippincott, 1957.

HARRISON, GORDON. *United States Army in World War II: Cross-Channel Attack*. Washington: U.S.G.P.O., 1951.

HART, B. H. LIDDELL. *Defense of the West*. New York: Morrow, 1950.

——. *Strategy: The Indirect Approach*. New York: Praeger, 1954.

——. *The Other Side of the Hill*. London: Panther, 1956.

HASSELL, ULRICH VON. *The Von Hassell Diaries, 1938–1944*. London: Hamilton, 1947.

HATTORI, TAKUSHIRO. *A Complete History of the Greater East Asia War*. Vols. I–IV. Toyko: Masu Shobo, 1953.

HEIDEN, KONRAD. *Der Fuehrer*. Boston: Houghton Mifflin, 1944.

HENDERSON, NEVILE. *Failure of a Mission: Berlin, 1937–1939*. New York, 1940.

HESSE, FRITZ. *Hitler and the English*. London: Wingate, 1954.

HEUSINGER, ADOLF. *Hitler et l'OKH, 1923–1945*. Paris: Berger-Levrault, 1952.

HIGGINS, TRUMBULL. "East Wind Rain," *United States Naval Academy Proceedings* (Annapolis), November, 1955.

——. *Winston Churchill and the Second Front*. New York: Oxford Univ. Press, 1957.

HILGER, GUSTAV, and MEYER, ALFRED. *The Incompatible Allies: A Memoir History of German-Soviet Relations, 1918–1941.* New York: Macmillan, 1953.

HILLGRUBER, ANDREAS. *Hitler, Koenig Carol und Marschall Antonescu, 1938–1944.* Wiesbaden: Steiner, 1954.

HINSLEY, F. H. *Hitler's Strategy.* Cambridge: Cambridge Univ. Press, 1951.

HITLER, ADOLF. *Mein Kampf.* New York: Reynal and Hitchcock, 1939.

———. *Hitler's Table Talk, 1941–1944.* Edited and introduced by H. R. Trevor-Roper. London: Weidenfeld and Nicolson, 1953.

———. *Hitler's War Directives, 1939–1945.* Edited by H. R. Trevor-Roper. London: Sedgwick and Jackson, 1964.

———. *My New Order: Speeches, 1922–1941.* Edited by R. de Roucy de Sales. New York, 1941.

———. *The Testament of Adolf Hitler: The Hitler-Bormann Documents, February–April, 1945.* Edited by François Genoud. London: Cassell, 1961.

Hitler Directs His War. Edited by Felix Gilbert. New York: Oxford Univ. Press, 1951.

HOFFMAN, GENERAL MAX. *The War of Lost Opportunities.* London: Paul, French, Trubner, 1924.

HOLBORN, HAJO. "Origins of Nazi Ideology," *Political Science Quarterly* (New York), December, 1964.

House of Commons Debates. Fifth Series. London: 1919–42.

HOWELL, EDGAR. *The Soviet Partisan Movement.* Washington: Dept. of the Army, U.S.G.P.O., August, 1956.

I.M.T.F.E., cited as. *International Military Tribunal for the Far East.* Tokyo, 1948.

Ironside Diaries, 1937–1940, The. Edited by R. MacCleod and P. Kelly. London: Constable, 1962.

ISMAY, MAJOR GENERAL HASTINGS. *The Memoirs of General Lord Ismay.* New York: Viking, 1960.

JACOB, GENERAL SIR IAN. "Churchill as a War Leader," in *Churchill by His Contemporaries. An Observer Appreciation.* London: Hodder and Stoughton, 1965.

JACOBSEN, HANS-ADOLF. *1939–1945: Der Zweite Weltkrieg in Chronik und Dokumenten.* Darmstadt: Wehr und Wissen, 1959.

JAKOBSON, MAX. *The Diplomacy of the Winter War: An Account of the Russo-Finnish War, 1939–1940.* Cambridge: Harvard Univ. Press, 1961.

Japanese Special Studies on Manchuria. Washington: Office of the Chief of Military History, undated.

JODL, GENERAL ALFRED. *Diary.* MS in Princeton Univ. Library, undated.

JOHNSON, CHALMERS. *An Instance of Treason.* London: Heinemann, 1965.

JONES, F. C. *Japan's New Order in East Asia: Its Rise and Fall, 1937–1945.* London: Oxford Univ. Press, 1954.

KAMENETSKY, IGOR. *Secret Nazi Plans for Eastern Europe.* New York: Bookman, 1961.

KASE, TOSHIKAZU. *Journey to the Missouri.* New Haven: Yale Univ. Press, 1950.

KENNAN, GEORGE. *Russia and the West Under Lenin and Stalin.* Boston: Little, Brown, 1961.

——. *Russia Leaves the War: Soviet-American Relations, 1917–1920.* Princeton: Princeton Univ. Press, 1956.

KENNEDY, MAJOR GENERAL SIR JOHN. *The Business of War.* London: Hutchinson, 1957.

KENNEDY, MAJOR ROBERT. *The German Campaign in Poland, 1939.* Washington: Dept. of the Army, U.S.G.P.O., April, 1956.

KESSELRING, ALBERT. *The Memoirs of Field Marshal Kesselring.* London: Kimber, 1953.

KHRUSHCHEV, N. S. "The Crimes of the Stalin Era," *The New Leader* (New York), July 16, 1956.

"Khrushchev Calls Attack by Chinese Reds 'Crazy'," *New York Times* (New York), April 6, 1964.

KILMARX, ROBERT. *A History of Soviet Air Power.* New York: Praeger, 1962.

KITTREDGE, CAPTAIN T. B. "A Military Danger," *United States Naval Proceedings* (Annapolis), July, 1955.

KLEIN, BURTON H. *Germany's Economic Preparations for War.* Cambridge: Harvard Univ. Press, 1959.

KLEIST, PETER. *Zwischen Hitler und Stalin.* Bonn: Athenäum, 1950.

KOCHEN, LIONEL. *The Struggle for Germany, 1914–1945.* Edinburgh: At the Univ. Press, 1963.

KONOYE, PRINCE FUMIMARO. "The Memoirs of Prince Konoye," *Asahi Shimbun* (Tokyo), December 20–30, 1945.

KORDT, ERICH. *Wahn und Wirklichkeit,* Stuttgart: Union Deutsche Verlaganstalt, 1947.

KOT, STANISLAW. *Conversations with the Kremlin and Dispatches from Russia.* London: Oxford Univ. Press, 1963.

Kriegstagebuch des Oberkommandos der Wehrmacht, 1940–1945. Collected and edited by Percy Schramm *et al.* Vols. II and III. Frankfurt am Main: Bernard and Graefe, 1963.

LABEDZ, LEOPOLD. "1939: A Backward Glance," *Encounter* (London), December, 1964.

LANGER, WILLIAM, and GLEASON, S. V. Vol. I: *The Challenge to Isolation, 1937–1940.* Vol. II: *The Undeclared War, 1940–1941.* New York: Harper and Row, 1952–53.

LAQUER, WALTER. "Hitler and Russia, 1919–1923," *Survey* (London), October, 1962.

———. *Russia and Germany: A Century of Conflict.* London: Weidenfeld and Nicolson, 1965.

LEASOR, JAMES. *Rudolf Hess: The Uninvited Envoy.* London: Allen and Unwin, 1962.

———. *War at the Top: The Experiences of General Sir Leslie Hollis.* London: Joseph, 1959.

LEE, ASHER. *The German Air Force.* New York: Harper and Row, 1946.

L'8 Armata Italiana nella Seconda Battaglia Difensiva del Don, December 11, 1942–January 31, 1943. Rome: Ministry of War, 1946.

LEIGHTON, RICHARD, and COAKLEY, ROBERT. *United States Army in World War II: The War Department; Global Logistics and Strategy, 1940–1943.* Washington: Dept. of the Army, U.S.G.P.O., 1955.

LEITES, NATHAN. *A Study of Bolshevism.* Glencoe: The Free Press, 1953.

LENIN, V. I. *Sochineniya.* Second and Fourth Editions, published in 31 and 35 volumes respectively. Moscow, 1930–35, 1941–45.

Le Operazioni del C.S.I.R. e dell'Armir, July, 1941–October, 1942. Rome: Ministry of Defense, 1947.

Les Lettres Secrètes Echangées par Hitler et Mussolini. Paris: Pavois, 1946.

LOSSBERG, MAJOR GENERAL BERNHARD VON. *Im Wehrmachtfuehrungsstab.* Hamburg: Nölke, 1950.

LUKACS, JOHN. *The Great Powers and Eastern Europe.* Chicago: Regnery, 1953.

MCNEILL, W. H. *America, Britain and Russia: Their Cooperation and Conflict, 1941–1946.* Royal Institute of International Affairs. New York: Oxford Univ. Press, 1953.

MAISKY, IVAN. "Stalin Hid As Nazi Attack Began, Ex-Envoy Recalls," *New York Times* (New York), January 7, 1965.

———. *Who Helped Hitler?* London: Hutchinson, 1964.

Makers of Modern Strategy, Military Thought from Machiavelli to Hitler. Edited by E. M. Earle and others. Princeton: Princeton Univ. Press, 1948.

MANNERHEIM, BARON KARL GUSTAF VON. *The Memoirs of Marshal Mannerheim.* New York: Dutton, 1954.

MANSTEIN, FIELD MARSHAL ERICH VON. *Lost Victories.* London: Methuen, 1958.

———. "The Development of the Red Army, 1942–1945," in *The Red Army.*

MARKOFF, GENERAL ALEXEI. "How Russia Almost Lost the War," *Saturday Evening Post* (Philadelphia), May 13, 1950.

MATLOFF, MAURICE. *United States Army in World War II: The War Department.* Vol. II: *Strategic Planning for Coalition Warfare, 1943–1944.* Washington: Dept. of the Army, U.S.G.P.O., 1959.

MATLOFF, MAURICE, and SNELL, E. M. *United States Army in World War II: The War Department.* Vol. I: *Strategic Planning for Coalition Warfare, 1941–1942.* U.S.G.P.O., 1953.

Military Improvisations During the Russian Campaign. Washington: Dept. of the Army, August, 1951.

MINNEY, R. J. *The Private Papers of Hore-Belisha*. London: Collins, 1960.

MORISON, SAMUEL ELIOT. *Strategy and Compromise*. Boston: Little, Brown, 1958.

MOTTER, T. H. VAIL. *United States Army in World War II: The Middle East Theater*. Washington: Dept. of the Army, U.S.G.P.O., 1952.

MOURIN, MAXIME. *Les Tentatives de Paix dans la Seconde Guerre Mondiale, 1939–1945*. Paris: Payot, 1949.

NAMIER, SIR LEWIS. *In the Nazi Era*. London: Macmillan, 1952.

N.C.A., cited as. *Nazi Conspiracy and Aggression*. Vols. I–VIII, "Supplements," and "Opinion and Judgment." Washington: Office of the United States Chief of Counsel for Prosecution of Axis Criminality. U.S.G.P.O., 1946.

N.S.R., cited as. *Nazi-Soviet Relations, 1939–1941: Documents from the Archives of the German Foreign Office*. Edited by R. J. Sontag and J. S. Beddie for the U.S. Dept. of State. Washington: U.S.G.P.O., 1948.

Operations of Encircled Forces: German Experiences in Russia. Washington: Dept. of the Army, January, 1952.

Pearl Harbor Attack. Hearings Before the Joint Committee, Seventy-ninth Congress, Second Session. Washington: U.S.-G.P.O., 1946.

PERTINAX. *Les Fossoyeurs*. Vols. I–II. New York: La Maison Française, 1943.

PHILIPPI, A., and HEIM, F. *Der Feldzug gegen Sowjetrussland*. Stuttgart: Kohlhammer, 1962.

PLAYFAIR, MAJOR GENERAL I. S. O. *et al*. *History of the Second World War: The Mediterranean and the Middle East*. Vols. I–III. London: H.M.S.O., 1954–1960.

POTEMKIN, V. P. *Histoire de la Diplomatie*. Edited by him and cited under his name. Paris: *Libraire de Medécis*, 1947.

POTTGIESER, HANS. *Die Deutsche Reichsbahn im Ostfeldzug, 1939–1944*. Neckargemuend: Vowinckel, 1960.

Raeder, Grand Admiral Erich. *Struggle for the Sea.* London: Kimber, 1939.

Rauschning, Hermann. *The Revolution of Nihilism.* New York: Longmans, Green, 1939.

——. *The Voice of Destruction.* New York: Putnam's, 1940.

Reitlinger, Gerald. *The House Built on Sand: The Conflicts of German Policy in Russia, 1939–1945.* New York: Viking, 1960.

Reverses on the Southern Wing, 1942–1943. National Archives MS. Heidelberg: Historical Division, H.Q. U.S. Army Europe, undated.

Reynaud, Paul. *In the Thick of the Fight, 1939–1945.* New York: Simon and Schuster, 1955.

——. *Mémoirs.* Vols. I–II. Paris: Flammarion, 1963.

Ribbentrop, Joachim von. *The Ribbentrop Memoirs.* London: Weidenfeld and Nicolson, 1954.

Robertson, E. M. *Hitler's Pre-War Policy and Plans, 1933–1934.* London: Longmans, Green, 1963.

Rommel, Erwin. *The Rommel Papers.* Edited by B. H. Liddell Hart. London: Collins, 1953.

Roskill, Captain S. W. *History of the Second World War: The War at Sea, 1939–1945.* Vol. II: *The Period of Balance.* London: H.M.S.O., 1956.

Rossi, A. *The Russo-German Alliance: August, 1939–June, 1941.* Boston: Beacon, 1951.

Ruge, Vice Admiral Friedrich. *Der Seekrieg: The German Navy's Own Story.* Annapolis: U.S. Naval Institute, 1957.

Schapiro, Leonard. "The Great Purge," in *The Red Army.*

Scharndorff, Werner. "The Bukarin Trial and Marshal Tukhachevsky's Rehabilitation," *Bulletin for the Study of the U.S.S.R.* (Munich), June, 1963.

Scheibert, Horst. *Zwischen Don und Donez: Winter, 1942–43.* Neckargemuend: Vowinckel, 1961.

Schellenberg, Walter. *The Labyrinth.* New York: Harper and Row, 1959.

Schlabrendorff, Fabian von. *They Almost Killed Hitler.* Edited by G. S. Gaevernitz. New York: Macmillan, 1947.

SCHMIDT, PAUL. *Hitler's Interpreter.* New York: Macmillan, 1959.

SCHORSKE, C. E. "Two German Ambassadors: Dirksen and Schulenburg," in *The Diplomats, 1919–1939.*

SCHORSKE, C. E., and FORD, F. T., "The Voice in the Wilderness: Robert Coulondre," in *The Diplomats, 1919–1939.* Edited by G. Craig and F. Gilbert. Princeton: Princeton Univ. Press, 1953.

SCHROETER, HEINZ. *Stalingrad.* London: Joseph, 1958.

SENGER UND ETTERLIN, GENERAL FRIDO VON. *Neither Fear nor Hope.* London: MacDonald, 1963.

SERGE, VICTOR. *Memoirs of a Revolutionary, 1901–1914.* London: Oxford Univ. Press, 1963.

SETH, RONALD. *Operation Barbarossa.* London: Blond, 1964.

———. *Stalingrad–Point of Return, August, 1942–February, 1943.* London: Gollancz, 1960.

SHABAD, THEODORE. "Soviet Military Experts Upgrade Stalin and Make Khrushchev an Unperson," *New York Times* (New York), April 18, 1965.

SHERWOOD, ROBERT E. *Roosevelt and Hopkins: An Intimate History.* New York: Harper and Row, 1948.

SHIRER, WILLIAM L. *The Rise and Fall of the Third Reich: A History of Nazi Germany.* New York: Simon and Schuster, 1960.

SHULMAN, MILTON. *Defeat in the West.* New York: Dutton, 1948.

SIMONI, M. L. *Berlino Ambasciata d'Italia, 1939–1943.* Rome: Migliaresi, 1946.

SIMONOV, KONSTANTIN. *Victims and Heroes.* London: Hutchinson, 1963.

SOKOLOVSKY, MARSHAL V. D. *et al. Military Strategy: Soviet Doctrines and Concepts.* Cited under his name. New York: Praeger, 1963.

Soviet Partisans in World War II. Edited by John Armstrong. Madison: Univ. of Wisconsin Press, 1964.

STALIN, JOSEPH. *Problems of Leninism.* New York: International Publishers, 1934.

"Stalin's Absence as Nazis Attacked in 1941 Recalled," *New York Times* (New York), November 4, 1965.

———. *Stalin's Correspondence with Churchill, Attlee, Roosevelt and Truman, 1941–1945*. London: Lawrence and Wishart, 1958.

STANDLEY, WILLIAM, and AGETON, ARTHUR. Cited under Standley. *American Ambassador to Russia*. Chicago: Regnery, 1955.

STERN, FRITZ. *The Politics of Cultural Despair: A Study in the Rise of the German Ideology*. New York: Anchor, 1965.

STETTINIUS, E. R., JR. *Lend-Lease: Weapon for Victory*. New York: Macmillan Pocket Books, 1944.

STEWART, GEORGE. *The White Armies of Russia*. New York: Macmillan, 1933.

STIMSON, HENRY L., and BUNDY, MCGEORGE. Cited under Stimson. *On Active Service in Peace and War*. New York: Harper and Row, 1948.

TANNER, VAINO. *The Winter War: Finland Against Russia, 1939–1940*. Stanford: Stanford Univ. Press, 1950.

TAYLOR, A. J. P. *The Origins of the Second World War*. London: Hamilton, 1961.

TAYLOR, TELFORD. *Sword and Swastika: Generals and Nazis in the Third Reich*. New York: Simon and Schuster, 1952.

———. *The March of Conquest*. New York: Simon and Schuster, 1958.

TELPUCHOWSKI, BORIS. *Die Sowjetische Geschichte des Grossen Vaterlaendischen Krieges, 1941–1945*. Frankfurt am Main: Bernard and Graefe, 1961.

The Diplomats, 1910–1939. Edited by G. A. Craig and Felix Gilbert. Princeton: Princeton Univ. Press, 1953.

The Fatal Decisions. Edited by S. Freidin and W. Richardson. New York: Duell, Sloan and Pearce, 1956.

The German Army High Command O.K.H. Synopsis. Washington: Office of the Chief of Military History, December, 1959.

The Great Patriotic War (Geschichte des Grossen Vaterlaendischen Krieges der Sowjet Union). Vols. I–III. The Marx-Lenin Institute of Moscow. Berlin: Deutscher Militaerverlag, 1962.

The Initial Triumph of the Axis. Edited by A. and V. M. Toynbee. Institute of International Affairs. London: Oxford Univ. Press, 1958.

The Red Army. Edited by B. H. Liddell Hart. New York: Harcourt, Brace and World, 1956.

The United States Strategic Bombing Survey: The Effects of Strategic Bombing on the German War Economy. Washington: Overall Economic Effects Division, October 31, 1945.

TINCH, CLARK W. "Quasi-War Between Japan and the U.S.S.R., 1937–1939," *World Politics* (New Haven), January, 1951.

T.M.W.C., cited as. *Trial of the Major War Criminals*. Vols. I–XLII. Nuremberg: The Allied Control Authority, 1947.

Total War and Cold War: Problems in Civilian Control of the Military. Edited by Harry L. Coles. Columbus: Ohio State Univ. Press, 1962.

TREVOR-ROPER, H. R. *The Last Days of Hitler*. New York: Macmillan, 1947.

TROTSKY, LEON. *My Life*. New York: Grosset and Dunlap, Universal Library, 1960.

———. *Stalin*. Edited by Charles Malamuth. New York: Harper and Row, 1941.

U.S. Dept. of State Bulletin. Washington: March 17, 1946; July 16, 1946; Sept. 29, 1946.

VOZNENSKY, N. A. *The Economy of the U.S.S.R. During World War II*. Washington: Public Affairs Press, 1948.

Warfare in the Far North. Washington: Dept. of the Army, October, 1951.

WARLIMONT, GENERAL WALTER. *Inside Hitler's Headquarters, 1939–1945*. London: Weidenfeld and Nicolson, 1964.

WEDEMEYER, GENERAL ALBERT C. *Wedemeyer Reports!* New York: Holt, Rinehart and Winston, 1958.

WEINBERG, GERHARD L. *Germany and the Soviet Union, 1939–1941*. Leiden: E. J. Brill, 1954.

———. "The Yelyna-Dorogobuzh Area," in *Soviet Partisans in World War II*.

WEIZSAECKER, ERNST VON. *The Memoirs of Ernst von Weizsaecker*. London: Gollancz, 1951.

WERTH, ALEXANDER. *Russia at War, 1941–1945*. London: Barrie and Rockliff, 1964.

WHEATLEY, RONALD. *Operation Sea Lion: German Plans for the Invasion of England, 1939–1942.* Oxford: Clarendon, 1958.

WHEELER-BENNETT, JOHN. *Munich: Prologue to Tragedy.* New York: Duell, Sloan and Pearce, 1948.

——. *The Forgotten Peace: Brest-Litovsk, March, 1918.* New York: Morrow, 1939.

——. *The Nemesis of Power: The German Army in Politics, 1918–1945.* New York: St. Martin's, 1954.

——. "Twenty Years of Russo-German Relations: 1919–1939," *Foreign Affairs* (New York), October, 1946.

WILLOUGHBY, MAJOR GENERAL CHARLES. *Shanghai Conspiracy: The Sorge Spy Ring.* New York: Dutton, 1952.

WISKEMANN, ELIZABETH. *The Rome-Berlin Axis.* New York: Oxford Univ. Press, 1949.

WOLFE, BERTRAM D. "Titans Locked in Combat," *Russian Review* (Hanover), January, 1965.

WOODWARD, SIR LLEWELLYN. *British Foreign Policy in the Second World War.* London: H.M.S.O., 1962.

YEREMENKO, MARSHAL A. I. *At the Beginning of the War.* Moscow: Nauka, 1964.

——. *Stalingrad: Notes du Commandant-en-Chef.* Paris: Plon, 1963.

ZAWODNY, J. A. *Death in the Forest.* Notre Dame: Notre Dame Univ. Press, 1962.

ZEITZLER, GENERAL KURT. "Stalingrad," in *The Fatal Decisions.*

ZIEMKE, E. F. *The German Northern Theater of Operations, 1940–1945.* Washington: Dept. of the Army, 1959.

ZOLLER, ALBERT. *Hitler Privat.* Dusseldorf, 1949.

Index